On Mountains

John Jerome

Every valley shall be exalted, and every mountain and hill shall be made low: and the crooked shall be made straight, and the rough places plain.   Isaiah 40:2–3

On Mountains

McGraw-Hill Book Company

New York   St. Louis   San Francisco   Bogotá   Düsseldorf   Madrid
Mexico   Montreal   Panama   Paris   São Paulo   Tokyo   Toronto

Portions of this book originally appeared, in a slightly different form, in
Skiing magazine. Copyright © 1974, 1975, 1976, Ziff-Davis Publishing
Company.

The author wishes to thank the following for
permission to quote from the sources listed:

Edward W. Cronin for "The Yeti," copyright © 1976
by Edward W. Cronin; John Murray (Publishers) Ltd.,
for *The Avalanche Enigma* by Colin Fraser; and Oxford
University Press, Inc., for *Collected Poems* by Conrad
Aiken, copyright © 1953, 1970 by Conrad Aiken.

PHOTO CREDITS:
Title page, courtesy of U.S. Geological Survey; Book One, courtesy
of U.S. Forest Service; Book Two, courtesy of Swiss National Tourist
Office; Book Three, courtesy of U.S. Forest Service.

Library of Congress Cataloging in Publication Data

Jerome, John.
On mountains.
Reprint of the ed. published by Harcourt Brace
Jovanovich, New York.
Bibliography: p.
1. Mountains. I. Title.
[GB501.2.J47   1979]   910'.02'143   78-24273
ISBN 0-07-032535-9

This book is for Gwen,
for Jud,
and, always,
for Chris.

Also by John Jerome

The Death of the Automobile

Truck

The Sports Illustrated Book of Skiing

Contents

BOOK THREE

The Mountain Life

ILLUSTRATIONS

My special thanks to Al Greenberg and the staff at Skiing magazine, who first raised the possibility, and then helped me get this done.

Introduction

"Gradient is the elixir of youth," says Jerome Wyckoff, in *Rock, Time, and Landforms.* He is applying this poetic sentiment to the development of streams, rather than to mountains, but the sentence jumped off the page at me when I first read it. Gradient. Indeed. No wonder Ponce de León, floundering around in the bogs and flats of Florida, failed to find the Fountain of Youth. Gradient, that's the stuff. Yes. This book grows from that brief quotation.

Mountains are mysteries. They stimulate man's imagination as powerfully as do the seas and the skies, and have traditionally been the repositories of myths and religions. The attempt to understand them has given birth to entire new sciences. Any mountain—indeed, any gradient at all—triggers our curiosity: what caused this? Why is it here? But there is also something deeper, more elemental than studies or the prick of idle curiosity: mountains are an experience. There is something that happens in the flesh, *to* the flesh, in the mountains. It makes mountain addicts. I'm not sure it can be explained.

I didn't grow up as a mountain boy, and I'm not a mountain man—and if I were, I doubt a book would result. True mountain people comprehend mountains differently than we late-comers do, which is a rude truth I sometimes have difficulty assimilating. While this book is not in any sense my story, I too spent my time in the bogs and flats, came to the mountains late, and have never quite recovered from the wonder of that first encounter. Such a background has necessarily colored the way I've thought about mountains ever since.

Houston, Texas, where I grew up, is fifty miles inland and fifty feet above sea level (and sinking, by the way). One foot per mile is not a gradient that spawns mountain boys. We played in the nearby bogs and flats, but there was one "hill" beside a bayou near my home, thirty or forty vertical feet of what could only have been channel dredgings. Dried muck. It was, of course, our favorite place: height, relief—gradient—even then had its charm. We struggled up and down that hill, dug dangerous caves in its sides, pushed and shoved over occupancy of its pip-squeak summit. Otherwise the country-side was so flat that the farmers hardly bothered with dikes for their rice fields. No question about it, I was a flatlander.

Upon graduation from high school, two friends and I took off in an old station wagon to go see Colorado. Just that: to go see it. (It's a tradition for Texans to go to Colorado in summer, mostly in an attempt to cool off.) It was a miserable trip, driving nonstop across the hot June deserts of west Texas, and we were in darkness long before we got to the splendors of Raton Pass. Barely across the Colorado border at dawn, we turned left for what the map indicated was high country. More endless driving, now along a dusty dirt road between scraggly pines, twisting and turning and never revealing more than two hundred yards of its desolate self at a stretch. Just about the time the level of adolescent bickering within the car reached an unbearable pitch, the car conked out. Vapor lock. My friends elected to wait it out.

Screw that, said I, and continued on foot. It didn't take many steps up that unpleasant road before I dived for the woods, primarily to escape the heat. Instant peace. Dry pine scent and springy footing and—my God!—patches of dirty snow in the deepest shade. In June. (Snow was not a familiar substance to me in those days.) Then I topped a minor rise, the trees parted, and . . . mountains. A clear little opal of a lake and a wall of rock behind rising to heights that I could not quite take in. Timberline. Snow on the peak. Mountain meadows, wild flowers—all those little mountain clichés—but I was *in* them, breathing them, for the first time. A texture to the light that made it all new, unlike anything I'd ever dreamed of.

I can't remember what I did, confronted with that sight, but I vaguely recall flopping onto my belly on the pine needles for a while. Mostly I must have stared. Seventeen is a tough age for dealing with wonder, and I felt it necessary to be deliberately callous. Protective seventeen-year-old aplomb and all that: I would have nothing to do with that bursting feeling in the back of my throat. But I do remember thinking, *This is where I'm supposed to be.* I haven't quite managed to stay in such surroundings ever since, but I've never gotten over that notion.

Years later I moved my family to Colorado, to live in Denver and flee into the mountains every chance we got. That was terrible: to drive into the mountains on weekends, to walk around and breathe and gawk, and then to come back out again, city-bound in both senses. I couldn't afford to stay in the mountains, and couldn't stand to stay out of them. Colorado drove me crazy.

There was a frustration involved that I think is peculiarly American: I couldn't find anything to *do* with mountains. I didn't hunt or fish (I'd done that, and didn't want to anymore). Climbing wasn't for me (that's another long story). Camping seemed silly, particularly with small children—complex efforts to get into an uncomfortable environment in order to test one's skill at reducing that discomfort. I couldn't find any logical way to use the mountains. Which meant that I didn't seem to be able to get *at* them.

Economic considerations took me out of the mountains for a while, and then, for the time when I still needed a rationale to get back in, I found one in skiing—a weak excuse, but sufficient. Skiing, and writing about skiing, put me onto a lot of different mountains and put me in touch with their intimacies, down there among the hummocks and vales and particulars of mountain topography, snow-covered though it almost always was.

Skiing force-fed my curiosity about mountains, but only in the vaguest and most ill-focused ways. I was as stimulated, I think; as anyone to wonder about mountains—why they are the way they are, what it is that so attracts us to them—but I seemed to be asking the wrong questions. I certainly wasn't getting any answers that were very satisfying. (One of the things that has always bemused me about mountain country is the general lack of curiosity among its residents. People who spend lifetimes in the mountains, who know every conceivable scrap of practical detail—where the spring freshets come down, when the valleys are safely frost-free, where the deer go to yard up—seldom seem to wonder why. It is amazingly consistent. It is as if the home mountains represent not much more than that gradient out there that makes things a little more beautiful, but also a little more difficult whenever any physical task is involved. Nevertheless, those mountain people wouldn't move away from the gradient for all the available ease in the civilized world.)

Mysterious as mountains are, the answers are available, once you get the questions right. This book is an attempt to do just that, to ask the right questions, and then to collect the answers—as many as I have been able to find—in a single place. It is the book I wanted to read, and couldn't find, when I first began looking for those answers.

The more questions I've asked about mountains, the less I've needed any excuse for staying in them. That tendency is, I hope, only my small personal version of an encouraging worldwide trend. I think we are all learning not to require use from our mountains, or for that matter from every other scrap and particle of the natural world. Mountains *are* useful, in hundreds of ways. But to go into them with use in mind is a guaranteed method of violating the experience. Of losing the wonder. In any event, for people bent on using the mountains, this book should very likely prove useless. I like to think there's a kind of poetic justice involved.

Instead, this book is for people like myself, who have never quite gotten over the thrill of having something huge and solid and natural out there making the horizon interesting (many of us, I suspect, are bored by the sea), who have an irresistible urge to seek high ground, not to have conquered it or to dissect it or to get beyond it, but simply in order to see farther from it. *Seeing* is the key. My own reward has been that in learning more I've found that familiar mountains, mountains I thought I knew as well as the faces of my children, now make my eyes pop. I am seeing them in a new way—new, at least, for me. I can hope for no more from this book than that in some way it may help you to experience a similar pleasure. Old things seen with new eyes. Mountains being just about the oldest scenery we recognize as such.

One more such personal note: I did get back. A medium-sized New Hampshire mountain of very great age looms in my study window as I write these words. It's called Kinsman Mountain (elevation 4,363 feet), named, not out of pride in local fellowship, but in honor of Nathan Kinsman, who settled our valley in 1782. I've been gazing at it for nearly ten years now, and I find something different to see in it every time I look. It's not the Rockies, no, but that's the great thing about mountains: any one will do.

Book One

Mountain-Making

Simple races, as savages, do not climb mountains—their tops are sacred and mysterious tracts never visited by them.—HENRY DAVID THOREAU, *The Maine Woods*

Chapter 1

Warts, Wens, Blisters

It is impossible to talk about mountains as we know them now without reference to time periods of hundreds of millions of years. Yet the argument can be made that mountains weren't really "invented," as distinct topographical features, until about three hundred years ago. Even then, we didn't like them.

Mountains were simply another kind of wilderness, another one of earth's many forbidding areas into which one did not go for frivolous purposes. There were exceptions, of course. Many a primitive people regarded their local range as a sacred place, "the center of the earth." Holy mountains were everywhere to be found. The ancients revered Sinai (7,497 feet)*

---

* Altitudes above sea level are given throughout the text (where I've been able to determine them), in feet, usually on first mention only.

and Ararat (16,946 feet). Vesuvius (4,190) and Etna (10,902) loomed large in early history; Olympus (9,550) and Parnassus (8,064) housed the gods, however mythologically. But between Hannibal's crossing of the Alps in 218 B.C. and Petrarch's ascent of Mount Ventoux (6,273) in A.D. 1335, there is scant record of any great curiosity about mountains. Saint Augustine used mountains allegorically in his little moral lessons before the fifth century. Some obscure eleventh-century German texts describe rudimentary mountain expeditions. Dante tells of his climb up a Mount Bismantova about the turn of the fourteenth century. He didn't like it very much; later he would refer to mountains as the gates of hell.

It was not an uncommon reaction. The poets of the time were also the only practicing scientists and theologians (that is, all learning tended to get recorded in poetic form—it was up to the Romantics a couple of centuries later to turn poetry into a trade), and those poets spoke of mountains as "warts, wens, blisters, imposthumes" on the fair face of Nature. The Devil's Arse was a feature of the English landscape—a hill, naturally. Dealing with mountains was worse, bringing even more anguish. Fear and fatigue. A hundred years after Dante, travelers who were forced by circumstances to journey through the Alps were often blindfolded; it was seriously believed that the horrors of the mountain scenery might drive them mad. The souls of the dead were believed to inhabit a ruined city on the summit of the Matterhorn. As late as 1723, a scientist named Scheuchzer, who was a Fellow of the Royal Society, opined that while most dragons were nothing but fables, nevertheless, "from accounts of Swiss dragons, and their comparison with those of other lands, such animals do exist." Charles Cotton, in his addendum to Izaak Walton's *Compleat Angler*—in the late 1600's—quotes a stranger from London who was escaping from the hill country after a har-

---

Metric equivalents aren't given, despite my sympathy for the metric movement, simply to avoid cluttering the text with numbers. Metric fans can multiply by 0.3048 to convert feet to meters.

rowing visit: "I'll no more on thee; I'll go twenty miles about first. Puh. I sweat, that my shirt sticks to my back." It might be considered the eternal oath of all dedicated nonclimbers of mountains ever since.

Mountains were barriers, problems, to be avoided. Hannibal's epic journey went not over the Alps but through them. Historically, an *alp* is not a peak; it is a high mountain meadow, and Hannibal's great accomplishment was to connect those meadows, to find the route that avoided as many of the mountains as possible—although he still had to build roads in virgin territory to make it possible for his elephants to descend. The inhabitants of mountain country had the same goal of avoiding their own mountains whenever possible, however strange it may sound. In Europe the mountain people historically grazed their livestock on those alps in summer, then withdrew in winter to huddle in the valleys, dodging avalanches. The only forays into the mountains that were not connected with agriculture or trade were occasional hunting trips after chamois or to collect "crystals"—any of various interesting mineral formations that eventually could be sold to the crazy English as souvenirs. (Smuggling, that other traditional pastime of mountain people, had to await the establishment of more substantial national boundaries.)

Among the rare early uses of the mountains was the establishment of medicinal baths, where flatlanders came for the cure. By the sixteenth century such baths were well established at Leukerbad, St. Moritz, and Pfäffers. Perhaps one reasonable explanation for the horrible reputation of mountain country is found in the history of Leukerbad, in the Valais. In 1518 an avalanche killed sixty-one citizens; in 1717 another killed fifty-five; and when an undetermined number were wiped out by another slide in 1758, the spa was abandoned.

The crazy English would finally come, inventing tourism and mountain climbing almost simultaneously, but not before we had radically altered the way we thought about mountains. This great change grew quite naturally out of the intellectual and social ferment of the post-Renaissance period, when Western man was changing the way he thought about everything else as well. After the oceans had been "conquered" in the Age of Exploration, Europeans finally noticed these pockets of relatively unexplored territory right in their midst—islands of mystery surrounded by civilization. New inventions—the telescope, the microscope, the printing press—brought on an explosion of scientific investigation. Yet the application of scientific thought to the earth itself came surprisingly late and ran into surprising resistance, not solely from the conservative Church. The Comte de Buffon, the great French naturalist, found sea shells embedded in rock in French hillsides far from the sea and contrived a remarkably prescient theory—that somehow the sea had once been where the mountains now are—to explain them. No less a rationalist than Voltaire wrote off the theory as mystical nonsense, preferring to believe that "pilgrims" had for some reason brought sea shells to the mountaintops, where the shells had become stuck in the mud. Their dispute took place only two hundred years ago.

Science makes a dignified rationale, but it can't be credited entirely for our change of attitude about the mountains. By the 1700's the Grand Tour was the tradition for young English gentlemen, an almost formalized step in completing one's education. Geneva was a regular stop on that tour, and a side trip to the "Ice Alps," the *glacières*—Mont Blanc, via Chamonix—was mandatory, a phenomenon one simply had to go see. The gentlemen were often young rakehells at loose ends while they awaited full possession of their inheritances; Geneva was the scene of much English mischief. Their backgrounds and education had prepared them only to be terrified by the mountains, so of course they flocked to them. Go up to the glaciers and scare hell out of oneself. Bracing. Have to do until a suitable war came along.

The English had a difficult time finding a way to make proper use of the mountains—self-induced fright was a suspect rationale, and one couldn't just go *look*, could one? The

6

drill, then, was to scour Geneva for whatever available scientific instrumentation one could find, throw it into one's kip, and go take some measurements. Journals and dispatches to patrons back home became full of interpretive speculation. It was hardly science in any modern sense, much of it being the airiest nonsense, but it was the beginning of real curiosity about just what these ice-covered warts and wens really were.

The largest difficulty for early theorists about mountains was the same faced by all the other rapidly developing sciences: what to do about Genesis? The Greeks had known about high-altitude fossils, and Aristotle's *Meteorologica* had laid down the basis of most geological thinking. Aristotle's brilliance, however, required an unlimited time span. Standard chronicles, if not the Scriptures themselves, were much more specific: the earth was created in 4004 B.C., with the sea and land separated on the third day and animal life not added to the mix until the fourth. How could Aristotle and Moses be resolved? Orthodoxy led to some strange postulations.

Fossils were presumed not to be animate at all, but "sports of nature," minerals gone berserk, perhaps as a result of planetary influences. The earth itself was theorized to be an animate object with its own life, its own growth and decay processes. Many objected to the notion that the Creator would bother with a "craggy" earth in the first place and held that the earth must originally have been a perfectly smooth sphere, in the best neoclassical tradition; the present state of "ruin" was the product of man's sin and the resulting Deluge (dated precisely by one thinker at 1770 B.C.). Classical symmetries were sought everywhere: as man's two halves matched, left to right, so on earth there must be a hump for every hollow. When the Creator scooped out the seas, he dumped his dredgings on Switzerland—and, in fact, by measuring the highest mountains one might accurately determine the depths of the seas.

There were, incidentally, some problems with that measurement. Estimates of the height of the tallest mountain—an honor claimed for, among others, Tenerife in the Canaries,

Atlas in North Africa, and something called Mount Perjacca in America—ranged from 1,250 paces to seventy-eight miles. As we will see, it is a dispute that will pop up again over Mount Everest, albeit on a much narrower gauge.

There was no shortage of theories. The analogy with man was pursued: mountains were obviously the bones of earth, and therefore must grow as bones grew. Considerable effort was devoted to finding a living basis in minerals, thanks to the invention of the microscope, which revealed "invisible worms" in virtually everything, living down there among their own little mountains and valleys. Similarly, the telescope had revealed mountains on the moon, which launched yet more new theories for the origin of earthly mountains. With these two inventions, biology and astronomy had been given new tools by which men could actually observe whole new worlds. Geology had no such tool and was consequently retarded—although a Jesuit named Athanasius Kircher was exploring caves and having himself lowered into volcanoes, and as a consequence came up with theories of mountain formation later characterized as "subterraneous Wildfire, Flatus, or Earthquakes."

Another theory had it that wind, driven into the earth somehow by coldness, thrust up the mountains in its efforts to get free. Edmund Halley, discoverer of Halley's comet, naturally posited that the cause of the Deluge, and thus of the formation of mountains, was the earth's passage through the tail of a comet. John Beaumont opined that "hills and mountains might be occasion'd by fermentation, after the manner of leaven in dough." Isaac Newton observed that if one poured beer into milk, the resulting curd did resemble mountainous structures in miniature, so perhaps the clue lay there. Jonathan Swift, of course, satirized them all.

But by the 1700's men were going into the mountains just to go into the mountains. It was a development with far-reaching implications in both literature and science. These new mountain adventurers discovered that indeed they did not go mad from gazing upon the awful sights; quite the contrary, the effect was inspirational, uplifting, transcending. The awful had become the awesome. Behind the change were simply a developing familiarity with at least the fringes of the terrain, and growing curiosity. But there was also the growing awareness—again thanks to such inventions as the microscope and telescope—that man might look at the ordinary with new eyes, might be able to see in new ways. Even without "Galileo's tubes." Before this time, men looked only for confirmation of classical and theological orthodoxies. The power of the mountains shook them out of that orthodoxy, and they began to look at the mountains themselves, at what was. They began to see what Marjorie Hope Nicolson has called "the attraction of the vast," which led to an "aesthetics of the infinite": seeing the heavens, the seas, the mountains, the unreachable distances as proper vehicles for celebration of God *and* the world. Men began to see, and to feel, for themselves. The process turned out to be surprisingly unblasphemous.

It doesn't do to give too much credit to the crazy English. Mountaineering scholars credit a Benedictine monk from Disentis, Brother Placidus á Spescha, with the first ascent of many peaks in his region of Switzerland (Grisons) in the late 1700's, and call him the "father of mountaineering." He may have been inspired by Albrecht von Haller of Zurich, yet another scientist-poet, who wrote of the beauties of the mountain regions in 1732 in a long poem, *Die Alpen.* Jean Jacques Rousseau's sentimental return-to-nature philosophy is credited directly to the influence of Swiss mountain literature. Rousseau in turn is believed to have been the inspiration for a Swiss named Horace Benedict de Saussure, who might be considered the first big-time Alpinist. He began trying to climb Mont Blanc (15,781 feet, highest in Europe) in 1760, at first so naïve about mountain conditions that he carried a parasol and wore a veil against sun blindness. He failed four times. Another Swiss team consisting of a crystal hunter named Jacques Balmat and Dr. Michel Piccard succeeded in

1787, and Saussure was the first to follow them to the summit. In the service of science Swiss climbers then ascended the Titlis (10,627) in 1791, the Jungfrau (13,642) in 1811, the Finsteraarhorn (14,022) in 1812, and the Schreckhorn (13,379) in 1842.

These ascents were the stuff of high adventure as well as of scientific advancement. Englishmen watched; it may be assumed that Englishmen fumed. The English have a long history of inventing new games, teaching them to foreigners, then getting soundly whipped at them. Here was a new game—never mind the science—and all of the adventure and glory were being grabbed by these taciturn Swiss. Foreigners. It wouldn't do. Englishman Edward Whymper began trying to climb the Matterhorn (14,685) in 1861; he was to make seven unsuccessful attempts before succeeding in 1865. Then, on the descent, after "one crowded hour of glorious life" on the summit, in the most notorious incident in mountaineering, "the rope broke," and Swiss Michel-Auguste Croz and Englishmen Douglas Hadow, Charles Hudson, and Lord Francis Douglas fell to their deaths. It would be hard to determine which event —the successful ascent or the disaster thereafter—more vividly inflamed English imaginations. What had been only one stop on the Grand Tour now became an English obsession, and Englishmen flooded the Alps. Between 1854 and 1870, Englishmen stood on the summits of every major Alpine peak. It is not to be assumed that they kept these exploits a modest secret. The tourist industry, ski resorts, and other dubious social inventions were the direct result of the flood of Englishmen. And mountains—glorious, inspirational, challenging, but above all accessible—were firmly fixed in the intellectual fashions of the world.

There is clearly a Western bias built into this narrative. It is absurd to consider that mountains are a recent "invention" when whole cultures have inhabited the mountainous areas of the globe ever since we first came down from the trees. We have, however, little indication of how those cultures have regarded their own mountains. It is hard to imagine that all those Incas and Tibetans and Native Americans could have gazed upon their own mountains without feeling some measure of the same awe and wonder experienced by the English tourists of the nineteenth century. The mountain heights could have been just another condition of life, like drought in the desert or shade in the jungle, as dulled by everyday familiarity as any other permanent environmental fact of life. But it is hard to conceive, because we do have this Western bias.

We'll never know, and that's the point. They didn't record those attitudes, didn't leave us any accessible history of a mountain aesthetic—except perhaps, cryptically and metaphorically, within their theologies. It was only in Western Europe that the sensibility, as well as the machinery, developed to preserve the record, to spread the attitudes. It was the Europeans, especially the English, who performed a kind of press agentry for the mountains. They changed men's minds about the mountains.

The Romantic poets were the premiere press agents. It may seem quite a leisurely time frame, from warts and wens in the late 1600's to the first serious ascents of the Alps in the mid-1700's to the English onslaught of the latter half of the 1800's. In fact the change in the public's understanding of mountains was considerably more compressed than that list of dates indicates. The Romantic poets either recorded the changing attitudes, or actively promoted the change, depending upon how much historical force one wants to credit to the fashions of poetry. In either case, it is in their work that the changing attitudes are clearly documented.

All of them wrote mountain poetry. All of them tramped the Alps, glorying in what they saw. That's what they wrote about: what they *saw*, and that, too, is the point. Their predecessors had firm classical backgrounds and looked within those backgrounds to find understanding of what they saw, letting the ancients tell them what their eyes beheld. The Romantics had the same classical training but they understood the new science as well, and the scientific revolution told them to look afresh, with their own eyes. They needed no other rationale for going into the mountains. They created a whole new literary movement out of scenery. The view.

Amazing change. William Wordsworth—who in 1793 included an account of a walking tour of the Alps in his first published work, *Descriptive Sketches*—tells us succinctly just how quickly the change took place. He quotes a "shrewd and sensible woman" in whose house he lived during part of his rural youth. "Bless me!" said the good woman, "folks are always talking about *prospects;* when I was young there was never sic a thing neamed!"*

* For this quote, and for much of the interpretation in this chapter, I am indebted to Marjorie Hope Nicolson, *Mountain Gloom and Mountain Glory: The Development of the Aesthetics of the Infinite* (New York: W. W. Norton, 1963).

The highest mountain on the globe is not, as is generally
supposed, Mt. Everest, that honor belonging to a lofty peak
on the Isle of Papua, or New Guinea. This monster . . .
was discovered by Capt. A. J. Lawson, of London, in 1881.
According to Lawson . . . [it] is 32,763 feet in height,
being 3,781 feet higher than Mt. Everest, which is only
29,002 feet. . . . This New Guinean giant has been
named Mt. Hercules.
—Littleton, N. H., *Journal,* July 19, 1889

Chapter 2

Where–and What–
the Mountains Are

So we have the Alps, which turn out to be more or less mis-
named—named for their meadows rather than for the peaks
which so obviously distinguish them—and, let's see, what else?
The Himalayas, the Rockies, the Andes. Some dormant minor-
league offshoots like the Pyrenees, the Caucasus, the Appalachians. That about does it. Using the tattered little geography
book in my head, I find myself hard pressed to come up with
much more than that in the way of mountains. Yet this abbreviated list, upon which we base most of our romantic ideas
about mountains, overlooks the bulk of the world's mountain
regions.

Those regions lie primarily in two great, sweeping *mobile
belts,* one making a complete encirclement of the Pacific
Ocean, the other traversing Eurasia on a roughly east–west

line. These regions are "mobile" in the sense that they are areas of great geologic turmoil in which mountain-building is still going on; they are in "belts" because they form clear dividing lines, albeit broad ones, that segment the globe into distinct sections.

The Pacific belt starts in Antarctica, where Mount Tyree thrusts up 16,290 feet above the frozen sea, and the Vinson Massif looms to 16,860 feet. The belt sweeps up along the western edge of South America (the Andes contain fifty peaks higher than anything in North America), through the Sierra Madre of Mexico (Citlaltepetl, 18,696), through the Rockies and Sierra Nevada of the American West (Mount Whitney, 14,495), on up through the Cascades, the Coast Range of Canada and Alaska, the Alaskan Range (Mount McKinley, or, as the Indians know it, Denali, 20,320 feet), and out across the Aleutian Islands.

It then curves downward through Russia's Kamchatka Peninsula (Klyuchevskaya Sopka, 15,584), the Kurile Islands, Japan (Fujiyama, 12,389), Taiwan (Yu Shan, 13,113), the Philippines, Indonesia (Djaja, 16,503), and, swinging east of Australia, into New Zealand (Mount Cook, 12,360, and sixteen other peaks above 10,000 feet). Thus back to Antarctica. This belt, which contains most of the world's active volcanoes and witnesses 80 percent of its earthquake activity, is popularly known as the "Rim of Fire."

The Eurasian mobile belt is more complex. It rises as a western spur off the Rim of Fire near Indonesia, curves up into south-central Asia, through the Himalayas (Mount Everest, 29,000, give or take a hundred feet) to the Caucasus (Mount Elbrus, 18,468), then splits again. One branch curves down into eastern Africa, containing several great peaks including Kilimanjaro (19,340). Authorities don't quite agree whether this spur is a true mobile belt or not, but it is one of the most interesting geologic areas in the world, intimately linked to the Great Rift Valley and the Dead Sea region of the Middle East. The main belt continues west through the Alps

(Mont Blanc), the Pyrenees (Pico de Aneto, 11,168), and the Atlas Mountains of northwest Africa (Toubkal, 13,665). The belt dwindles out in the Canaries, where Tenerife, that source of seventeenth-century wonderment, turns out to be neither 1,250 paces nor seventy-eight miles high, but 12,172 feet.

There are sound geologic reasons for lumping all our mountains tidily into mobile belts, but to do so overlooks their huge numbers and inexhaustible variety. That hip-shot description of the mobile belts identifies eighteen or twenty specific groups of mountains but still ignores, for example, the view out my study window. That view is of a tiny piece of the Appalachians—a mobile belt which, like the Urals in west-central Russia, is dormant, no longer the scene of appreciable geologic activity. For now.

Grouping mountains into belts also leaves out most of the familiar local names by which we know our home hills. Omitted, for example, in the region I know best, are the White Mountains (where I live), the Green Mountains, the Adirondacks, the Catskills, the Berkshires, the Poconos, the Alleghenies, the Blue Ridge, the Great Smokies—each a major mountain group, each a discrete segment of the dormant belt which is the Appalachians. There are dozens more. In the Rockies there are more than a hundred different mountain ranges large enough to have their own names. One-fourth of the earth's land area is "mountainous"—above three thousand feet. Fourteen million square miles of mountains. And 10 percent of that mountainous area is high enough (or cold enough) to be above the permanent snow line.

Mountain taxonomy can be distressingly vague, but a few definitions will help sort out the confusion. Kinsman, the mountain outside my study window, has a north and a south peak, but it is clearly recognizable as a single mountain. If I lean out the window a bit, however, I can see the next peaks north and south (Cannon Mountain and Mount Moosilauke, respectively) in the long ridge that is identified as the Fran-

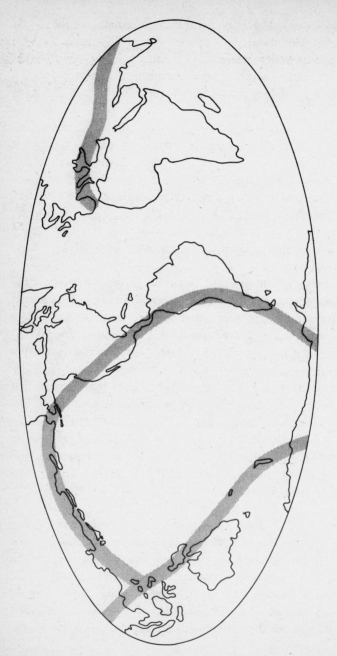

THE MOBILE BELTS

conia Range. A *range* is the next unit up in mountain labeling, next largest after a single peak; it can be a single complex ridge or a series of ridges of the same general age and form.

The Franconia Range runs into the Presidential Range, which culminates about thirty-five miles north of Kinsman in Mount Washington, at 6,288 feet the highest point east of the Mississippi and north of the Mason–Dixon line. The Presidentials and several other ranges make up the White Mountains, which are properly denoted as a mountain *system*—a parallel alignment or chainlike cluster of ranges. A series of mountain systems taken together are a mountain *chain:* the White, Green, Adirondack, Allegheny, and Blue Ridge systems, plus others, make up the Appalachian chain. An extensive complex of mountain chains more or less geologically lined makes up a *belt* or *cordillera.* As in mobile belts.

The difference between mountain chains and belts—as in the Appalachians and Urals—can be a bit fuzzy. The Rockies, for example, are clearly a chain extending from the Canadian Rockies to the high desert country of southern New Mexico. But if you extend that classification to include the Davis Mountains of Texas or the Sierra Madre of Mexico, or extend it northward to include the Coastal and Brooks ranges, then that chain becomes a cordillera. The Appalachian chain extends from northern Alabama into the hills of Newfoundland, but the belt that once included these mountains probably must be extended, in one's imagination at least, to include the mountains of Greenland, or even the Scandinavian Alps.

The timberline on Mount Washington is at about four thousand feet, and the mountain is so spectacular, particularly in winter with twenty-three hundred feet of snowcap, that most New Englanders just assume it is the highest point east of the Rockies. Not so: Mount Mitchell, in the Blue Ridge escarpment of the Great Smokies in North Carolina, is the highest point east of the Mississippi, at 6,684 feet. (Forty-three peaks in the Smokies exceed six thousand feet; except for Mount Washington, nothing in New England comes close to that mark.) And the highest point east of the Rockies is Harney Peak, 7,242 feet, in the Black Hills of South Dakota. Thus the Black "Hills" are a thousand feet taller than the White "Mountains."

Altitude is relative, of course, unless you're trying to breathe in its upper reaches. The snow line—the level above which snow never melts—can be anywhere: it is above twenty thousand feet in the Andes, at sixteen thousand or higher in the Himalayas, not much above eighty-five hundred feet in the Alps—where it has risen by about three hundred feet in the past fifty years. On California's Mount Shasta the snow line varies between 13,000 and 14,162 feet; five hundred miles to the north on the Olympic Peninsula, it comes down to six thousand feet. In the Arctic and Antarctic, of course, it is at sea level.

The impressiveness of the altitude depends on the location of the viewer's feet, I suppose. I love my view of Kinsman because my house sits in a valley at about eleven hundred feet above sea level, so I am gazing at nearly thirty-two hundred vertical feet of relief. Tenerife achieved its unwarranted early reputation as the highest mountain in the world because it stands on an island and every inch of its twelve thousand-plus feet was visible to every approaching ship. The most famous mountains have always been the spectacular ones that sit near a coastline, like Fujiyama, or on the edge of a range, usually overlooking a level plain, like Pikes Peak (14,110), towering over Colorado Springs, or the startling vertical abruptness of the Grand Teton (13,766) of Wyoming.

To get some sense of how mountain altitudes run, consider this: put another Pikes Peak on top of Pikes Peak, and you begin to approach the altitude of a Mount Everest. This is not to denigrate that Colorado tourist attraction, as benign and beautiful as any mountain with an automobile road to its top, but to establish a relative scale. Fourteen thousand feet is the magic number, a kind of benchmark of American superlatives, for big mountains in the forty-eight contiguous states. The highest peak in the United States outside of Alaska is Mount Whitney in California, at 14,495. Pikes Peak is only 385 feet lower, yet it is far from the tallest peak even in Colorado, which has no fewer than fifty-four mountains that pass the fourteen-thousand-foot mark. At 14,433 feet, Mount Elbert, the highest peak in Colorado and the second highest in the forty-eight states, is only sixty-two feet shorter than Whitney. There is a lot of competition for the honors in that last 495 feet.

In the Himalayas, by startling contrast, the magic number is eight thousand—but that's *meters:* roughly 26,250 feet. There are fourteen eight-thousand-meter peaks in the Himalayas (and none comes close to that height anywhere else in the world). Tibet, however, has an *average* altitude of over sixteen thousand feet, including a plateau a thousand miles wide that is higher than any peak in the continental United States. Himalayan peaks really do begin where American peaks leave off. Altitude *is* relative.

It is also tricky. I am pulling these altitude figures from a dozen generally trustworthy sources, and very few of them agree. Mount Whitney is 14,495, 14,494, or 14,491 feet high, take your pick. Mount Elbert is either 14,431 or 14,433. Mountain measurements are taken in a variety of ways, none of them terribly reliable. Early-day "scientific" climbers used boiling-point thermometers to guesstimate altitudes. More modern altimeters are merely fancy barometers, and barometric pressure varies so much that we use its daily changes to predict the weather. Serious surveyors use theodolites, which require optical sighting from a base that is absolutely level (and at an absolutely known altitude to start with). Mountain masses themselves exert enough gravitational pull to skew plumb-bob readings, making establishment of a level base problematical. Optical readings depend on light rays, which behave predictably in the laboratory and then go crazy out in the mountains, at the whim of atmospheric pressure, humidity, temperature variations, smog and dust levels, and the like. The possible error is exaggerated by distance; mountain terrain seldom allows close-up sightings.

Satellite observation, with laser beams and other assorted

technological wizardry, will eventually provide us with more accurate measurements. But it will take some time, in these data-explosive years, for that accuracy to be applied to all our peculiar curiosities and to become generally available after that. Meanwhile, we pick up and reprint each other's dubious numbers.

I have not given an altitude figure for Mount Everest, and I will not: that mountain provides the premiere case in point. A British surveying party first "officially" measured the world's highest mountain in 1852 and found its peak to be 29,002 feet above sea level, a figure that went into every schoolbook. Years later members of the British party confessed. They had taken several measurements from several different locations and had gotten readings ranging all the way from 28,990 to 29,026 feet. In the interest of a kind of consensus accuracy, they simply averaged their readings. But to their dismay the average came out to precisely twenty-nine thousand feet. Nobody, they felt, would believe *that*—so they threw in another two feet just for verisimilitude. It sounded more scientific.

A hundred years later, a party of Indian surveyors went back for another look. They spent two years taking measurements from six different locations. They emerged with the figure of 29,028 feet, and since 1954 that has been accepted worldwide as the new gospel. The Indian measurement was also an average; their measurements had varied by as much as sixteen feet.

Twenty-one years later a Chinese expedition climbed Mount Everest and announced that their scientists had determined, among other things, that the mountain was 29,029.24 feet high, a figure which raised the Indian standard by just about fifteen inches. The British, who have felt a kind of proprietary interest in the mountain since it was first climbed by a British expedition in 1953, objected. Nonsense, said Brigadier Richard Gardiner of the map section of the Royal Geographic Society. "It is ridiculous to pretend anyone can measure Everest to within a decimal of a foot—or even to the nearest fifty feet."

Ah, but Everest could be that high, and the Indian figures from 1954 could also have been correct. Geologists feel certain that the Himalayas have been uplifted by about six thousand feet in the past 600,000 years, or about a foot every hundred years. Some feel that the rate of uplift may be accelerating. Russian biologists report finding high-altitude meadows that have risen so rapidly that lowland grasses still survive on them at over thirteen thousand feet. A meter a century might not be unreasonable, says a spokesman for London's Geological Museum. "It's also possible that other points in the surrounding area might be falling at the same time, which would complicate things even more."

Shortly after the Chinese announced their measurement, another British expedition left to attempt the previously unclimbed southwest face of Everest. A member of that group, Nick Estcourt, provided a little more perspective on the dispute. "The Chinese themselves may have made the mountain higher before measuring it," he said. "At least one Chinese expedition has left behind a bust of Chairman Mao. Perhaps that is a foot high. Anyway, if Everest is bobbing up and down, we must just hope to catch it on a low day." They must have: the British attempt succeeded, surmounting Everest's last unclimbed face in 1975.

There's even a way to make it all more relative than that. There is a science called *geodesy*, which attempts to determine the precise dimensions and form of the earth. If you could extend the sea-level configuration of the earth underneath the lands, the sphere that would result would be the *geoid*, as compared to the ellipsoid that is the earth's actual shape. To look at the mountains geoidally is to measure them from the center of the earth, rather than from sea level. The editors of the *Guinness Book of Records* asked the Smithsonian Astrophysical Observatory to look at the world's mountains that way, with the help of satellite observations. Geoidally speaking, the world's tallest mountain is Mount Chimborazo in Ecuador, 20,577 feet above sea level, but, located as it is near the bulge of the earth's surface at the equator, some 7,058 feet farther from the center of the earth than the summit of Everest.

All this talk about altitude presupposes that there is general agreement on just what a mountain *is*, which isn't necessarily justified. (See the Black Hills versus the White Mountains.) The government of Nepal doesn't require mountain-climbing expedition permits for ascents of peaks up to twenty thousand feet high. Such peaks are regarded as "viewpoints" rather than mountains (as well they might be, with nearby peaks towering nearly ten thousand feet over them). The state of Kansas, that national symbol of unrelieved flatness, has its own Mount Sunflower, towering to a mighty 4,039 feet—towering, that is, over surrounding thirty-five-hundred-foot plains.

The definition of a mountain is one of those subjects that invites elegant discussion, and I've found none more so than that published by the charming old geographer Roderick Peattie, in 1936:

A mountain, strictly speaking, is a conspicuous elevation of small summit area. A plateau is a similar elevation of large summit area with at least one sheer side. An essential and yet indefinite element in the definition of a mountain is the conspicuity. Conspicuity, like height, is a relative matter, and depends upon the personal evaluation or the standard by which it is measured. Many eminences but a few hundred feet high are termed mountains by dwellers on flat plains. One writer arbitrarily states that a mountain must be a quarter of a mile high. If this relief be measured from the surrounding country rather than from sea level, then certainly one would have a mountain. Seldom is relief as great as on the coast of Formosa, where there is a precipitous cliff of 4270 meters. The Great Plains of the Western United States are a mile high. A slight eminence upon these plains would hardly be termed a mountain. Pikes Peak is, in truth, a mountain not because it rises more than 4270 meters but because its relief over the surrounding country is so great (2440 meters) [8,000 feet]. Also it has steep sides. Its conspicuity is great. For days, in the era of traveling by ox cart, its white summit was a guide to the early settlers, who bore upon their covered wagons the slogan "Pike's Peak or Bust." It was a symbol, a goal, and it played a great part in the imagination of the plodding, hopeful travelers. Mountains should be impressive; they should enter into the imagination of the people who live within their shadows. Unfortunately, it is next to impossible to include such intangibles in a definition. Mountains have bulk; mountains have also individuality.*

The figure for the Formosan cliff must be a misprint—it actually rises about 2,500 feet, or 760 meters. Taiwan's highest peak is under four thousand meters: Yu Shan, at either 13,113 or 13,064 feet, depending on the source. But then, that's what I mean about altitude.

Nevertheless, Professor Peattie's sentiments are good enough for me. Small summit, conspicuity, bulk, individuality —yes. Relief. All relative values, but they'll do. I would add Wyckoff's gradient, the elixir of youth. Of course. It doesn't matter that these attributes are all relative. I know a mountain when I see one, and so do you.

* Roderick Peattie, *Mountain Geography, A Critique and Field Study* (New York: Greenwood Press, 1936), p. 3.

The road had the merit of all savage trails, and of all the
tracks a man still makes who is a-foot and free and can
make by the shortest line for his goal; it enjoyed the
hills.—HILAIRE BELLOC, *The Old Road*

Chapter **3**

Field Notes

Let us not rush into this with fourteen-, or twenty-, or thirty-
thousand-foot mountains. Better to examine, for now, a single
(small) mountain. I am not a geologist or a naturalist, but
come with me up Mount Kinsman. I'll show you whatever I
can on my home mountain.

It's eight miles or so of walking; we can do it as an energetic
long afternoon, but it's more enjoyable to start early and carry
lunch to eat on top. We could bushwhack from the back door,
but that means an extra couple of hours of getting smacked in
the face with fir branches. If we drive three miles down the
valley, we can go in at the Kenney place, on a perfectly civilized Appalachian Mountain Club (AMC) trail that is maintained just for strollers such as us. We have lucked into a crisp
August morning—after two days of rain a cold front has come
through and now a northeast breeze is drying out the atmosphere. The peak is in clouds, but the cloud line is rising, hour
by hour, on the shoulders of Mount Kinsman: the summit will

be in bright sunshine by noon. Great walking weather, although the trail will be sodden in places. (It always is. There's so much water trying to come down off the mountain, in all seasons, that there are always muddy spots in the trail. Except in dead of winter.)

The trail starts at the Easton town line, at about eleven hundred feet above sea level, on an old logging road. We start in, and half a mile into the woods we come across the ruins of the old Andrew sawmill. All our New Hampshire forests are second or third growth by now. This valley feels as woodsy and forested as anywhere, and half of it is national forest preserve, but turn-of-the-century photographs show it cleared back almost to ridge line on both east and west. Skinned and barren-looking from the combined demands of lumbering, charcoal-making, and wood heating.

The Andrew mill was built in 1892, first for dimensional lumber, later—when the hardwoods ran out—for softwood lath. Now the ruins are almost indiscernible in the summer undergrowth, but the original installation had a boarding-house and company store, and steam power. The owner's son finally convinced the old man in 1903 that horses were faster in the woods than oxen, and the mill switched from sleds to wagons about the same time. (A similar switch from horses to bulldozers was not too many years away. And mechanized lumbering was so "efficient" that these mountains, which had withstood the onslaughts of men, oxen, and horses for over 150 years, were then logged out in about twenty years, before World War II.) The Andrew mill has long been abandoned, and the forest that has grown up over it is of so uniform an age that the occasional giant tree that predates the lumbering years is a startling sight. We'll come across one now and then along the trail, three feet thick and standing half again as tall as the surrounding woods. It's a sight that does magnificent things for the imagination: what must these woods have been like in, say, 1477 A.D.?

Just as we get to the Andrew ruins, there's a change in the

quality of the forest. I can't really say what causes it. Before the change the forest is very . . . yang: pine-needle floor; dry, brown, sandy soil; prickles and cones; harsh sun penetrating the woods; hot, dusty air in your nostrils. Buzz of insects. Dense undergrowth on both sides of the trail, walling us off. Then the transition comes and the woods go yin: soft, damp, ferny, with lush mosses and low cushions of princess pine (seeming to invite dalliance; lie down and get instantly soaked to the skin). Cool wet air, boggy, breezeless, nonscratchy. Quiet—no birds and few insects. It's a *mood* change: what causes this?

The logging road leads on. Ghosts of old logging roads infest these woods. When we get to the summit of Kinsman, we'll spot the old roads with field glasses, ten and twenty miles away, switchbacking their way up the sides of other mountains. We can also spot them from ten *feet* away, disappearing into the undergrowth. But at any range between ten feet and ten miles, they dissolve in the fecundity of the surroundings. Ghosts.

Similarly, you have to intuit the shape of the land, at least in the green of full summer. From the trail it's hard to see far into the woods, to get any notion of what the terrain is doing out there. But we're getting into the sugarbush now, and sugaring tends to clean up the woods, taking out most of the understory stuff, removing the lesser trees (burned to boil off sap), maintaining the big maples in the best possible health. We pass Zeke Kenney's collecting tub, the horse-trough-like container where sap is held before boiling, now collecting nothing but dead leaves; it'll be cleaned up and back in action next March. The woods are almost parklike here, European in feel, a supremely pleasant place to walk. The openness leads me to unaccustomed thoughts. That perhaps wildness is overrated? That I've oversold myself on the healthy chaos of wild places? It is a mood that passes quickly enough.

So far the trail has been alternating between low ridge and shallow gulley, the natural terrain providing ribbed fingers that point up the mountain, showing the way we want to go, always gently rising. Now, in the sugarbush, we come upon an unexpected flat, a kind of implicit meadow—if only the tree cover were removed and the topsoil beneath allowed to sprout in meadow grasses. Anyway, that's what the terrain leads me to imagine. Then, as soon as I'm led to that speculation, the trail turns to pure rubble, a solid collection of football-sized stones chockablock in the path, cobblestones for giants. (Guaranteed ankle-breakers if you don't watch your step.) Why is this?

The path is carrying so much water downhill that it has become virtually a running creek, and the rubble provides welcome stepping stones. Now and then, where the stones run out, the path has been corduroyed with short traverse lengths of log, like railroad ties, by the ever busy AMC. But nobody could have carried all these stones in here and placed them so regularly and neatly. This must be what underlies all that flat. Divert the mountain runoff from the miniature gulley that holds the trail—a creek-bottom path, really—and it would instantly strip off the six or so inches of topsoil of my "meadow" and convert it into a rockfield. (Just like all the rest of New Hampshire, says the farmer.) Our rubbled path is really the rocky underside of this peculiar flat place on the side of the mountain. But what put all these rocks here, virtually sorted by size? I don't know; perhaps we can find out.

("Creek-bottom path" is not too farfetched a description. Some hikers—mostly locals who prefer not to share their walks with visitors—disdain the formal trails entirely. They pick out a creekbed and go straight up that, rock by rock. It's much slower and more slippery, but there's drinking water every step of the way, and besides, how else is one to discover his own private skinny-dipping holes? Most of the local hiking trails, if they are not specifically laid out to link mountain summits, have as their ultimate goals the more spectacular waterfalls, potholes, and cascades of the mountain streams anyway. Using a creekbed as a trail just cuts out all the stuff in between. I can be persuaded. . . .)

A mile and a half up the trail we come to the Kinsman Cabin, a two-roomer maintained by the White Mountain National Forest for overnighters. (Most of the graffiti on its walls seem to be authored by visiting Green Berets, who regularly drop into these mountains—by parachute—on training missions.) In this first mile and a half we have climbed only a little more than eight hundred feet (out of three thousand, total, to the summit), but we're passing out of the hardwoods and into softwood forest. The line of demarcation is not clear. From a distance, gazing up at one of these New England mountains, you can pick up the subtle line in summer, with the brighter green of hardwoods below, the darker, almost blue above, where the conifers take over. In winter, the distinction is much more obvious from a distance, since the leafless hardwoods then appear only as a grayish haze on the hillside. But up on the mountain, on foot, we wander in and out of both kinds of forest, and there seems to be no discernible pattern, not even one of altitude.

Shortly before two thousand feet we start seeing the first glacial erratics: great boulders left standing free, isolated, by the withdrawal of the ice sheets. Some of them now wear semiformal wild flower patches on top, rooted in the six to eight inches of humus that has collected there, looking almost like man-made rock gardens. Others of these boulders sprout twenty-foot fir trees on top, with root structures that wrap around them like macramé nets for holding hanging flowerpots. Just past the cabin, the trail makes its first sustained steep rise, and once on it, we can look back and see that the erratics rim the bottom of the steep section, where the steepness flattens out; they must have rolled to a stop there at some time in the dim past. The steep pitch is the rough equivalent of a third of a mile of staircase—easy enough if we don't sprint it, but decidedly more demanding than the gentle grade we've been climbing so far. We'll sweat before the trail levels out again, and have more appreciation for the air-conditioning breeze.

Back at the cabin, we passed one fork of Kendall Brook, tumbling across the trail, beginning to cut its way down into the granite to make the cool, dark hollow of a minor-grade flume. I wasn't familiar with the term *flume* when I first moved to the White Mountains—it's what the locals call a deep, narrow-walled gorge with a stream cutting through its bottom. Some flumes hereabouts are famous, including one in Franconia Notch State Park (just over the mountain from Kinsman) so popular that it's a bus-served tourist attraction. The first fork of Kendall Brook doesn't quite qualify, but at the upper end of our steep rise, perhaps six hundred yards above the cabin, there's another flume that is more substantial, that has made its way into the AMC guidebooks. It's a four-hundred-yard-long notch between nearly vertical stone walls, twenty to thirty feet deep, varying between eight and fifteen feet in width. It is full of tumbling, tangled waterfalls and shallow pools, jumbles of log waste, and fractured rock. If it were sunlit it would be a splendid picnic spot, but it is so deep and its shoulders so well forested that it is a dark and spooky place, in permanent shade, thick with mosses and dripping springs. After one particularly late spring, I found ice still clinging to the south walls near the end of June.

The flume is a spectacular piece of scenery, but after the quiet pleasures of the trail that preceded it, it seems almost gaudy. True, that's why most people walk up here, to see the flume. But it is an anomaly, almost a disruption. It doesn't seem to fit in with the rest of the mountain. The flume descends at right angles to the trail as the trail traverses the pitch of the mountan, and it deepens as it goes downhill, away from the trail. Above the trail Kendall Brook descends through a much gentler depression in the side of the mountain; a short distance above the trail there is a rocky spur, a pseudo-ridge that sticks out of the mountainside like the hipbone of a fashion model. The flume is only an eight-foot-wide interruption in the downward curve of that ridge, which culminates a quarter of a mile below the trail in Bald Knob, a polished granite protrusion that offers the most panoramic views of the valley of any spot around. Bald Knob is another magnet for walkers on Kinsman, a half-mile of side trip that leads to the sunny picnic spot the flume never quite delivers. A great percentage of Kinsman climbers never go any higher than the twenty-five-hundred-foot overlook that is Bald Knob. We'll go on up and see what they're missing. They're missing a great deal.

After the flume and Bald Knob, the trail enters an area of ancient blowdowns and recent sawdowns, the former probably from the hurricane of 1938 (or our local mythic wind, the Bungay Jar), the latter from scurrying AMC crews maintaining trail. It's a strange area with a strange feeling to it: scattered firs, perhaps twenty to thirty feet tall, which seem to be dying out, turning scraggly and brown. The understory growth is also balsam fir, but—perhaps because the dying trees allow too much sunlight to reach them—fir gone crazy, of a uniform two-foot height but much too thickly established ever to survive. What caused this infestation of surplus growth? Disease? Fire? I need a forester to explain the mountain to me.

Then suddenly the fir scrub stops, the trail continues its gentle climb, and we pass into a forest of yellow and white birch with no underbrush to speak of. The previous steepness—or rubble in the path, or any other hindrance to rapid movement—serves a useful purpose on walks like this. It makes you keep your head down, watch your footing, and thus keeps you from looking up and overdosing on the splendor of the forest. Dappled light of bright sun filtered through maple woods, beech woods, birch woods: staggering. Now, in predominantly yellow and white birch, there is no choice; it is no longer possible to walk with eyes down, ignoring the glories of the light. The forest floor here is clearly the product of old storm or fire damage—all broken stumps, fallen trees, giant jackstraws—so long in place that it is all covered with foot-thick, brilliant green, utterly voluptuous mosses. It is a pillowy, billowy forest floor that cries out to have nymphs and dryads romping over it, a boy's dream of Sherwood Forest, totally wild but still benign. A Maxfield Parrish dreamscape.

Part of the enchanted effect is the look of the forest floor, but more of it is the summer sun through birch trees. Here one realizes that in any woodland the type of tree absolutely determines the sensory quality of the forest. The species determines the amount and quality of light admitted, the texture of the footing underneath, the degree of underbrush, the kind of wildlife, even the sounds the wind makes and the resonance of the echoes. I don't know my trees yet, am just learning them; now I understand why I have to know them better. If you don't know the trees, nothing I can tell you about the quality of light in a yellow birch forest will make any sense; if you do know what a yellow birch forest is like, that is all I need to say—that it is a yellow birch forest—to set off a whole sequence of associations and sensory images of beauty and quiet and peace in your head. That's worth knowing the trees for.

Nothing bad could possibly happen in a yellow birch forest, I think (watch me sprain an ankle the moment I think it). Meanwhile, it is easy to see why the forester falls in love with his forest. And this wonderland we are in, this ferny forest extending in a gentle climb from twenty-five hundred to thirty-six hundred feet, is that dread cardinal sin against the Protestant ethic which the lumber industry refers to as a cellulose cemetery. All these fine trees up here, and nobody *using* them for anything. Except to look at, to walk through, to absorb peace from. Sorry, U.S. Forest Service, you can't have these.

(They'll get them, they'll get them yet. The next ravine to the north on Kinsman contains a fine forty-foot waterfall known—not unexpectedly—as Bridal Veil, in the middle of a thick fir forest. Rumor has the National Forest types proposing to log off all the firs around the falls—to be used for pulp, I'm sure—and to replant the area with high-altitude apple trees. The ostensible purpose is to provide a better habitat for deer, which have had some hungry years locally in recent times, and on that basis they'll sell the notion to the defenders of wildlife. It'll only take about forty years to restore Bridal Veil to some semblance of stability, to get the silt out of the stream, et cetera.)

The enchanted forest part of our climb stretches on and on, as we gain a gradual thousand feet. It's a very benign mountain; I keep saying that, but it's true. The coniferous trees do begin to reassert themselves, of course, and we continue to get alternating stripes of yin and yang forest. The yin is full of ferns and moisture, mini–rain forest, soft; the yang comes back with the prickly needles and cones and sticky sap of the conifers, the harshly sandy soil they love, the brownness. As soon as the trees overhead block out enough sun, the understory growth thins completely and the view opens out so you can see across the hillside underneath the forest cover. When something interrupts the canopy overhead, the view closes in again.

Suddenly at about thirty-six hundred feet, we pop out into scrub fir forest, the trees gone waist-high, miniaturized on us, and we can see . . . everything. We are not at timberline, but the effect is the same, since we are now taller than the trees. The trail turns into solid granite, broken and tumbled and irregular underfoot, but solid nevertheless, almost sidewalk-ish: the granite core of the mountain exposed, to be trod upon. It always surprises me. I know well enough in my head that mountains are all, always, made of rock. But there's a permanent naïveté down inside, the product perhaps of those years of digging holes in the back yard and daydreaming about reaching China. I still occasionally catch myself regarding mountains as piles of "earth"—soil, dirt, rather than solid rock with topsoil spread as thinly over them as verdigris on a statue.

The diminished height of the trees means that now the breeze gets at us, and the damp shirts on our backs feel almost icy. There is so much moisture in the air that, from about three thousand feet upwards, so long as we have been in deep shade we could see our breath. On a seventy-five-degree day in mid-August! Now, in sun, there is a whipping breeze as we stop to gawk: views. Mountains, everywhere. This, too, is always surprising, every time I come up.

Living up against one side of Kinsman, I have this feeling of an isolated ridge running due north and south, surrounded by low foothills. There are perhaps five substantial peaks on the ridge: Layfayette (5,242 feet), Cannon (4,114), North Kinsman (4,293, of which we've now climbed about 4,200), South Kinsman (4,358, half a mile of easy ridge away), and Moosilauke (4,802). And then thirty miles to the north there's Washington (6,288) and, over in Vermont, another north–south range, not quite so high as the White Mountains. That's about it. It comes as a shock, then, to pop out on top of any of the local mountains and see peaks stretching into the distance in every direction. There are forty-six peaks in New Hampshire that reach four thousand feet or better, five in Vermont, twelve in Maine, and from the top of the White Mountains you can see over the Green Mountains of Vermont and 140 miles into the Adirondacks—where there are dozens more. Four thousand feet makes an appreciable mountain when the base altitude is one thousand feet or lower, as it is in most of New England. For every four-thousand-footer there must be two more that reach three thousand feet. Hundreds of mountains within a hundred-mile radius. New England is much more mountainous than life in its cozy valleys would ever indicate.

North Kinsman doesn't quite reach above timberline. It flirts with it, but there are scrub firs right to the very top of the peak—scrub, but tall enough to block the view. Accordingly, although there is a breathtaking lookout to the east, north, and south from a six-hundred-foot cliff overhanging Kinsman Pond, the view back into my home valley is frustratingly obscured. We have to walk another half mile over to South Kinsman—and climb sixty-five more feet—to be able to see the valley where we started out. Ah, yes—there's my house, right there.

We sit on a granite shelf overlooking Kinsman Pond and eat our lunch, tired legs tingling with relief at the chance to sit down, sweaty clothes blowing dry in the breeze. I try to bushwhack to a western viewpoint on North Kinsman and discover that the gnarled and twisted fir scrub is almost literally impenetrable. We pick out as many peaks as we can with the AMC maps and guidebook, use field glasses to look for beavers in Kinsman Pond below us (and don't see any), repack our orange peels and plastic baggies into the small day pack we brought up with us. We stretch out full-length on the rocks in the bright sun—out of the wind—and almost doze for a few minutes before starting back down. And then we head down the trail, stiffened legs protesting at being put back to work, toes threatening to blister from being driven forward in our boots as we teeter against the pull of gravity. Pause to relace our footwear more tightly Off we go.

As gravity crumples our toes in our boots and punishes our knees and thigh muscles, so it works inexorably at the trail we follow down the mountain. Despite what appears to be thick mulch and humus in the tangled spaces in that impenetrable scrub at the peak, there is obviously little topsoil to speak of anywhere on the upper reaches of the mountain. The bared granite of the trail is crisscrossed in a frantic patchwork of roots and rootlets, tendrils of growth scrabbling for purchase on the impervious stonework of the upper mountain. Every rootlet holds back its own tiny, perfectly level paddy of silt, its uphill side topped up with powdered rock. Eventually this rock dust will mix with the organic wastes that collect on the mountain to make something like soil—at the rate of about an inch every hundred years. For now, it is a fine, sterile paste puddled in the crook of every rootlet. Of a consistency like automobile rubbing compound. Or jeweler's rouge.

Looking at that paste, I am driven to consider the height of the mountain. Three thousand feet of granite, to be reduced by gravity—by that same paste-making process—to level ground. (Although the valley below will, of course, slowly fill, and thus rise to meet the subsiding peak.) I consider that the geologists estimate that these mountains have been worn down to flatness (by that paste-making process) and thrust back up again three or four times in the history of the earth. It is a thought that bolsters patience when the trail back down seems too long, when it is taking too many steps with my aching thigh muscles to get back to the car.

Idle thoughts on an idle walk. Too many steps in the softening, slanting light of early afternoon, too easy to fog out, become dazed with mild fatigue, and stop paying attention on the way down. I try to stimulate myself with my own unanswered questions. What makes these bands of forest species, the gross changes from hardwood to softwood and back again, that we keep walking through? What causes the sharp shifts in terrain, from flat to steep pitch? Why are there flat places on the sides of the mountains, level meadows, when gravity and erosion are supposed to be cutting everything back toward the solid core of the mountain? What put the rubble, so neatly sorted by size, in the creek-bottom path? Why, in this wild place, have we seen so little wildlife, so few birds? My questions are easily diverted to vegetation, forest type, tree species; these are phenomena that involve processes observable within a single lifetime, and therefore seem more answerable than questions aimed at the ponderous implacability of the mountain itself.

But we've been to the top of the mountain and back again, and now must realize that we've barely gotten a glimpse of the basic shape that it represents. It is hard to tell from a walk up its spine; one must piece it together from contour maps and different viewing angles. Kinsman is gentle and gradual on this side, and sharply gouged out into a cliff face on the other. It's a long ridge of a mountain, with one side that is an extremely regular inclined plane, virtually a straight line from the valley floor to the ridge line. Between the north and south peaks there is a huge glacial cirque leading down to the southwest, descending from a bowl shape above into a sharp ravine with bare rock slides on its sides; lower down it is known as Slide Brook. To the north and south Kinsman segues into more mountains; it is in effect only a pair of peaks on a wandering ridge. A few miles to the north the ridge plunges into Franconia Notch; to the south it drops into Kinsman Notch.

These two notches are only ten and a half air miles apart; in between them is a wall of granite that forms the terrain, the lay of the land, the very character of our entire valley, that has undoubtedly shaped the lives of everyone who has settled here since the 1770's. It is that great granite presence that seems to give the valley its stability. (Never mind about those three or four times it has been worn down and upthrust again.) I don't know how it is formed, why it is shaped the way it is, what makes it such a benign and beautiful peak. My assumption at this point is that it is possible to find all those answers, and as this process goes on, perhaps I will. If I do, maybe then I'll understand why all of us who live in Kinsman's morning shadow love it so.

Plumb down the middle of the Atlantic Ocean runs a
majestic range of submerged mountains—the Mid-Atlantic
Ridge. No mountain range on land can compare with it,
not only in size, but in the stark outline of its peaks and
rocky terraces. . . . It is a silent world, unbroken even by
the descent of myriads of radiolarians falling softly like
snow from the surface waters above.
—RONALD FRASER, *The Habitable Earth*

Chapter **4**

Mountain-Building's Missing Links

What *makes* mountains? The question threatens to stop the
imagination in its tracks. That mountains could actually have
been made—manufactured, thrust up, raised by whatever inconceivable forces—is almost impossible to envision. One can
only picture it through a kind of time-lapse photography in the
head, allowing billion-year processes to take the appearance of
uninterrupted flow. One must transmute physical characteristics in the inner eye, seeing the earth not as a chunk of rocklike
solidity but as something closer—in composition if not in
shape—to a very thin-shelled egg. Most particularly, our sense
of scale must be juggled, to see that, as Harvey Manning puts
it, "the highest mountains and deepest valleys are nothing
more to the earth as a whole than the scratches and dust on a
billiard ball."

That, too, is hard to imagine, particularly in relation to some of the mountain world's more awesome scenery, but it is important to get the true scale in mind. Most relief maps, globes, and other model representations of the earth's surface exaggerate the vertical relief, usually by at least forty to one. Thus on a crinkly-surfaced relief globe a ten-thousand-foot mountain is represented by what is really, in scale, a four-*hundred*-thousand-foot rise—a distortion necessary to give us some feel, some clear indication that relief exists. An accurate scale representation would be too subtle to be believable to eyes accustomed to gazing up at real peaks and down at real valleys.

To understand an accurate scale, imagine drawing a twenty-one-foot circle on a gym floor with chalk.* Ignore for the moment the earth's not quite perfectly round profile: the chalked circle twenty-one feet in diameter could be considered a reasonable representation of the earth on a scale of one to two million. Now, if your piece of chalk left a line three-eighths of an inch wide, that line would blot out a scale distance representing not only the highest mountains (twenty-nine thousand-plus feet) but also the deepest known ocean depths (more than thirty-five thousand feet). Put another way, on a globe twelve inches in diameter, an accurate scale representation of Mount Everest would make a spike less than a hundredth of an inch tall. If you spun such a globe under your fingertips, you very likely could not differentiate between the continents and the oceans. An eggshell is rougher, in scale, than the surface of the earth.

To understand where mountains come from, it is necessary to know something of the composition of the earth that thrusts them up—to know what the raw materials for the mountains are. They are represented on our gym floor. The center of the chalked circle would be ten and a half feet from the chalk line. In the classical model of the earth's internal structure, the first

* For this graphic demonstration of true earth scale, I am indebted to Arthur N. Strahler, *Physical Geography* (New York: John Wiley & Sons, 1975).

five and a half feet from the center outward would represent the earth's *core;* the next five feet of radius would represent the *mantle.* The final structural layer, represented in our scale model by only the outside inch or so of radius, is the *crust*—that good solid ground under our feet.

That's the classical model, circa 1900. A rush of scientific discoveries in the past twenty-five years has added much complex detail to this picture. These discoveries have established the validity of *plate theory,* sometimes referred to, not quite accurately, as "continental drift." Simply put, the source of all our mountains is the collision of massive plates in the earth's outer layer—structural entities that are not even reflected in the classical model. But before plates can make much sense, it is necessary to grasp at least the broad strokes of the old-fashioned version of the earth's composition.

On our gym floor the inner five and a half feet represent the innermost twenty-two hundred miles of the earth's radius. This core is the heavy, hot, partially molten ball that is the center of the earth. It is composed mostly of iron, with a small amount of nickel, and, possibly, sulphur or silicon—the composition is still being argued. Its temperature is four to five thousand degrees Fahrenheit (2200–2750° C.), under pressures three to four million times those at sea level. Since melting points are raised by increased pressure and lowered by its decrease, pressure overcomes temperature in the first eight hundred miles or so from the center of the core, and that portion is solid. In the outer fourteen hundred miles of the core, lessening pressure allows the earth's internal heat to keep the core liquefied. While the earth has an average density of about five and a half, and most surface rocks average three or less in density, the core has a density of from ten to fifteen. It takes up about one-sixth of the earth's volume.

The mantle, comprising the next eighteen hundred miles or so of the earth's radius, is almost entirely composed of a rock known as olivine, the densest silicate material known, of a density ranging from three to six. If the core represents a sixth of the earth's volume, the mantle takes up most of the remaining five-sixths. The crust itself, including all the continents, mountain ranges, and ocean floors, is an almost insignificant portion of the total volume.

Under the pressures and temperatures within the mantle, the olivine may at some levels change into other forms, particularly as it works its way closer to the surface, where reduction in pressure allows the crystal structures to expand to less dense forms. Although we have no way of knowing precisely the composition of materials more than forty miles below the surface, scientists have deduced a great deal about the structure of those materials and about their changing forms. The perplexing question is not the *what* of the material, but the *how*—how it finds its way from level to level in order to undergo these changes. As best we can determine, the mantle material, when hit by the sudden shock of an earth tremor, reacts with near perfect rigidity. Yet when force is applied to it over long periods, that material . . . adjusts. Geographer Arthur Strahler likens it to cold tar, which shatters at an abrupt blow but if left alone will actually flow—slowly— downhill. The process within the mantle is still something of a mystery. It is known that the internal heat of the earth melts the rock of the mantle in small pockets here and there, and when it does, the molten rock is known as *magma* while it is below the surface, *lava* when it reaches ground level. It is assumed that some kind of convection currents bring mantle material to the crust level.

Magma can also cool and resolidify while it is still within the earth's crust; when it does, basaltic rock is formed in the lower layers of the crust, granitic rock in the upper layers. Thus the basic building material of the earth's crust underneath the ocean beds and deep down below the continents is basalt, and the basic material of the continents—and the mountains—is granite. The crust under the oceans is fairly thin, three to five miles in thickness, but very dense. The crust that forms the continents can be twenty-five or more miles thick, but it is considerably lighter, of an average density of only about 2.8. Basalt, in other words, is the underlayer of all the earth's crust; granite is the overlayer only in the land areas. Continents in effect "float" on top of the basaltic layer, and mountains in turn float on the continents—as Jerome Wyckoff puts it, "no more a load on the continents than icebergs are a load on the ocean." And like the icebergs, the mountains show a small part of their bulk above the surface while concealing the great portion of that bulk within the base structure of the continents they rest on. "Under mountainous areas the basalt layer may either follow the profile of the peaks far above it, or may be so thickened that it actually offers a convex surface to the earth's interior," according to Ronald Fraser.*

Earthquakes are the sound of mountain-building going on. Almost all our information about the interior of the earth comes from the monitoring of earth tremors, including the identification of the *Moho,* one other feature of the classical model of the earth's structure. Because shock waves travel at different rates in different materials, scientists have been able to determine from them that there is a curious division between the solid and liquid portions of the earth's core. The phenomenon was first demonstrated by a Croatian seismologist named A. Mohorovičić, in 1909, when he discovered that shock waves traveling deep into the earth and then returning to the surface undergo an abrupt change of speed about thirty miles down. This point, called the Mohorovičić Discontinuity, or the Moho for short, marked what was thought to be the clear dividing line between the earth's crust and the mantle.

The theory proved to be more important than its first experimental fruits. Earthquake tremors travel completely through the earth, no matter where their apparent focal point is located. Earthquakes also set the earth ringing like a gong, although at frequencies as low as one oscillation every fifty-four minutes. After the Chilean quake in May, 1960, for ex-

* *The Habitable Earth* (New York: Basic Books, 1964), p. 40.

ample, the earth "rang" for a solid month—time for seismologists to build up a tremendous body of data which, computer-analyzed, began revolutionizing our notions of the earth's structure.

Science does have an ironic capacity for taking bad news and getting good data out of it. Disastrous earthquakes provided much information, but another kind of disaster—man-made—provided even better raw earth data. A nuclear test, particularly of the underground variety, produces a sharper, more distinct shock wave than does a rumbling earthquake, and of course is more precisely timed. During the periods of heavy nuclear testing before 1970, those tests—whatever they may have done to the atmosphere and defense budgets—inundated the seismologists with new and better information about what was going on within the earth. In addition, efforts to develop monitors to enforce the various proposed test bans led to the worldwide installation of a whole new generation of sophisticated seismic equipment.

All the new data from all the new equipment showed quite clearly that the Moho had been a valid principle only dimly grasped. The original Moho concept was simply a point of demarcation, without much elaboration on what that meant: basalt down to here, olivine thereafter. In fact between the rigidity of the crust and the semirigidity of the mantle lies nearly a hundred and fifty miles of varying layers and discontinuities, transitional zones, and other seismic anomalies. The most important of the newly discovered layers is one of crystalline rock starting about forty miles down, a little below the original Moho, and extending another ninety miles. It happens to have a structure that at that depth's temperature and pressure allows it to flow. One writer characterizes it as "crystal slush." It is more formally known as the Gutenberg Channel, after its discoverer, the late Beno Gutenberg of Pasadena, California. It is the crucial element to plate theory, and thus to an explanation of our major mountain belts.

The term "crust" was first applied to the earth at a time

when it was assumed that the planet had gone through successive gaseous, liquid, and solid stages, and the crust was imagined to be the hardened froth bubbled up by the liquids boiling below. The term stuck, but "crust" turns out to be not too accurate a description of the superficial layer of the globe. Instead, current models describe an external structure called the *lithosphere,* which includes the crust but extends downward about forty miles toward the center of the earth. This outermost layer is of reassuring rigidity, but it happens to be fractured into six to eight major *plates* (plus some smaller pieces)—the vehicles of plate theory, which fit together more or less like the pieces of a jigsaw puzzle but which are in ponderous geological motion. The crust, whether in three-mile-thick sea beds or thirty-mile-thick continents, rides on top of the plates.

Below the lithosphere is the layer of crystal slush, called the *asthenosphere,* from *asthenes,* Greek for "weak." It is the Gutenberg Channel. It extends downward to about 130–150 miles. There are additional transitional zones, about which not a great deal is yet known, at 240 and 430 miles. Also, at about 2,950 miles there is a very large transitional area three hundred miles thick, in the vicinity where the core turns from liquid to solid.

Revising our mental picture of the number, composition, and location of the layers of the earth beneath our feet would hardly seem to constitute a scientific revolution, but that is precisely what the conception of an earth layer composed of plates floating on a kind of crystal slush has done. Actually, the idea of forty-mile-thick rigidities with whole continents on their backs is only a refinement of a body of speculation with which science has been toying for hundreds of years. It is the idea that the continents had at one time been joined to each other and had somehow moved apart. Sir Francis Bacon proposed theories in this area, as did Ben Franklin and, very likely, almost anyone else who ever noticed the peculiar "fit" implied by the shape of the west coast of Africa and the east

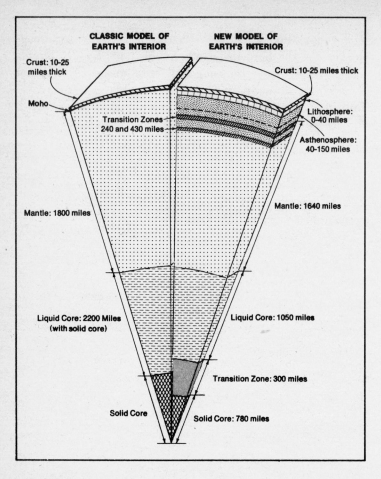

CLASSIC MODEL OF EARTH'S INTERIOR

NEW MODEL OF EARTH'S INTERIOR

Crust: 10-25 miles thick

Crust: 10-25 miles thick

Moho

Transition Zones 240 and 430 miles

Lithosphere: 0-40 miles

Asthenosphere: 40-150 miles

Mantle: 1800 miles

Mantle: 1640 miles

Liquid Core: 2200 Miles (with solid core)

Liquid Core: 1050 miles

Transition Zone: 300 miles

Solid Core

Solid Core: 780 miles

coast of South America. But nobody could suggest a force strong enough to move continents.

Of all the scientists seized by that tantalizing relationship across the South Atlantic, none was more taken than a German meteorologist and explorer named Alfred Wegener. He published his own theory of continental movement in 1915 and kept revising that work until his death in 1930. He didn't stop with South America and Africa but proposed that, with a minor juggling of contemporary coastlines, all of the continents could have been fitted into a single supercontinent. He called that prehistoric supercontinent Pangaea and maintained that at one time it contained all of the land area of the world. It began to break up, he said, about 150 million years ago, losing Antarctica, Australia, India, and Africa. Later, South America broke away from Africa, and it was only after that took place that the North Atlantic was formed, as North America split away from Europe.

Wegener became obsessed with his theory. He pulled together a voluminous array of scientific observations of much greater sophistication than mere matching coastlines. He found fossil remains and even living species which existed only on both shores of great oceans: how had they developed so similarly if those lands had not once been joined? He found evidence of massive climate changes—fossil palm trees in Spitsbergen in the Arctic, glacial scouring near the equator— that could only be explained either by vast changes in the spin axis of the earth or by continental movements. He found matching geological formations in Brazil and South Africa, in Scotland and the United States, so striking in similarity that they seemed to indicate that the oceans in between were recent interruptions of vast mountain ranges.

Wegener also pointed to the continental shelves, those areas of shallow sea extending miles beyond the fringes of all the world's land masses. These, he said, are the true continental boundaries. He pointed out that there are few intermediate depths in the oceans, that the earth is either continental land-mass (including continental shelf) or true ocean bed with depths of over a mile. These, he said, are the only two classes of earth surface. If the continents are not simply to sink into the ocean floors from their immense weight, then the material of the ocean floors must be much denser than that of the continents to provide isostatic balance. He found gravitational readings which tentatively supported this thesis, but accurate readings at sea, which would indicate the relative density of sea floor material, were beyond the technological capabilities of his time. When the technology was developed after his death, the readings he predicted were obtained.

It doesn't do to make a Galileo out of Wegener. There were other drift theorists with their own versions of landmass movements and their own collections of evidence to back up their theories. An explanation of mountain formation was not the first order of business for Wegener or for any of the others. In fact, the questions of distribution of species and historical climate changes attracted more scientific attention than did jigsaw puzzle work with coastlines. In time a considerable body of evidence accumulated which built a superstructure of valid scientific thought over the basic idea that the continents had indeed moved about. But the proof of that basic idea would not come clear. Wegener himself never came up with a force powerful enough to push continents through or over ocean floors, and he realized it. Drift theory, he admitted, was still looking for its Isaac Newton. He also made the mistake of mixing some dubious arguments among his sound ones, and by the time of his death the arch conservative hierarchy of the earth sciences had virtually dismissed his theories.

The key that continued to elude the early drift theorists lay in the ocean floors. The continents did not have to move through or over them; the ocean floors moved with the continents. Continents do not drift; plates do. Massive, rigid, forty-mile-thick plates, which may or may not happen to have continents on their backs, grind inexorably across the periphery of the globe. Inconceivable, of course: if the force to move continents through ocean floors could not be found, the force required to dislocate these infinitely more massive structures was beyond imagining. The early theorists had all the parts of a theory except one: the Gutenberg Channel. It was the missing link in drift theory. This "weak" layer, the "crystal slush," by its very softness and its ability to flow provided the lubricant on which the plates could ride.

Drift theory never did get its Newton; instead, it got half a dozen. The story of the post-1950 research in drift theory reads like a good detective novel, involving multinational investigations across disciplines as diverse as botany and archaeology, a brash piling of theory upon theory that would be scientifically scandalous if those theories had not proved out step by step with irrefutable scientific evidence. The current proof rests, interestingly enough for our purposes, on the discovery of the greatest mountain range of all.

That range is forty thousand miles long, a thousand miles wide, encircles the globe twice, and covers more area than all the continents combined: it is the mid-ocean ridge. In the mid-Atlantic it has peaks rising six thousand feet above the ocean floor and a rift down the center that makes the Grand Canyon look like an irrigation ditch—or would, if we could only see it. (The rift comes ashore at one end in Iceland's Rift Valley and at the other end—after looping around South Africa—in the Great Rift Valley of East Africa.) From that rift flows lava, underneath the sea. The lava, if it is not actually pushing apart the plates that lie on either side of it, is at least causing those plates to grow. The Atlantic is growing wider at a rate of about one inch per year; if Columbus were to sail today, he'd have about forty feet farther to sail than he did in 1492.

Perhaps the single most telling line of proof of plate theory derives from magnetism. Archaeologists have known for some time that when the clay for pottery or brick is fired and then cools, it becomes magnetized—faintly but measurably so—along the same alignment as the earth's magnetic field. It has also been known for some time that the earth's magnetic poles have moved about from time to time and that the magnetic field has even "flipped," reversing south and north, several times in the past. This knowledge has been useful in helping archaeologists date their findings: when kiln-fired material from antiquity is found "in place," its magnetic alignment can be checked against the established dates for shifts in the earth's magnetic field. For a long time the most recent known field reversal was one that occurred seventy thousand years ago. But discoveries in the 1960's uncovered a reversal that happened only about thirty thousand years ago and lasted perhaps a thousand years. Very handy for archaeologists. It was also discovered that the same kind of magnetic alignment that affects bricks and pottery also takes place during the cooling of volcanic rock, although much more faintly. Very handy for drift theorists.

Originally it was assumed that this phenomenon showed only that the poles had moved. Then a British group found that material from different continents pointed to completely different "tracks" for what should have been the same polar movement. The wandering progress of the North Pole could not be different for Scotland than it was for India. The only possible deduction, therefore, was that it was not the poles but the continents themselves that had done the moving. Aha! But further proof was sought.

Drift theorists such as Arthur Holmes of the University of Edinburgh had for some time believed that new material from the interior of the earth was quite possibly coming to the surface in the mid-ocean ridges. There is another kind of ocean floor anomaly found well away from the mid-ocean ridges: the ocean trenches, narrow but immensely deep gorges (up to thirty-five thousand feet deep), such as those off the coasts of Chile and Japan. Perhaps, proposed Holmes, old, cold crustal material was sinking back into the interior of the earth at the bottoms of those trenches. A Princeton University scientist named Harry Hess elaborated the theory in 1960, suggesting that the new material surfacing as lava in the ridges was indeed making new ocean floor, then gradually traversing the ocean width to be devoured, millennia later, in the trenches. Hess's work provided a clear and coherent picture of what was actually happening, but it was lacking the kind of hard physical evidence required by so conservative a discipline as geology.

Meanwhile, oceanographers were carrying on work suggested by Wegener thirty years before: they were trying to measure the magnetic characteristics of the ocean floor from seagoing research ships. They were puzzled by their findings. The earth's magnetic field in many ocean areas seemed to change from very strong to very weak and back again. The ocean floor seemed to be made up of alternating bands or stripes of strong and weak magnetism. It made no sense.

Two researchers at Cambridge University wrung the sense out of it, however, and in September, 1963, they finally nailed into place the last loose element in plate theory. Suppose, said Fred Vine and Drummond Matthews, that—just as Hess had proposed—new crustal material has been surfacing in the rifts that mark the centers of the mid-ocean ridges throughout the immense stretches of geologic time. That new material would spread in both directions away from the center of the rift. It would cool as it spread. As it cooled, it would take on—in effect "record"—the changes in the magnetic field of the earth, just as did the archaeological potsherds which led to the discovery of the phenomenon of magnetic imprinting. Those alternating "strong" and "weak" magnetic readings obtained from the ocean floor would in fact be readings of the reversals of the magnetic poles, and would provide the same kind of historical time check on the process. More important, if the ocean floor is spreading evenly away from the ridges, then the same record will be laid down on both sides of the rift, each side a mirror image of the other.

Just such magnetic patterning was found, not only in connection with the mid-Atlantic ridge but also in similar rises in the Indian Ocean. As Nigel Calder puts it, "The ocean floor turns out to be like a gargantuan version of the column of rocks of different ages that can be seen in a cliff face on land, only laid on its side with the youngest rocks at the mid-ocean ridge and the oldest rocks thousands of miles away towards the margins."* Clear confirmation of the Vine–Matthews hy-

---

* *The Restless Earth* (New York: Viking, 1972), p. 41. For a more technical treatment of the development of plate theory, see Walter Sullivan, *Continents in Motion* (New York: McGraw-Hill, 1974). This chapter depends heavily on the information and clear explanation provided by both books.

pothesis of 1963 didn't come until the late 1960's and early 1970's, primarily from data gathered by the research ship *Glomar Challenger*. Meanwhile J. Tuzo Wilson of the University of Toronto had published a paper in 1965 which first clearly proposed that the mobile belts—where the mountains are—are the dividing lines between rigid plates. Dan Mc-Kenzie of Cambridge and Jason Morgan of Princeton worked out geometrical laws that explained the location and movements of those plates. The laws were published in 1967 and 1968. That work brought a flood of new support for and confirmation of plate theory, much of it from the biggest names in theoretical geology.

By the mid-1970's geology had passed through the scientific equivalent of a religious conversion so far as plate theory was concerned—although there were a few distinguished holdouts, notably among the Russians. As a geologist told Nigel Calder, "Ten years ago, you couldn't become professor at a U.S. university if you believed in continental drift; now the opposite's true."

So the plates move. But what does this signify for mountains? Finally, after this long scientific suspense story, we come to the force that pushes the mountains up. A few principles of plate behavior can be established. As the plates move, powered by ponderous convection currents within the mantle, they necessarily bump into each other. Along the edges, where the bumping happens—where mountain-building takes place —is where all the geologic action is: nothing much goes on in the center of a plate. Therefore, these active edges can be located, even under continental mass or deep ocean, by studying earthquake activity, which occurs most regularly and frequently along the junctures where plates meet.

There are no gaps between plates. Two plates can draw away from each other. But if they do, molten material from the layer of slush—magma, or, if it makes it to the surface in the molten state, lava—will simultaneously fill the gap. When it does, a ridge is formed, as has been happening in the ocean beds for millions of years. Plates rarely separate in land areas; when they do, a rift valley is formed, such as those in Iceland and East Africa.

The plates also do not overlap. In the event of a head-on, plate-to-plate collision, one plate slips under the leading edge of the other, then bends immediately downward, sharply so, and passes slowly on down to be reabsorbed into the slush layer of the Gutenberg Channel. As the plate bends downward it also pulls the leading edge of the superior plate slightly downward, so that the meeting place of the two plates forms an ocean trench. This trench thereafter functions as a repository for the massive quantities of sediment that will spill off from both downward-curving plates.

As the advancing plate curves downward, its passage into the softer layer below causes earthquakes. The true focus of these quakes is well down within the asthenosphere, but the effect is felt most severely at the point on the earth's surface directly over that focus—the *epicenter*. The friction of the plate's passing generates a great deal of heat, as well as earth tremors; when the heat generated is sufficient to melt the rock of the crust above, the result is volcanic activity. The volcanoes will always arise on the landward side of the ocean trench—that is, on the stationary or superior side of the juncture of the plates.

There is one other kind of plate motion. One plate can also slide alongside another, like a ship leaving a parallel pier. This motion results not in mountains but in a *transform fault:* the San Andreas fault in California is the typical example. There, the plate that carries the western fringe of California, its continental shelf, and a huge chunk of Pacific Ocean floor is moving north in relation to the plate that holds the rest of California—and the rest of the United States—on its back. Transform faults also commonly occur as transverse lines across both mid-ocean ridges and ocean trenches; they are caused by different rates of movement in various parts of a single plate structure.

The boundaries of a given plate will thus be a combination of ridges, trenches, and transform faults.

Continents ride on the plates. A continent cannot sink, no matter what happens to the plate on which it is located. (Sorry about that, Atlantis fans.) Continental rock is too light in weight to sink and the material of the ocean floor and the asthenosphere much too dense to accept it. When two plates which both have continents on their backs collide, something has to give. Flatland does: mountains are thrust up. One of the two plates will slip under the other, bend, and begin descending into the layer of slush; but an ocean trench cannot be formed by such a collision—too much material is being thrown into the juncture, and that material is too light to sink. Instead, the continental material on both plates is skimmed back from the advancing edges like butter on a knife blade. Jammed together, piled up, tripped and folded, faulted, broken, overthrust. Geologists have long been able to trace the history of just such motions in the naked strata of mountain ranges. But

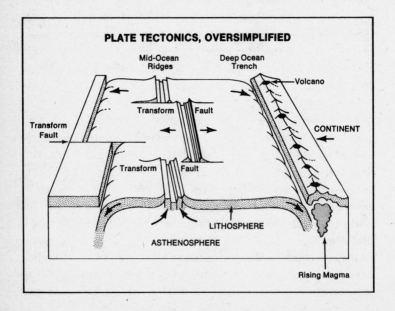

PLATE TECTONICS, OVERSIMPLIFIED

the incredible complexity of the movements always sowed confusion in any attempt at formation of a coherent theory of mountain-building. Only with understanding of plate action has all that complex motion become comprehensible.

Because continents cannot sink they are very old, older than the oceans. Although a plate without a continent can disappear entirely, completely consumed in the asthenosphere, a continent goes on "forever," perhaps being crumpled up from time to time into mountains, then being eroded down again into featureless plain. The only way a continent can "die" is to be eroded away entirely, deposited in the sea as sediment. Chances are good that it will then be uplifted again to form a new continent.

Plates can also change shape, of course, easily and in various ways. They can break along new lines by such mechanisms as transform faulting. One plate can weld itself onto another, particularly when there is a continental collision; in such a case the mountain range thrown up by the collision acts as a kind of surface flux to help bind the weld. Where plate edges run under continents, as they occasionally do, the continental overload will vastly confuse our neat picture of the plate's shape. Earthquake zones in such a situation are much broader and less well defined than they are when the plates carry only ocean floor. Changes in the shape of a plate are most apt to occur at three-way junctures, where three plates meet, all of them moving in different directions.

While continents do not die and plates do, it cannot be assumed that the descending plates disappear immediately. Seismographic records resulting from nuclear testing came up with peculiarities that for a while seemed to contradict not only plate theory but a lot of other clearly established notions of the earth's structure. The anomalies were finally explained as being caused by "cold" plates which had descended beneath ocean trenches right on schedule but had maintained their rigidity, or some degree thereof, well down into the asthenosphere. One such plate lies directly under the Soviet nuclear test ground in the Arctic and played hob with seismographic records for years before it was finally explained. It is the remains, scientists have decided, of a plate that began to descend hundreds of millions of years ago, at the time Asia crashed into Europe in the meeting that pushed up the Urals, one of the oldest mountain ranges in the world. The asthenosphere turns out to be, in Nigel Calder's elegant phrase, the graveyard of ancient plates.

Wegener's Pangaea, which began to break up 200 million to 150 million years ago, is practically current events as far as the earth's 4.6-billion-year history is concerned. Most of the continental movements that have been traced took place within the most recent 10 percent of that history. The Appalachians were formed perhaps 200 million years before Pangaea, when an earlier version of the Atlantic Ocean was squeezed dry as parts of what are now North America and Europe crunched into one another. There was also an ocean between Europe and Asia, which disappeared perhaps 225 million years ago in the collision that thrust up the Urals, now lying as a north–south stripe across Russia. That was when Pangaea started forming; it lasted only about twenty-five million years, splitting into two major ancestral continents that the geologists call Laurasia and Gondwanaland. Part of what would become North America stayed stuck to what is now Europe; part of what is now Africa and Europe split away with North America.

Gondwanaland started breaking up about 130 million years ago. South America split off from Africa, its westward-moving plate overriding the Pacific plate, causing the geologic havoc that resulted in the Andes—just as North America's split from Europe fifty million years later would eventually lead to volcanic activity in the Cascades and elsewhere along North America's western edge. Another piece of Gondwanaland that would become Australia and Antarctica broke away, losing India in the process. Australia and Antarctica separated less than sixty million years ago; India began crushing into the underside of Asia a little later in the crunch that would raise the Himalayas. Africa butted into the bottom of Europe, first forcing Greece and Yugoslavia into it and throwing up the Carpathian Mountains, then jamming Italy in, forcing up the Alps. That all started only about twenty-five million years ago; both the Alps and the Himalayas are still growing, as those puzzled surveyors of Mount Everest can attest. In the meantime the Mediterranean Sea has disappeared and been re-formed a couple of times, the land bridge between the Americas has submerged at least once (and should again), and such minor upheavals as the formation of the Red Sea and the Gulf of California have taken place.

The Rim of Fire around the Pacific presents a textbook illustration of the working of plates. The whole series of island arcs that marks that rim—the Aleutians, the Kuriles, Japan, the Marianas, the Philippines—all are marked by seaward ocean trenches and are alive with just the earthquake and volcanic action that is expected when one plate collides with another, then bends and plunges toward the center of the earth. These island arcs are all volcanic in origin, and they are all formed of andesitic lavas. Andesitic lava is formed when lava picks up a high content of silica by surfacing through the granite of the continental crust. Mid-ocean islands, by contrast, are formed of basaltic lavas, which have bubbled up through the basalt of the ocean bed. Inside the Rim of Fire geologists identify another circumferential Pacific line, called the andesite line. Seaward of that line the lavas are all basaltic; shoreward, the lavas are all andesitic. Thus the island arcs of the Rim of Fire are all in effect outgrowths of the continents to which they are, however subtly, attached.

Theoretical analysis has shown that a sphere with its upper layer under compression (as in the crust) and its next under-layer under tension (as in the mantle) will fracture, and that the fractures that result will be conical in shape, with the apex lying deep within the sphere's interior. The form such a fracture will take where it reaches the surface will be an arc-shaped depression—as in the ocean trenches that lie just seaward of all those island arcs around the Rim of Fire. The arcuate shape is the key, not only to these island arcs, but also to mountain ranges everywhere: there are none that do not lie in a gentle curve across the face of the earth.

The Hawaiian Islands almost seem to make plate action visible to the naked eye. They are not located at a plate boundary but are clearly the product of volcanic action. Plate theorists propose that they mark a hot spot in the earth's understructure, hot enough occasionally to melt through the moving plate above and pour up a mountain. (One of the mountains is probably the largest in the world. Mauna Loa rises only 13,680 feet above sea level, but over 30,000 feet from the ocean floor where it originates. It contains over ten thousand cubic *miles* of rock.) The islands are arranged in a northwest-to-southwest chain. By atomic dating it has been determined that the islands have surfaced at about one-million-year intervals. The eldest is at the northwest end of the chain; the youngest, Hawaii, is the southeasternmost, and current eruptions occur in the southeast corner of that island. The plate under the Hawaiian Islands continues to move to the northwest. The hot spot remains in place. Eventually those islands should grind against Japan or the coast of Russia—where the next great mountain range, very likely overshadowing the Himalayas, should be thrust up.

Continental bumper cars, push-'em-and-dodge-'em among land masses. Ireland was once part of Greenland, Boston in the Sahara, North Africa at the South Pole, the Appalachians in Eastern Europe. It will continue. Chunks of California will break off from the mainland—probably forming into our own little Western version of Madagascar—then move up to join the coast of Alaska, pushing up more coastal mountains as they do. Turkey is being spit out from between Europe and the Middle East like a watermelon seed, with devastating earthquakes a regular occurrence; it may well eventually lodge against the north coast of Africa. In fact, if the spread of the Atlantic and the corresponding shrinkage of the Pacific continue, it seems likely—two hundred million years or so hence —that the continents will move completely around the globe, and rearrange themselves into another Pangaea-like single continent in what is now the Pacific Ocean. I can hardly wait, says the would-be plate theorist in me: it will confirm all these theories.

Science is continually yanking the solid ground out from under our feet. It wasn't enough that "Galileo's tubes" put mountains on our beloved moon (and turned it into mere rock), put "invisible worms" in all the common stuff of our lives. The man kicked us out of the center of the universe, tossed our earth into the void. We used to stand on our stable earth and watch the sun and moon spin around us. Now we know better: we stand on drifting rafts, spinning on our own, and watch mountains heave—geologically—toward the sky.

The term "geologic" seems to imply glacial slowness, ponderous motion, and in that sense the science of geology can itself be called geological. The earth science has finally, however, begun to accept the dislocations and revisions necessitated by the drift theorists. Plate theory is really only one more link in a string of ideas that runs right through Galileo's rotating earth to such exotica as quantum physics. Ideas that say that reality is, roughly, the opposite of what we experience. We aren't the center of anything. Solid objects are made up of little pieces of electricity. Mountains float, and continents set sail. Forget geography as too impermanent; what we seem to need is a kind of geologic navigation, to find out where we really are.

In the incantatory language of convention, [mountain-building is] an orogene preceded by a geosyncline, receiving an immediate influx of bathyal sediments, followed by the accumulation of synorogenic flysch sediments preceding the first folding phase.—RONALD FRASER, *The Habitable Earth*

Chapter 5

The Heave and Surge of the Crustal Sea

Plate theory nicely explains the gross movements of the crust of the earth that have resulted in major mountain chains. But for the next level of detail—to understand why a given group of mountains is as it is and what makes it different from the next group—it is necessary to go back to older and less dramatic ideas. Scientists spent centuries studying mountains before the clarification of plate theory came along. The earlier conceptions—"incantatory" though their "language" may be—are not without their value, and plate theory does not necessarily invalidate them.

The search for the source of mountains has always been a search for uplift. What is it that moves these rocks, strata, masses *upwards?* Plate theory concerns itself primarily with movements parallel to the surface of the earth but does describe one source of uplift, that which occurs along the edges of continents in the crumpling together of landmasses. This uplift is called *orogenic,* a term which simply means "mountain-making."

But landmass within the continental boundaries can also be uplifted. The uplifting and subsidence of the earth's crust over broad areas—without breaking, crumpling, or other severe distortion—is properly known as *epeirogenic* movement, from the Greek *epeiros,* "mainland" or "continent." The term is of little use to anyone but geologists, but the movements are among the most massive that ever occur on earth: the gentle, deliberate epeirogenic uplift results in a *shield,* or *kraton,* that is, the great broad plain that forms the heartland of a continent. Just as Wegener divided the earth's surface into two types, continents and ocean beds, so geologists now further divide the landmass into two categories: shields and orogenic belts.

The shields are the oldest and most stable areas of the earth's surface. North America's is known as the Canadian shield, that of Eurasia is the Russian–Baltic shield. There are similar shields in Greenland, Africa, South America, Australia, India, and Antarctica. Rocks have been found in the shields that have been radiation-dated at 3.5 billion years of age. The oldest known ocean floor, by startling contrast, is only about seventy-five million years old.

These great shields may have had mountain ranges rising in their midsts in their past, but if so, it was during periods beyond the scope of current geologic analysis. The mountain-building that we understand with any certainty at all has taken place within the last 10 percent of the earth's history. It seems likely that in all the previous eons there would at times have been mountains within the areas which are now represented by shields. But the evidence long ago eroded away. The shields are solid, stable *peneplains*—the geologists' term for the flat, unrelieved plains that are the end product of erosion on land.

But still these shields move. They are, in some cases, even

now rebounding from the weight of the ice that pressed them down more than ten thousand years ago. Central Scandinavia is rising at about thirty-eight inches per hundred years. Hudson Bay has risen 1,175 feet by the same process and is still rising; another thousand feet should empty it. All of Canada is in fact rising and should eventually tip Lake Michigan sufficiently to dump its contents into the Mississippi River. It has also been estimated that all the continents—complete with the mountain ranges on their backs—respond to the gravitational pull of the moon just as the tides do, gently rising and falling as much as six inches a day.

The force that pushes Canada and Scandinavia upward is called *isostasy*. It is the same physical phenomenon that allows continental masses to "float" on the earth's crust only because they are counterbalanced by markedly denser crustal material elsewhere. If the crust is depressed by its load in one place, as with an ice cap, then it must bulge somewhere else to counterbalance. Remove the ice cap and the depressed area will rebound—and the bulge that balanced it will subside. Isostasy supplies the uplift—and subsidence—for the slow, gentle, continentwide epeirogenic movements. But pre–plate theory geologists credited isostasy with the narrower and more abrupt uplift that takes place within the orogenic belts—uplift now laid primarily to continental collisions. The reasoning is interesting, and the mechanism described is not discounted by later developments of plate theory. In fact, there are some mountain-building movements that seem to be explained no other way.

When a mountain range is eroded entirely away, as we suspect must have happened on the shields, the enormous weight is carried off by wind and water. It must be deposited somewhere, of course, and ends up in the nearest low place—just off the continental shelf on the ocean floor. That floor, much denser than the nearby continent to start with, now has the weight of the mountain range added to it in sedimentary form. Finally this great weight of sediment depresses the ocean floor into a down warp known as a geosyncline. When it does, the crustal pressure on each side eventually crumples the geosyncline. The sediment within it is compressed, melted, metamorphosed into other forms of rock by the pressure exerted by this folding. Some of it is folded downward, to form the roots of mountains; some of it is folded upward, to make rudimentary mountains. Then isostasy shoves the whole mass upward, like a cork popping to the surface after it has been poked under. *Voilà*, mountains.

This was the mechanism that historically was credited with the formation of the Appalachians, the Atlas, the Urals, and the Alps—until the clarifications and refinements of plate theory came along. It was particularly attractive in its time because it explained those perplexing marine fossils so often found at high altitudes in mountain rock. Geosynclinal theory and isostasy correctly put the birthplace of mountain ranges in some former sea, no matter how those theories had to strain to put them there. Plate theory makes the process a little simpler: for two continents to collide they must first be separate, and to be separate they must have a sea between them. The squeezing out of the ocean collects the marine fossils to decorate the mountaintops. Nevertheless, geosynclinal–isostatic theory is still helpful in thinking about mountain formation.

A particularly useful portion of that theory has been the identification of *folding* as one of the four major motions of the earth's surface that result in mountains. Folding is simply the bending of strata, layers of rock, in order to accommodate the forces and dislocations at work in the crust. Sometimes the folding can be so severe that whole loops, hairpin curves, of strata are formed, which then topple over or even turn upside down. More commonly, convex folds are pushed up to form ridges, and concave folds sink to provide the foundation for the valleys between. Exposed as sensuous curves in roadside cuts, these folds set our minds to imagining great phantom mountain ranges arching miles above the hills we can see. The exposed strata also provide an object lesson in the patience of geologic processes. It is hard to conceive that the stratified material is not liquid at the time it is folded, but it is not. It is solid rock, able to deform to those striking patterns without shattering only because no matter how unimaginable the amount of force applied by crustal movement, the rate at which that force is applied is so very gradual that the rock can actually manage to bend.

It can also break—in more precisely identifiable ways and at much earlier stages than in the toppled fold described above. When hot magma cools and shrinks, fractures occur; when there is no movement of the resulting adjacent rock faces, the resulting break is a *joint*. When the faces do move in relation to each other, the fracture is a *fault* (just as in the transform faults that occur in plate movements). When a fold is thrust upward so sharply that the strata break and slide over adjoining material, the action is called an overthrust fault. Overthrust faulting is what can turn folds topsy-turvy. Early geologists became skilled at identifying rock strata, but weren't so good at analyzing the mechanisms behind the location of those strata. They were continually being driven to distraction when they found rock of one established age sitting placidly atop other rock that was known to be millions of years younger. Overthrust faulting is usually the explanation.

Sometimes the uplift breaks segments of strata into integral blocks which can move up, down, or transversely in relation to surrounding strata. Block faulting frequently undergoes pronounced tilting. The Sierra Nevada of California is formed out of one such tilted block that is four hundred miles long, sixty miles wide, rises two miles above sea level on the east—including Mount Whitney—and plunges five miles beneath the sea on the west. The Tetons in Wyoming mark the spectacular uphill edge of a similarly tilted block. So do the Wasatch, which rise above Salt Lake City—although in the last case the tilt is in the opposite direction, western edge raised.

A third form of crustal deformation which makes mountains—along with folding and faulting—is the *dome*. Note:

deformation, not movement. A dome is formed well beneath the surface of the earth, when a pocket of molten rock collects beneath strata that it can't quite penetrate. Before it cools it will push that strata up into what is in effect a huge underground blister, with a skin of solid rock on top, magma beneath. This blister is a *batholith*. It does not work its way to the surface to make mountains. Instead, the entire area is uplifted by epeirogenic movement, then the surface of the uplifted area erodes until the cap of the batholith is exposed. Since that hard cap erodes more slowly than the softer surrounding material, eventually the dome is exposed. Erosion continues, cutting through that dome and leaving a jumble of crystalline mountains. The Adirondacks of New York are cut from a batholith almost a hundred miles in diameter. The Idaho batholith covers an area about the size of New Hampshire and Vermont combined—sixteen thousand square miles —that contains the Clearwater, Coeur D'Alene, Salmon River, and Sawtooth mountain ranges. The Coast Range batholith is even larger, stretching a thousand miles from British Columbia up into the Yukon.

While the batholith itself does not work its way to the surface (except in the negative, erosional sense), it may send up a *pipe* or vent to the surface to relieve its internal pressure. When the pipe reaches the surface, the fourth type of mountain-building occurs: a volcano is formed. Volcanoes can flow quietly, in which case they form the *shield* type of mountain— broad, gently sloped, like Mauna Loa. Or they can erupt explosively, forming a *cone* volcano, such as Japan's perfect holy mountain, Fujiyama. In either case, volcanism is the fastest form of mountain-building there is, the only form that is observable within a human lifespan. Fault action, the next fastest method, is so abrupt and disruptive when it happens that its occurrence is usually associated with earthquakes. But while the San Andreas fault slipped some twenty-one feet transversely during the San Francisco earthquake of 1906, and displacements of up to forty-seven feet were recorded in the

Good Friday earthquake in Alaska in 1967—one of the strongest shocks ever recorded—most land displacements along fault lines are on the order of inches per each movement.

Compare that with the fantastic history of the volcano of Paricutín, which was born in 1943. Reports of its rate of growth vary wildly, but it does seem to have gone from a smoking vent in a cornfield in Mexico one day to a hundred-foot cone erupting ash and cinders the next. Within two weeks it was over four hundred feet high; it reached a thousand feet—and wiped out two villages in the process—within the year. When it went dormant nine years later it was 1,350 feet high, and had spread flowing lava six miles from the crater.

What goes swiftly up can even more swiftly come down, of course. The most devastating natural phenomenon known is a form of volcanic eruption that can be characterized as nothing less than the explosion of an entire mountain. That's what happened in 1883 when Krakatoa exploded, just west of Java, blowing out more than four cubic *miles* of rock in a single blast. The eruption in 1902 of Mount Pelée on Martinique in the Caribbean is generally regarded as one of the worst volcanic disasters of modern times, but its death toll of thirty thousand was more the result of poisonous gases than of the explosive force of an eruption. Katmai, on the Alaskan peninsula, blew out in 1912, leaving a *caldera*—the depression formed when a volcano either blows up or collapses on itself—that was two miles wide and thirty-seven hundred feet deep. One of the biggest such explosions of all must have been that of ancient Mount Mazama, in what is now Oregon, about sixty-six hundred years ago. That eruption blew away the top four thousand feet of the mountain and left lovely Crater Lake, five and a half miles in diameter and, at two thousand feet, the deepest lake in North America, to fill its caldera.

Crater Lake is in the Cascades, a string of volcanic mountains stretching from Mount Baker in the north to Shasta and Lassen Peak in the south. There are extinct volcanoes in the

Datil and Jemez mountains of New Mexico, the San Juans of Colorado, the San Franciscos of Arizona—as well as massive lava flows, cooled since ancient times, in Washington and Idaho. Yellowstone Park shows active volcanism, of course, and there are areas of geothermal activity in most of the western states. But for active volcanism, nothing in North America compares with the western half of the Rim of Fire: Russia's Kamchatka Peninsula, for instance, has 127 active volcanoes in its six-hundred-mile length.

Although folds, faults, domes, and volcanoes are the four basic mechanisms for mountain-building, it is seldom possible to credit any single form of uplift with the creation of a mountain range, except in the case of isolated volcanoes. For an example of the complexity of geologic process, it is instructive to look at the lower Hudson River Valley in the region above New York City.

Perhaps 400 million years ago there was a shallow sea in the area, inland of the current coastline. That sea collected enough heavy sediment—thousands of feet of it—to sag into a geosyncline. About 230 million years ago, a continental collision started mountain-building in the area. Massive overthrusting and faulting built quite a large mountain range there, and caused enough rippling, parallel folding inland to lay down preparation for what would eventually become the Poconos and the Catskills.

The mountain range was, in the next forty million years, eroded flat again, creating a peneplain. Then block faulting created a series of slightly tilted ridges—steep on the east, quite gentle on the west. Those, too, were eroded back into peneplain status. Until the beginning of the Ice Age less than a million years ago, the region probably existed as a relatively featureless peneplain marked only by a flat and sluggish Hudson River.

The Ice Age scoured out the countryside thoroughly, one glacier coming down the Hudson itself, scraping it into the familiar U-shaped glacial trough, leaving a terminal deposit —a *moraine*—at the mouth. Then isostasy lifted everything back up again, high enough to power much more rapid erosion rates. There was down-faulting to the east of the Hudson and, sharply, along the west bank of the riverbed, leaving the Palisades, which still tower on the Jersey shore. Up-faulting throughout the region left the country on both sides of the river quite hilly, in what is now known as the Hudson Highlands. Between the Highlands and the Shawangunk Mountains there remains what is left of the peneplain; west of that the Shawangunks mark the ghost of a tilted block long ago washed away to sea. Farther west lie the Poconos and the Catskills, which are actually formed from a plateau—not so much thrust up as eroded down, the current peaks marking the original surface layers of the plateau that has been eroded away between them.

The area is complex now, with folded overthrust fault structures, block-fault ridges, eroded plateaus, and glacial bulldozings. Yet it has been reduced to flatness at least three times in history—or rather prehistory. The complexity now exhibited is the result, not of the dramatic movements that our imaginations associate with mountain-building, but of the different rates of erosion of harder and softer rock. All of the drama is still there, in the understructure, but it takes a geologist to see it.

The Hudson Valley is far from the most complex geologic region in the world, of course; by a geologist's standards it might even be considered dull compared to "real" mountain regions. The Alps, for instance, represent an area originally a hundred and sixty miles wide, now compressed down to ninety miles, with overthrust faults shoving strata thirty and forty miles over the surrounding countryside. The Alps have been studied for generations and still defy consistent interpretation in every facet. If the Alps defy interpretation, the Himalayas—distant, forbidding, often inaccessible for political as well as physical reasons—are simply an unimaginable jumble.

We are not about to run out of mountains for the geologists to interpret. To try to interpret.

In spite of just about anything we can do, we mislead ourselves about mountains by conjuring up *catastrophism*, which is one idea that held up development of a coherent body of geologic theory for centuries.We still slip into it: it is the idea that major landscape features must have been created by catastrophic events. Early geologists just couldn't avoid thinking in terms of earthquakes, tidal waves, floods, and eruptions on a scale that far surpasses anything recorded in history. See the scale of movement achieved by the San Francisco and Alaskan earthquakes.

The opposite view is called *uniformitarianism*, which holds that processes that operate in the present also operated in the past and produced the same general results. These processes need not have operated at the same rate in both past and present. All of the processes of the past may not be observable today. But in general, as a working method for understanding the earth, the present holds the key to the past. It is a view that is considered irrefutable by current geologic thinking.

It is difficult to avoid slipping back into catastrophic thinking, however, when we contemplate a jumble such as the Himalayas—or when we blithely skip hundred-million-year periods in describing some of these geologic processes. The best way to avoid that slip is to get a firmer grasp on the immense blocks of time about which we so blithely speak. Epeirogenic movement can help provide the grasp.

The Colorado River has not sawed its way "down" to the bottom of the Grand Canyon, for example, no matter how we may experience the landscape there. Instead, the Colorado River has existed since before the Kaibab Plateau through which it now cuts was uplifted by epeirogenic movement. Undoubtedly the river has been tipped and tilted from time to time, given more velocity and force on its trip to the Gulf of California. When it was so tilted, it had a greater capacity to erode, and thereby managed to keep its own kind of balance. Even more graphic is the Arun River, which cuts a magnificent canyon across the Himalayas between the highest and third-highest mountains in the world, Everest and Kanchenjunga (28,168 feet). The Arun demonstrates not so much the cutting power of a mountain river as the gradual nature of the mountain-building process, even when that building is the clear result of continental collision: the Arun got there first, and has held its own as the Himalayas have risen about it.

The crustal matter of the earth can be moved about in three ways: en masse as solid material; as a liquid when it gets hot enough to melt; or as particles, as in erosion. En masse, the process is called *diastrophism:* folding, faulting, uplifting through isostasy or epeirogenic movements, geosynclinal activity, and the like. Whenever the crustal material is melted, it is called *igneous activity:* the extrusion of lava flows and volcanoes, the intrusion of liquid rock into strata beneath the crust to form batholiths. When crustal material is moved from place to place in particle form, it is called *gradation:* the weathering of rock and erosion of rock or soil. Each kind of crustal movement is associated with its own kind of rocks. Gradation produces *sedimentary* rocks—the accumulation of erosional material in combination with various organic substances, cemented into rock by time, pressure, and chemical changes. Sedimentary rock is, in its classic form, laid down on the bottoms of oceans and lakes. When it accumulates enough weight to form a geosyncline, then folding may start—the beginning of diastrophism. Diastrophism uses heat and pressure to change the sedimentary rock, thus making it into *metamorphic* rock. If in the process of folding or other crustal movement, sedimentary or metamorphic rock gets melted, then *igneous* rock is formed—magma below the surface, lava when it reaches the surface of the land. Identification of rocks—all the schists and gneisses and feldspars, as well as the gemstones and other stuff of boyhood dreams—is a whole other subject, far beyond the scope of this book. But these three categories of rock—sedimentary, metamorphic, and igneous—represent the first and most important gross classification in that identification.

He thought, not for the first time, that it would be his idea of heaven to sit on an observation platform somewhere and watch the earth change—watch mountains heave and fold, seas shrink, rivers wear down their valleys, continents drift and collide, forests dry into deserts and deserts burgeon into forests. The process, the constant flux, enthralled him. Man's life span was too short to be interesting: he wanted to see all the great slow events, right to the final cinder, the black hole.—MARGARET DRABBLE, *The Realms of Gold*

Chapter **6**

The Bare Bones of the Land

What we're after here is the reason for the shape of the land. Each of the four major kinds of mountain-building—folding, faulting, domes, and volcanoes—has a distinctive topographical signature. But any given piece of mountain terrain is usually the result of a mixture of these mountain-building processes, so the signature is seldom easy to recognize. The clues lie in the bedrock. If you can see the bedrock, it is possible to deduce how the land over that structure is being formed. For every piece of landscape there is a fairly orderly sequence of change. Once you know how the land is being shaped, it is sometimes possible to estimate at which stage in its development it is. You can't ascertain the actual age of the area without geological information about rock composition—and, perhaps, the help of radiation dating. But you can gauge relative development, which makes it possible to understand the past and predict the probable future of the landscape.

The classic example of folded mountains is provided by the Alleghenies of Central Pennsylvania, where parallel ridges and valleys succeed one another as regularly as waves in the sea. Even the oil company highway maps of the area show how the parallel slashmarks characterize the center of the state, as both streams and roadways all run down the center of the valleys between the folded ridges. Those valleys are fertile farmland, comfortably settled; the ridges between are heavily forested, mostly uninhabited, and provide a view of more, similar ridges, all of the same relative height, stretching away in wave-like succession. The roads that run down the valleys only cross ridges in the occasional water gap, where a stream has eaten through, or by long, traversing climbs that make manageable the steepness of the ridges.

The underlying structure of these folded mountains is very like the surface character, a succession of smoothly curved layers of rock—strata—folded into parallel waves. Where the sedimentary layers in this area have been gently folded, bituminous coal is often found; where the folding is severe, the compression extreme, that coal has been pressed into its anthracite form. Despite the seeming regularity of those folds that we can see, there are broken folds in these mountains that have been thrust twenty to forty miles to the west of their original location. But then, like the Alps, the Alleghenies themselves represent perhaps a hundred miles of original coast that has been crushed to approximately sixty-five miles of width, which is precisely how the folding took place—folding severe enough to leave sedimentary strata as much as eight miles deep.

Folding is just about impossible to recognize if there hasn't been some form of layering of the underlying rock. For layers to be present, the rock must originally have been formed from sediment, although it may then have been metamorphosed into another form. Sediments are laid down in horizontal layers, so any tilting shows that the rock has been folded or undergone other diastrophic movement. Geologists are forced by the niceties of their science into complex definitions of types of folds: synclines (downfolds), anticlines (upfolds), homoclines (strata that fold in one direction only, the other part of the curve cut off), and the like, but the distinctions are too fine for our needs. Generally, in a regularly folded region such as the Alleghenies, anticlines and synclines alternate with reassuring regularity, and the topography follows the underlying strata. It is possible, however—particularly in aged regions where erosion has had ample time to revise the landscape—for this orderliness to be reversed, so that the upfolds of the strata don't correspond to the upfolds of the terrain. It's a curious stage of development of folded landscape.

It happens this way. The instant that a fold starts pushing a ridge up, erosion starts trying to pull it back down again, working to reduce the mountain and fill the valley. If erosion on the side of one of those long, low, folded ridges cuts a ravine to the top—at a right angle to the ridge line—it will then begin to widen at the top, pulling erosional material from farther and farther back along the ridge. Finally it will cut completely through the convex cap of strata (anticline) on top of the ridge. As it continues to cut, it will make a narrow groove of valley running right along the length of what was once the ridge summit. Lo, the anticlinal mountain has become an anticlinal valley—concave in shape but with convex strata underlying it.

Meanwhile the material eroded from the ridge has been carried into the conventionally concave valley below, building it up. The steep sides of the ridges erode much faster than the stable, concave valley bottom. Eventually the land on each side will be cut away below the level of that concave bottom, and lo, the synclinal valley has become a hill, albeit with concave strata underneath. Mountain and valley have in effect changed places as the entire folded structure has been reduced. The process will be repeated again and again, so long as the folded understructure keeps causing varying rates of erosion—until the whole region has been reduced to peneplain.

If this sounds a complex and confusing jumble, that is only proper, since that's exactly how most chunks of landscape turn out: jumbled. Add to the above process the fact that most strata *plunge*—that is, the ridge and valley system they form is more or less tilted, end to end, one end of the ridge higher than the other—and the picture is further complicated. It may be almost impossible to dope out by casual observation, but it's worth having some notion of the processes at work, if only to explain the occasional direct contradiction you'll run across —such as the mountain ridge with strata that obviously run in curves totally contradictory to the shape of the mountain they underlie.

Under pressure to deform, rock can behave as an elastic or as a plastic—or it can simply rupture. If the response of the rock is elastic, it will snap back to its original shape when the

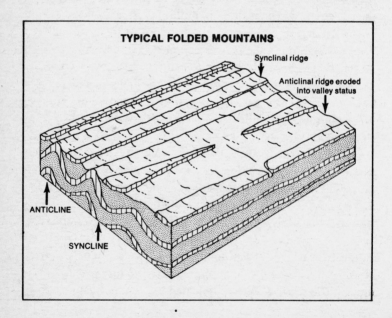

TYPICAL FOLDED MOUNTAINS

Synclinal ridge

Anticlinal ridge eroded into valley status

ANTICLINE

SYNCLINE

pressure is released; if it is plastic, the rock will deform by subtle internal recrystallization and will retain its deformed shape. If the rate of deformation is too abrupt for these adjustments, rupture will result: a fault or joint. Strictly speaking, there's no real distinction to be made between faults such as the notorious San Andreas, which is expected eventually to move Los Angeles north of where San Francisco now lies, and the little inch-by-inch displacements visible in any roadside cut. A fault is a fault: the movement can be in any amount, in any direction, so long as the opposing sides are displaced in relation to one another. (Joints, which have no relative movement between sides, don't build mountains.)

Faults can be categorized. A normal fault is a result of tension—pulling apart—at the earth's surface. One side is raised, the other lowered; the line of the break, called the fault plane, is steep, sometimes almost vertical, leaving a clean *fault scarp,* or cliff line. *Reverse faults* are the results of compression, with the upward-moving side riding over the side that descends, leaving an overhanging scarp. If the compression is strong enough, a reverse fault can become an overthrust fault —as in the Alps and the Appalachians, or for that matter in most other mountain ranges—with the overriding block thrust for miles over the lower material. Overthrust fault planes are almost horizontal; there's usually some folding in the immediate vicinity of the plane, caused by the same compressive force that makes the fault happen. Faults that have a horizontal rather than a vertical movement, such as the San Andreas, are *transform faults,* associated more with plate movements than with sheer uplift.

Sometimes normal faulting (under tension) will cause an entire block of strata to drop downward, making a long, flat-bottomed depression with uplifted fault planes along each side; the depression is called a *graben.* Its opposite movement, a block thrust up between normal faults, is called a *horst.* Faulting on a scale to produce mountains can be in the form of a gigantic horst—*lifted* mountains, of which the largest ex-

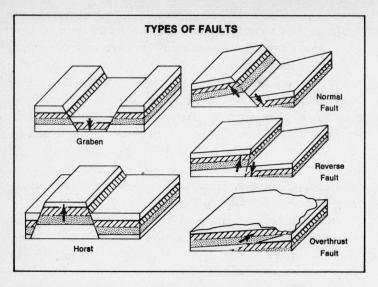

TYPES OF FAULTS

Graben

Normal Fault

Reverse Fault

Horst

Overthrust Fault

ample is the Ruwenzori Range on the Uganda–Zaire border, 16,763 feet high, rising ten thousand feet above the nearby plateau. But more common among fault-block mountains are *tilted* ranges, in which the block has faulted upward on one side, down on the other.

As with folded mountains, the force that makes fault-block mountains may manifest itself only in inches of displacement per year—or per century. And also as with folded mountains, erosion begins at the instant the faulting occurs. Thus the blocklike character doesn't last very long. Erosion gets to it too quickly, and the fault-block origin must be inferred from other characteristics. A dependable clue to the origin of a tilted block range is a vast difference in the angle of slope between the fault-line side and the remainder of the range. Approached from the west, the massive block that makes the Sierra Nevada of California has a sedate slope of three degrees; that side of the range is, in effect, the top of the tilted block. On the east, where the uplift occurred, the slope is a truly mountainous twenty-five to thirty degrees. But that eastern slope was originally on the order of *sixty* degrees. Erosion has cut back the Sierra that much, moving the crest of the range several miles to the west, causing the original fault line to disappear, and spreading the lowlands of the desert to the east with monstrous alluvial fans of erosional debris. Part of the depressed side of that fault—and thus the depository for much of that erosional debris—is Death Valley, at 282 feet below sea level the lowest point in the United States, with twelve-thousand-foot Telescope Peak towering immediately over it.

Death Valley doesn't hold a candle to the Dead Sea, of course, as far as lowlands go. There, a gigantic graben contains a lake the shoreline of which is 1,292 feet below that of the nearby Mediterranean. (At its deepest point the Dead Sea descends another thirteen hundred feet underwater.) The Dead Sea region has fault scarps on either side rising forty-four hundred and twenty-two hundred feet respectively, above sea level, for a total relief of well over a mile. (*Graben* may be a bit extreme for precise characterization of the Dead Sea area. It is more properly a rift valley, associated with the same spreading of crustal plates that created the Red Sea and the complex of rift valleys—and the Ruwenzori Range—in nearby East Africa.)

In addition to the Sierra Nevada, the Grand Tetons, and the Wasatch in the United States, and the Ruwenzori Range in East Africa, there are fault-block mountains everywhere else on the globe. The Harz Mountains in Germany, the Vosges in France, the Northern Pennines in England, the hills of the Gobi Desert in Central Asia—all are fault-block mountains. So are the Isles of Greece.

What happens with dome mountains is very similar to, and can best be understood in terms of, the development of uplifted plateaus such as the Kaibab, through which the Grand Canyon is cut. Plateau-country rock is laid down in horizontal strata, usually as an ancient seabed, later lifted by epeirogenic movement. Some of the strata, such as hard sandstone, are necessarily much more resistant to erosion than others, such as easily soluble shale.

When a stream begins to develop in the newly uplifted

terrain, its first cut will be a V-shaped notch. As the stream works through a resistant layer and reaches a weaker one, the rate of erosion accelerates. The weaker layer washes out and undermines the edge of the stronger layer above, which then breaks off, leaving a nearly vertical cliff face. Beneath the cliff the disintegrating weak layer crumples to a smooth curve down toward the stream below.

Meanwhile general erosion will have been reducing the overall surface of the plateau until a resistant layer is reached, so the uppermost layer in the canyon will always be a hard stratum of cap rock broken off in a vertical cliff. As the stream cuts deeper, that cap rock is continually undercut by the collapse of the weak layers below; it continues to fracture back away from the edge, widening the top of the canyon. As the stream uncovers more strong layers below, the process is repeated there on a narrower scale. Often a lower layer is stronger than the cap rock; both cap rock and lower layer continue retreating, but the lower layer at a slower rate. When the cap rock retreats far enough to leave a broad bench at the next strong layer, the result is an *esplanade,* familiar to any Grand Canyon visitor. Each resistant layer will form a shelf, and the weak layers in between will erode into smooth curves, giving the canyon wall the distinctive cap rock-slope-shelf-slope-shelf profile we associate with the canyon country.

A dome—a batholith—may be steep-sided or very gentle in its contour, but in the initial stages of its exposure to erosion its central portions are subject to mechanisms very like those that operate in plateau-and-canyon country. The material that overlies the dome is usually sedimentary, and erosion cuts through it in the familiar cliff-slope-shelf progression just described. Once the topmost layer of the dome proper is breached, however, the material revealed is a relatively unstratified crystalline mass; the orderly progression comes to a halt. The formation of mountains out of the body of the dome becomes quite free-form. The homogenous mass gets cut into peaks, ridges, canyons, and ravines that follow no discernible pattern—except where faulting or jointing within the dome has left lines of weakened rock for drainage to follow.

Around the periphery of the dome, landscape development is a little more predictable. The dome curves sharply downward toward its edge, and the sedimentary layer follows that curve. As the cap rock is eaten away from the center of the dome and toward its circumference, the angle of the dome increases. Mountains developed in the central core of the dome send spurs toward the periphery, following the ridge lines of resistant rock. Where these spurs run into the cap rock, they are abruptly terminated; the ends are in the form of triangular facets called *flatirons*—angled chunks of sedimentary rock arranged in a row around the circumference of the dome, pointing skyward and toward the center. These flatirons inevitably fill our imaginations with ghost mountains of immense height, since we have no visual reference to indicate how the steep angle at the periphery is quickly reduced to follow the contour of the dome. The mountain spurs that end in flatirons have triangular faces because the cap rock that ends the spurs is eaten through by the V-shaped canyons between the spurs.

Beyond the region of the flatirons, farther from the center of the dome, the upward-pointing strata are eroded into *hogback ridges* in concentric rings around the dome. These ridges alternate with steep, narrow valleys cut from the softer layers of sedimentary strata in between. These narrow valleys contain streams formed from dome runoff—part of a dome region's unusual drainage pattern. From the dome's center—at least in the early stages, before the mountains are formed—drainage is radial, like the spokes of a wheel. But when the runoff reaches the hogback ridges, the streams are forced to run in a great circle around the circumference of the dome. Where there is room for a stream, there is usually also room for a road, one that can be built without the expense of blasting or climbing ridges. Once human settlement reaches a dome region, then, the dome often acquires a peripheral road to go with its encircling stream systems. One such stream-and-road combination in the Black Hills is so distinctively circular that locals call it "the racetrack."

The shield volcano, that broad, gently sloped mountain built up by successive flows of liquid lava, will eventually erode into another form of dome mountain. After it becomes extinct, the shield volcano becomes, simply, a lava dome—but without the sedimentary layers above it. Thus the mountainous structures that erosion will cut out of it will not be apt to show the flatirons and hogback ridges that develop from sedimentary overlays. Roughly jumbled mountains are the only result.

The more familiar volcanic shape is the cone. Cone volcanoes are formed when the lava that surfaces is explosive. Lava can be acid, neutral, or basic in composition. It is generally basic where it surfaces only through ocean crust (basalt), and grows more acidic as more and more granite is encountered, landward. Lava that is basic in its chemistry flows quickly but relatively gently, spreading over large areas, such as the Deccan Plateau in India or the fifty-thousand-square-mile Columbia Plateau of the Pacific Northwest, where lava deposits miles thick have been laid down in prehistory.

Acidic lava, on the other hand, is highly viscous and flows slowly, bulldozing anything in its path—when it flows without exploding. More commonly, it encounters water on its way to the surface of the earth, and explosive gases and steam are generated. When the lava is depressurized at the surface, the result is the classic volcanic eruption, just like the ones in all those South Sea Paradise movies: lava, cinders, ash, and volcanic dust thrown high into the air, then settling back to earth around the original vent to build a mountain. If there are no periods of liquid lava flow between the eruptions, the mountain will be built as a smooth-surfaced cone with a slope of about thirty degrees—but it won't grow very high without some more solid assistance. What usually happens is that alternating explosive and liquid lava eruptions will build up a sequence of layers of ash and cooling lava, giving the cone more structural integrity than a mere pile of ash and cinders.

Temporary plugging of the neck of the cone can cause a buildup of pressure sufficient to blow the top of the mountain off, leaving a *caldera* composed mostly of the rubble that falls back in after the explosion. New cones can erupt through the floor of the caldera—that's what formed Wizard Island in Crater Lake. New vents can work their way to the surface on the sides of the cone, making smaller subsidiary cones, such as Shastina, on the side of Mount Shasta in California. Eventually the volcano will cool and the lava within the vent structures will solidify.

Ash and cinder deposits of the sort that make up a typical cone volcano erode quite rapidly. Over time various organic processes, plus erosion, turn its surface into surprisingly rich soil; the smooth contours of the cone get eaten away into more rugged and mountainlike terrain. The breathtakingly beautiful Mount Fuji is very young as volcanoes go.

After the period of mountain ruggedness, the cone will be eroded away entirely, leaving in its place only the vertical tower of solidified lava that cooled in the neck of the original cone. Then the lava skeleton of the volcano is bared, sometimes complete with subsidiary cones. Where fissures and fractures beneath the surface of the cone were filled by lava during the mountain's youth, *dikes* will remain—tapering, sharp-ridged walls radiating from the neck across the surrounding plain. Shiprock (7,178 feet), in New Mexico, is our own best-known example, an eroded volcano that exists now only as a tower of solidified lava with radiating dikes and surrounding mini-cones, like tree stumps in the desert. (Such towers of cold lava were the traditional favorite location for castles in Europe, and many still exist there, with cliffs for defense in place of moats.) There are other erosional volcanic leavings scattered through the Southwest, including far-flung spewings from erupting cones that have formed shallow but tumultuous sheets of lava far out in the desert, their surfaces so tortuous and impenetrable that the Spanish explorers gave all of them one common name: *malpais*-literally, bad country.

Generalizations about folds, faults, blocks, domes—or anything else found in mountains—provide only broad guidelines. Almost every mountain range is, in the end, a crumpled and broken mass of confused earth history, about which generalization is a shaky proposition. There are hulks of dead volcanoes in New England, and ridges folded neatly as piled laundry in the midst of that great tilted block that forms the High Sierra. Without access to the interior of the earth, the reasons for such mixture of landforms remain mysterious.

But generalization—categorization, really—provides some interesting clues, organizing principles to help guide our observation. Ways to look at a piece of land to see what it might have been, and yet may be. Look here, at the way this outcropping gets picked up again over there, down that ridge; it must have been all one piece once, with brontosaurs gamboling over its sides.

There's no intent here to discourage that kind of imagination; these generalizations should serve only to help control, to aim it more accurately. It is necessary to keep in mind those hogback ridges and flatirons, formations that point skyward like an index finger, asking us to believe that up there, miles above, mountains once towered beyond any human conception. It's an exciting thought, but wrong. Geologists say that the Uinta Mountains in Utah—which incidentally happen to be the Rockies' only east–west range—show signs of twenty thousand feet of uplift. Wow. Unfortunately for our imaginations, the Uintas also show inescapable physical evidence (in, for instance, their current relief of about six thousand feet) of fifteen thousand feet of erosion, almost surely occurring simultaneously with that fantastic amount of uplift.

The Appalachians, after all, have been thrust up and worn down again at least three times. They may have looked like the Rockies from time to time; they have also, now and then, looked like the plains of Kansas. The Himalayas, not only the highest but also the youngest and freshest mountains in the world, reach almost thirty thousand feet. But half of that immense altitude is beneath the fifteen-thousand-foot Himalayan plain they rest on. Something like fifteen thousand feet of relief would seem to be the realistic limit for earth structures as we know them.

Climate has a great deal to do with it, of course. The Peruvian Andes might just provide the exception to the rule of thumb I have now proposed: they rise to over twenty thousand feet within a hundred miles of the ocean (where the Peru–Chile trench drops off some thirty-five thousand additional feet into the Pacific, making a total of over nine miles of relief, the largest differential on earth). The Andes get almost no rainfall in the foothills; they stay brown and dry up to about five thousand feet, then turn green where the rainfall starts—a zone that extends all the way up to the very high snow line. The lack of rain in the foothills means that erosion there is quite slow. The foothills are nearly as steep as the peaks above them. This unusual erosion pattern, coupled with very rapid uplift from the collision of the South American and Pacific plates, may help explain the vivid relief.

By comparison, in southern California the erosion rates are ferocious, despite the region's reputation for sunshine and fair weather. The Los Angeles earthquakes of 1971 actually raised the nearby San Gabriel Mountains slightly, adding inches to their previous maximum altitude of about 11,500 feet. It won't last. "The San Gabriels," says Jerome Wyckoff, "would be as high as the Himalayas, and Hollywood a seaside Nepal, if the mountains were not being worn down almost as fast as they grow."

Rates of erosion are related to the availability of water. During the ice ages so much sea water was tied up in the polar regions that the continental shelves were exposed, and there was little free water available for erosion, especially in the northern hemisphere. (The ice itself eroded the land in somewhat different ways, as we will see.) Now our oceans are brimming full and water is relatively plentiful. Erosion is rapid; the scenery is changing fast.

Do not, however, mourn for mountains past. The shape of the land is the product of a struggle between internal forces of the earth and the forces that would reduce the contours of the land. When the reductive forces have had time to work, the land is brought relatively low; when the internal forces have been recently active, relief and gradient are high. Scenic splendor. The struggle between these two kinds of force has been going on since the earth achieved a solid state, and will continue so long as there is heat, water, and solid matter to work on.

As it happens, there is more land above sea level, and at higher elevations, in our present era than throughout most of the earth's history. We live in a time that follows closely on the heels of the most active era of internal forces that we've been able to discover. Or we are still living within that era, and the activity could even be increasing. The forces that make folds, faults, domes, and volcanoes must in large part be inferred from slim evidence—scientific measurements taken two or three steps back from the observable action. But what happens to those geologic forms after they've been pushed (or pulled, or intruded, or bubbled up) into place is directly observable, on a time scale that is comprehensible if a bit tedious.

It can be argued that man's widespread adaptability and the variety of his civilizations are products of the very variety of the landscape in which he dwells. The bare bones of that variety—folds, faults, domes, volcanoes—were mostly laid down before we began climbing out of the trees. But just the bare bones. Much of the rugged and beautiful detail that now delights us has developed, not just within the history of the various creatures lumped by anthropology under genus *Homo*, but within the span of post–Ice Age, civilization-building mankind. Us. That scenery is still developing; it is our privilege to be able to witness the process.

> All in all, it seems that the beauty of mountains is pro-
> portional to the rate at which they are being destroyed.
> —JEROME WYCKOFF, *Rock, Time, and Landforms*

Chapter **7**

Ultimate Forces and Universal Solvents

The forces that build mountains seem quirky, chancy, totally
accidental; the forces that pull those mountains down are
absolutely dependable. Forces within the earth keep shoving
portions of the crust upward, creating landforms, but another,
serenely all-pervasive force pulls them right back down again:
gravity. The biggest boulder ever split loose from the highest
mountain peak will, inevitably, someday end up as sand in the
sea.

Gravity. From the geologic point of view, the surface of the
land is always moving—downhill. The process may be as
microscopic as the rearrangement of organic compounds within
the soil, or as massive and dramatic as a landslide, but it is
continual. Any instability will always be resolved toward the
downhill. Soil creeps downward; hillsides slump and slide;

rock rubble trickles downhill stone by stone—or breaks loose in rock avalanches. Rockfalls and mudslides only demonstrate at high speeds and on gross scale what is going on all the time. The mountains are always coming down.

Consider that biggest boulder on the highest peak. For erosion to begin working on it, the boulder must either be broken free or broken up. *Weathering* is the process, which can be chemical or mechanical in nature. In chemical weathering, various naturally occurring compounds—carbon dioxide, carbonic acid, organic acids produced by vegetable matter—combine with the material of the rock, breaking it down into new forms. Iron-bearing minerals pick up oxygen to form the various iron oxides, for example, and other elements are similarly combined. Granite breaks down into quartz, mica, and clay.

Changes occur on the surface of the rock or along the joints and faults where moisture can penetrate. Some of the new compounds formed will have a greater volume than the old, and will break up the rock in their expansion. (Weathering can thus combine chemical and mechanical action.) Chemical changes can simply dissolve the rock away; the minerals are carried off in solution by the hydrologic cycle. Chemical weathering can result in rock surfaces that are either spherical or angular, depending on the type of rock and the chemicals at work on it. (Water working deep within the soil can produce rotten rock in underlayers far below the surface; such a rotted layer—*saprolite*—has been found at a depth of four hundred feet in the Brazilian jungle. Because of its structural weakness, any saprolite occurring around large building projects must be identified and removed to prevent foundations from crumbling after construction.)

Chemical weathering is the algebra of erosion, working to subtle, hidden formulae. But mechanical weathering is pure plane geometry, stubbornly logical, step by obvious step. Rocks can be worn down grain by grain by the forces of water and wind. More commonly, *frost-wedging* does the work, and it works on a larger scale. Water expands about 9 percent when it freezes. When it trickles down into the joints and planes of the rock mass, then freezes, it becomes a powerful wedging agent and pries the rock apart. At high altitudes—particularly in meadow areas above timberline, where the freeze–thaw cycle is pronounced—frost-wedging works over the exposed bedrock so thoroughly that the ground becomes littered with the sharply angular detritus, forming a *felsenmeer,* a "sea of rocks," which in turn becomes a snowfield in winter. Marvelous skiing there, when weather permits.

All of the joints of rock masses tend to run at right angles to the strata, or *bedding plane,* of the rock. The frequency of the joints—the closeness of their spacing—depends on many things, including how much pressure has been inflicted on the rock in the past. Deep within the earth, where the pressure is immense, jointing is sparse; as the rock is brought to the surface, by erosion or any other process, it expands. Large granite and marble blocks actually undergo measurable expansion after their removal from their bedding planes in the quarry. When the pressure on the rock is reduced, it can split, shatter, thereby increasing the frequency of the jointing.

Some of the great granite domes that occur in mountainous terrain are distinctly marked by a weathering process called *exfoliation.* Broadly curved joints form in a pattern concentric to the spherical rock surface. The joints may be a few inches apart near the surface, a hundred feet or more apart further within the rock. Frost-wedging or the unloading of pressure on the rock face (or both) causes the joints to separate, cleaving off great curved shells of rock, leaving behind after each cleavage a slightly smaller dome of the same spherical shape—reduced in size by degrees as each new layer of exfoliation falls away. The process is responsible for what look like concentric rings of ledge that curve across the surface of such famous faces as Yosemite's Half and Quarter Domes. The huge cliff that holds the Old Man of the Mountain—the famous granite profile in Hawthorne's short story—in Franconia Notch, New Hampshire, is a product of exfoliation. The profile, or rather the peculiar collection of planes and ledges that looks like a profile from the highway nearby, has been cabled and turn-buckled in place to protect it from the severe local frost-wedging which will eventually, inevitably, bring the Old Man crashing down.

The same exfoliation process, called *spalling*, can work on much smaller boulders, successively removing spherical sheets only fractions of an inch thick—but only if the structure of the boulder is spherical to start with. Rock that is broken loose by frost-wedging among joints and bedding planes generally comes out rectangular in shape. But rocks do tend to become round. On a rectangular rock, chemical and mechanical weathering can work on three adjoining surfaces at the corners. The long-term trend is for the corners to be knocked off and the rock to evolve toward roundness.

Salt crystals can shatter rock just as effectively as ice crystals can. In the rimrock country of the desert Southwest, water percolates down through the cap rock until it hits an imperme-able layer of shale, then flows toward the cliff edge. When it reaches the surface of the cliff-edge rock, it dries. The salts it carries crystallize in the superficial layers of sandstone at the lower edge of the cap rock. Eventually, this crystal growth shatters the sandstone surface, eroding a concave curve back underneath the cliff face at its lower edge. Native Americans used these niches for shelter, and where the niches were deep enough, as at Canyon de Chelly, built cliff dwellings in them.

The detritus chipped off the cliff surface by salt crystalliza-tion or by frost-wedging falls to the foot of the slope below and forms a *talus slope*—*talus* is a Latin root referring to the ankle joint, which seems particularly fitting for the soft piles of stone that fill the joint between cliff face and valley bottom. The loose rock debris of the talus slope piles up to the maxi-mum angle it can maintain without sliding—known as the *angle of repose,* a remarkably constant thirty-four to thirty-five degrees. The talus material is also known as *scree* (Norwegian for small stones), hence a *scree slope* (and scree guards on hiking boots). Larger chunks of scree will carom down to the bottom of the slope when they fall, while lighter pieces will lodge near the top. Thus, the contents of a talus slope are generally sorted by size, big chunks at the bottom, fine stuff at the top. If the cliff face is notched, the notch will funnel the falling rock into a narrow channel so the slope below acquires a talus *cone*. Cone or slope, the loose surface balanced just at the point of sliding makes for miserable walking, and most hikers will choose the long way around.

Once our mountaintop boulder is broken up by weathering, its pieces begin moving down the mountainside. (The bedrock mass can also break loose and slide, without benefit of preliminary weathering, if erosion makes the mountain too steep to support its own superstructure. That's what happened in 1970, when Mount Huascarán in Peru—22,200 feet high—dropped part of its peak, in the form of an avalanche of rock and ice, on the village of Yungay, causing the loss of some twenty thousand lives. The disaster was precipitated by an earthquake, but the damage was caused by the resulting avalanche. It's an instance that supports the idea that there's a limit to the height of relief features the earth can sustain on a long-term basis. More on Huascarán in Chapter 13.) When gravity moves any material downslope, be it bedrock or mere mountain dust, the process is known as *mass wasting*. It can occur with or without the assistance of water.

Eventually the rock particle loosed at the top of the mountain will make its way into moving water, and it will then pick up speed. The particles carried in a mountain stream grind away at each other (reducing their caliber) and at the stream bed (increasing the gradient, gouging loose more particles by abrasion) in their plunge toward sea level. If gradient be the elixir of youth, youth is powerful indeed; mountain streams use their extreme pitch to generate tremendous power. The load of particles turns the stream into a natural milling machine, grinding downward, ever downward—downhill, yes, but also down toward the center of the earth, following gravity's irresistible pull, notching and furrowing the mountain-side. Once that power has been generated, its effectiveness is staggering: witness the excavations of the Colorado and Arun Rivers, sawing through the Kaibab Plateau and the Himalaya Mountains respectively, keeping up with the uplift that raised the surrounding territory.

The steeper the gradient, the faster the stream; the faster the stream, the more abrasive material it can move; the more abrasive material it moves, the more deeply it cuts its pathway down the mountainside, increasing the gradient. According to Wallace Stegner, "There is a rough physical law to the effect that the carrying power of water increases as the sixth power of its velocity, which is to say that a stream moving two miles an hour will carry particles sixty-four times as large as the same stream moving one mile an hour, and that one moving ten miles an hour will carry particles a million times as great. A stream that in low water will deposit even its fine silt and sand, in high water will roll enormous boulders along its bed, and sometimes one can stand near the bank and see a rock that looks as big as a small house yield and sway with the force of the current."*

The same process can be looked at conversely: streams actually sort out the material they carry, just as—and more precisely than—talus slopes do. (Glaciers, as we will see, do not.) As the gradient lessens and the velocity of the stream is reduced, the larger particles, which may have been carried all the way from our mountaintop, drop out. At every lessening of gradient, the stream deposits everything larger than the maximum size it can carry at the new speed. Only the finest sand and silt make it to still water, remaining in suspension until the movement of the water actually stops, then slowly settling out.

Interestingly enough, this sorting phenomenon explains why and how streams curve. An initial diversion of the stream's

* Wallace Stegner, *Beyond the Hundredth Meridian* (Boston: Houghton Mifflin, 1962), p. 96.

course may be the result of a change in gradient, with the stream encountering enough of an upgrade that it seeks a lower bed line around the obstacle. But the stream's tendency is to increase the diversion. As soon as the stream changes direction, the water on the outside of the curve speeds up, and that on the inside slows down—for the same reason you need a differential in your car's rear axle. The slowly moving water on the inside of the curve can no longer carry as much sediment, and drops its particulate load; sand and silt bars always form on the inside of a curve in a stream. The faster water on the outside of the curve carries more abrasive material with more force, and therefore carves out the outside stream bank and carries those carvings away. Curves grow. Curves also migrate downstream by the same process. On a flat, as at a river delta or terminal moraine, a stream will silt up its bed so badly as it slows that it will eventually seek new routes, leaving a braided effect of intertwined abandoned channels. Often it will cut off and abandon an entire curve, forming the familiar oxbow lake. You can spot such lakes on the map of just about any area that includes a flood plain or tidal plain.

The stream of water that picked up our mountain particle at the peak may have started as a thin sheet of water pouring down a rock face, but quickly enough it will have sought out the nearest depression. It will find—or make—a funnel, a channel, a gully, a rivulet, a notch. A notch pulls other water sources to flow down its sides, eroding those sides, translating the notch into a V-shaped ravine. The mountain is beginning to get valley systems down its sides.

When the stream goes over a vertical drop such as a fault, creating a waterfall, it picks up speed and abrasive power. Most waterfalls form more gradually, when a stream flows over a break in a hard and resistant stratum and begins cutting away the softer underlying strata. The hard lip resists, stays in place, while the softer strata below are eaten away, so that the waterfall tends to grow in height. Abrasive rubble piles up at the bottom of the falls, and the swirling, eddying action at the base undercuts the lip material, which eventually breaks off, moving the waterfall upstream. As the waterfall migrates upstream, it leaves a gorge below, the steepness of the gorge sides maintained by the firmness of the same resistant strata that caused the waterfall to form in the first place. Eventually erosion will widen and finally remove the gorge. Similarly, the waterfall may cut its way back until it finds a less resistant path around the ledge; the stream goes elsewhere, and the waterfall is cut off and dies.

If the stream cuts its way down to hard bedrock, it will form one of nature's more delightful playgounds, with waterfalls, plunge pools, troughs, and chutes. If it can gather enough abrasive material into a depression in its otherwise swift course, it will begin to grind out a pothole, a cylindrical carving in the streambed with spiraling circulation that uses the abrasive material—often a single rounded boulder, called a grinder—like the pestle in a mortar, to deepen and widen the hole. Potholes make marvelous swimming holes, in the unusual case where the temperature of the mountain stream is bearable.

So long as the stream can continue to carry off all of the load it receives from its mountain source, plus that from erosion of the ever-widening V-shaped canyon it has cut for itself, it will continue to cut its streambed more deeply. Once it cuts its bed so deeply that it reduces the gradient that has given it the power to keep its bed cleaned, the cutting and deepening of the streambed stops. All of the subsequent erosional activity is transferred to the sides of the canyon; the V-shape is gradually widened. (The V-shape is maintained because the upper levels have been exposed to erosion for longer periods of time than have the depths, so more material is removed from them. Resistant strata will, of course, give the V-shaped profile a stepped appearance.) At this point the falls and rapids have been removed from the stream, and it can be said to be *graded,* the angle of its gradient having reached equilibrium with its power to erode. Its sedimentary load will now be carried to its mouth, there to be dumped into a slower moving or stationary body of water, usually to form a delta.

In the process of developing from a swift-moving mountain stream into a graded riverbed, the stream will often encounter larger depressions in which it forms ponds or lakes. The delta-forming process works here, too, as the heavily laden stream water slows immediately upon entering the pond and starts dropping sediment. Ponds and lakes are among the shortest-lived of landscape features; they get silted up very quickly, in geologic terms, and are turned into mere sluggish spots in the developing streambed, where the stream may loop and meander for a while before getting on with the serious pursuit of gradient.

What kind of valley system a mountain will develop can depend heavily upon which kind of crustal movement was responsible for lifting the mountain up in the first place. In plains-plateau and dome mountains, erosion is the main mechanism, cutting mountains out of the broad uplifted areas that were originally almost flat in appearance. In the early stages of that development, the country appears not so much mountainous as simply canyon-carved, as in the Grand Canyon country: flat plateaus divided by river channels. As the region matures, however, the V-shaped canyons are progressively widened, the plateau tops between them are gradually reduced in area, and the steep sides of the canyons are broadened out into something much more like mountain slopes. In effect the flat, plateau-top acreage is exchanged for canyon wall–slope acreage. The effect is as though the base level of the area is somehow switched from the plateau top to the valley bottom. At some point the region stops being a highland that happens to be dissected by canyons and starts being a mountain region that happens to have flat-topped peaks.

Theoretically the eventual fate of such an area is to be reduced to peneplain, but in actuality geologists recognize no true peneplain in existence today (with the possible exception of the Amazon basin—opinion is divided). There has been no recent period geologically stable enough to give erosion time to produce one. Which is perhaps a further argument that we live in a time of maximum scenic splendor, since there's nothing particularly scenic about a peneplain.

If a plains-plateau region were to be reduced to peneplain, however, it is only reasonable to assume that here and there on its broad surface a particularly resistant, isolated hump of rock would produce the peculiar type of mountain known as a monadnock—a mountain that rises conspicuously (and solitarily) above a surrounding peneplain. The typical example is Mount Monadnock, 3,165 feet, in southern New Hampshire, an area which itself rises about fifteen hundred feet above the surrounding rolling countryside. That countryside is not quite a peneplain: it has been uplifted from that flattened state, and erosion has again begun to cut some relief into its features. Such an uplifted peneplain is said to be rejuvenated; indeed, crustal movement has given it a shot of gradient to restore its youth.

The pattern of stream formation and valley development seems self-evident now, but it wasn't so until the 1800's. It was in 1802 that an English geologist named John Playfair finally disabused his fellow scientists of the notion that the valleys were somehow formed first, then streams came along to occupy them. Playfair's Law:

Every river appears to consist of a main trunk, fed from a variety of branches, each running in a valley proportioned to its size, and all of them together forming a system of valleys connecting with one another, and having such a nice adjustment of their declivities that none of them join the principal valley on too high or too low a level; a circumstance which would be infinitely improbable if each of the valleys were not the work of the stream which flows into it.

Playfair's Law isn't really susceptible to challenge, although there is the occasional exception to it, such as the small stream in a valley too large for it. There is always a consistent reason to explain the anomaly. Every streamlet has its own little watershed, giving it sufficient water to keep its own channel cleaned out. In very early stages, when streams are establishing drainage patterns, a stream will occasionally cut through the divide between it and its neighboring stream's source. The stream having the deeper bed already established will, in such a situation, overcome the other, "stealing" it—the process is called *stream robbery*—and adding the stolen flow to its own.

This consistency of development helps us understand the development of mountain ranges formed by the more complex crustal movements. Seen from directly above, a complex mountain region can be divided into a multitude of small basins locking together like pieces of a jigsaw puzzle, each with a system of divides separating it from the adjoining basins, each with a drainage stream that feeds into successively larger streams and rivers. (In arid lands the drainage streams may be dry washes for much of the year.)

As the region matures, the drainage basins are enlarged by the erosion of the slopes on either side of the divides; this gradually lowers the relief of the entire area while the basins evolve toward consolidation. Erosional material from the slopes may be dropped in the valleys well before it reaches a stream to carry it seaward. This deposit—*alluvium*—is the waterborne equivalent of the talus slope or talus cone. Alluvial deposits make up the topsoil of most mature valleys. In dry desert country, the distinctive *alluvial fan* is one of the most consistent features. Heavy seasonal rainfall erodes the arid land severely, because little vegetation survives between storms to hold the soil. Short-lived streams pour down the dry slopes with heavy sedimentary loads. Where the mountain slope meets the shallower plain below, the streams lose their velocity and dump their sediment. Alluvial fans in the American Southwest sometimes reach widths of several miles; artesian wells may be drilled at the downslope border of them, since they function as aquifers, holding water in their porous depths long after the surrounding arid countryside has returned to its naturally parched state.

Desert mountain country develops additional features because of the rapid but sporadic erosion. Depressions between mountain ranges quickly acquire alluvial fill, which may settle into flat spots in the central part of the depression. Under more temperate circumstances, such flat depressions would become lakes; in the desert they mark the beds of temporary lakes which usually dry up completely between storms. These lakebeds are known as *playas*. The lakes formed on them contain the mineral salts washed down from the surrounding mountain ranges, which evaporation then concentrates to salinity levels which far exceed those of the ocean. During dry spells nothing but a salt flat may remain. Utah's Great Salt Lake is the remnant of a much greater prehistoric Lake Bonneville, now existing as the immense playa that is the Bonneville Salt Flats, site of annual automobile and motorcycle speed records.

Frequently in desert mountain country, the juncture of the mountain slope with the plain below is marked by a smoothly sloping bedrock surface, which may or may not have a thin coat of alluvial material covering it. The bedrock strip running parallel to the base of a mountain range, between the foot of the mountains and the alluvial valley beyond, is a *pediment*. When such terrain—mountain, pediment, alluvial valley— reaches the end stage of the cycle of denudation, the desert mountain equivalent of a peneplain, then its form is known as a *pediplain*.

Pediplains and peneplains are geriatric landforms ripe for rejuvenation via uplift. Mountains are the adolescents of the land, even in such timeworn versions as the Urals and the Appalachians. (I haven't seen the Urals, but the Appalachians, everyone's typical example of ancient mountain topography, still abound with the tumultuous mountain streams which are the very symbol of youthful land. That's one reason why I live there.) Nevertheless, chaotic disorganization is the signature of a youthful mountain range. *Sierra,* as in Sierra Nevada and Sierra Madre, is the Spanish word for "saw" as well as for "mountain range." Its application to mountains refers not to the evenly spaced regularity one associates with a saw blade, but to the sharp-toothed disorder that a mountain range's profile marks off on the horizon. Penetrate the territory beneath that profile, and you'll find that mountains are indeed youthful places. Gravity would level everything—lowering the stream walls, widening the valleys, consolidating drainage basins and stream systems. But gravity takes time, geologic time, to do its work. Our mountains just haven't been there long enough.

Ice is the silent language of the peak;
and fire the silent language of the star.
—CONRAD AIKEN, *And in the Human Heart, Sonnet X*

Chapter 8

Mountain-Making's Finest Hour

Water is the dependable solvent that will, eventually, expose
the scenery beneath an otherwise undistinguished and amor-
phous landscape. No matter how arid the climate and sparse
the rainfall, water is the principal sculptor of the land. But for
the really spectacular detail—for the terrain we call *alpine*—
the primary sculptor is water in a singularly unwatery form.
Ice is what makes the mountains mountainous.

Ice is hard to think about. It is, in fact, rock. That is, it is the
compound water in its naturally occurring solid state—as diamonds, for instance, are a natural state of carbon. But ice is a
peculiar kind of rock—light enough in weight to float in water,
extremely hard and brittle in its unpressurized version, yet
capable when pressurized of flowing like a river. Ice does, of
course, take up more volume than water's liquid form, and by

virtue of this expansion alone it makes a powerful erosional tool, as in frost-wedging. But although the erosional effect of such things as freeze–thaw cycles may represent a greater force for changing the shape of the land, it is ice en masse—glaciers and their action—that perpetrates the really dramatic changes.

Glaciers form where more snow falls in winter than can melt away in summer. Snow is also ice—perfectly hard and full of knife-sharp, jagged edges, albeit on a microscopic scale. It's a physical fact that's hard to keep in mind in the face of that downy fluff that floats down out of the sky. (High mountain snow can be another sort of stuff entirely. Chris Bonington's account of an English assault on Everest tells how, in hundred-mile-per-hour storms above twenty thousand feet, snow would change on the instant of contact from the blowing, windspun state into something that had to be chopped with ice axes.) Once the snow has settled into place, it begins undergoing various structural changes, the last of which is called *melt metamorphism*. The ice crystals in the snowpack grow in size, sublimating moisture out of the air spaces between them, changing into *névé*, or *firn* snow (from a German term meaning "of last year," hence old snow).

Firnification on the surface of a snowpack can develop an upper layer that consists of ice pebbles, which weld together each freezing night, then melt into separate grains again in the sun: "corn" snow, a skier's delight. In colder temperatures, the grains remain bonded, but air spaces remain. Below this layer the air begins getting squeezed out of the interspaces: *nivation* compresses firn snow into solid ice. This compaction results in a completely bonded zone of perfectly rigid ice that can be two hundred feet thick and as brittle as the stuff you put in cocktails. This is the layer that fractures, developing *crevasses*, the gaping cracks that form as the entire glacial mass moves downslope.

Beneath that brittle layer lies the ice that can flow. Some of the downslope movement of the glacier comes simply from the squeezing out of air spaces. Some of it occurs when the glacier uses water like the grease at a ship launching. The immense internal pressure from the accumulated weight of ice raises the melting point of the ice, and the meltwater acts as a lubricant. If there are irregularities on the bottom of the glacial valley, pressure will be greatest on the uphill side of the irregularities, lowest on the downhill side. The meltwater runs between these two points; when it reaches the downhill side, it refreezes.

But much of the downhill movement of the glacier occurs simply because the ice itself becomes plastic in nature. The huge weight deforms the ice crystals so that they can slip over one another like the cards in a brand-new deck. Such deformation increases the size of the ice crystals, and crystals taken from the *terminus,* or *snout*—the downhill end of the glacier— will be measurably larger than those from near its source.

In polar regions snow accumulations and prevailing temperatures allow the formation of masses of ice that are continentwide. Greenland's ice cap is over eleven thousand feet thick, its weight depressing the landmass underneath to sixty-five hundred feet below sea level. Antarctica has over six million square miles of ice, averaging a mile in thickness. Ice caps are glaciers, and they move, flowing outward from a central high point to the edges. The rate of flow is quite slow, however, and it is doubtful we'll ever get to see the work they have done on the landforms they cover. The glaciers that we're interested in, however, are the alpine or *valley glaciers,* which form above the permanent snow line in the mountains, make a long, narrow ice field that descends along the bottom of a valley, and terminate in a snout that is below the snow line, often near an area temperate enough to be settled or even put into agricultural production.

Drive a line of stakes across the surface of such a valley glacier, come back a month later, and that straight line of stakes will now form a great U-shaped arc, with the curve pointed down the valley, the lowest stake in the center of the ice field. The rate of flow—which may reach several feet per day and will vary greatly from season to season—is slowest at the sides and bottom, where friction with the valley is greatest. It is fastest in the center of the glacier, where internal pressures converge. Crevasses are usually ripped open where the glacier passes over humps in the valley floor, when variations in the rate of flow produce tension cracks in the brittle upper surface. (But crevasse locations can't be predicted, and they are often bridged with insubstantial snow, so travel on a glacier's surface is always hazardous.)

Where crevasses intersect, tall ice pinnacles are formed, called *seracs*. Seracs will show horizontal stripes, alternating layers of ice and rock debris. The surface of the glacier gets a new coat of rock dust and dirt each summer, when accelerated freeze–thaw cycles occur. (Above eight thousand feet frost can form on any summer night.) Frost-wedging works on the valley sides and headwall to shower down a great deal of rock onto the ice field, and there is little new snowfall to cover the accumulation until the following winter. The debris forms a dark layer, a transverse "growth" line within the body of the ice, much like a ring in a tree trunk.

(This erosion by frost-wedging seems too slow and gradual a process to have much effect on landscape formation. Yet as the late mountaineer John Harlin pointed out, the fall of rocks on high peaks is virtually continuous; the rocks are dislodged not by climbers but by freezing and thawing on the mountain surface. Experienced climbers are particularly wary of the occasional vertical joint or notch which offers a direct route up but also collects and funnels the rock that comes down, much like the notches that deposit talus cones on the valley floor.)

Glaciers also have longitudinal stripes in them, running down their length. Where conditions for glacier formation are favorable, trunk glaciers are found that feed into the main glacier system. Each trunk glacier carries its own load of debris, which does not mix with that of the main glacier; the debris is squeezed into a line that turns and follows the main glacier downhill, forming a dark stripe. Count the lines running down the glacier's length and you can determine how many trunk glaciers feed into it.

The upper part of the glacier, where snow is still being transformed into ice, is the *zone of accumulation,* or *firn field;* in cross section, its upper surface will have a slightly scooped out, concave shape. Farther down the glacier, where the surface carries little new snow, the cross section will show a convex upper surface. This is the *zone of ablation.* Old, dying glaciers have a limited zone of accumulation at the upper end; growing, dynamic glaciers may be topped with firn snow well down their length.

Most crevasses are crescentic, forming arcs which aim down the valley. Where the surface irregularity of the underlying valley is severe—as at a fault line or cliff face—the crevassing action may make an *icefall,* a jumbled mass of seracs that are kept on the verge of avalanche by the movement of the glacier. The approaches to most of the major Himalayan peaks are guarded by massive icefalls, and most of the climbing fatalities associated with those mountains occur in avalanches within the icefalls. *Lateral crevasses* can also open up, pulled apart by the difference in rate of flow between the sides and the center of the glacier. A minor rock peak that protrudes high enough to poke up through the surface of the glacier, leaving an isolated rock island, is known by the Eskimo term *nunatak.* A nunatak can have its own network of crevasses around it. Nunataks usually occur near the sides of the glacier, where the ice sheet is thinner, so the crevasses there may not be as deep as they are elsewhere. Nevertheless, they are best avoided.

When a glacier manages to flow downward into a body of water, as at the ocean, the snout is buoyed upward, since the ice weighs less than water. The strain will break off chunks of the glacier in a process known as *calving.* No Walt Disney nature film is complete without some footage of this spectacular action, usually filmed in Alaska's Glacier Bay, near Juneau. A stupendous sight: great ice cliffs collapsing into the sea,

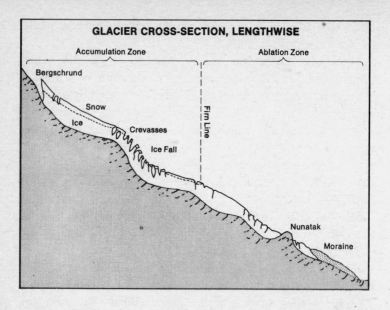

GLACIER CROSS-SECTION, LENGTHWISE

supplying the northern oceans with icebergs. (More icebergs are calved from the polar ice caps, of course, by the same uplifting action where the cap meets the sea.) Any glacier that terminates on dry land will serve as the headwaters for a glacial stream or river, which will have a milky green color to its water—at least in its upper stages—from the heavy load of finely ground rock dust, called *rock flour,* suspended in the flow. You can often spot that distinctive color in the water in mountain streams that you assumed were miles from any glacier.

The rock flour is there because the glacier is another one of nature's great milling machines, perhaps the most powerful of all. The glacier plucks rock out of the valley bottom and freezes it to its underside: a gigantic bulldozer for the cutting of valleys, the weight of the ice mass providing the horsepower to drive the machine. On their ponderous downhill journey, glaciers follow existing valleys, rather than carving their own. With their great weight and irreducible bulk, they carve the V-shape of an erosional valley into a giant U-shape. The Great Glacial Trough of Banff National Park is a perfect example; so are California's Yosemite Valley and New Hampshire's Franconia, Crawford, and Pinkham notches.

Glaciers straighten valleys out as well, because they are much too massive to follow every little zig and zag of a river's path. When sawtooth spurs and ridges intrude into the path, the glacier simply slices them off, leaving a triangular facet in the valley side, formed from a cross section of the truncated spur. Glaciers also polish the surface of solid rock where they slide over it, and the upper limit of an ancient glacier may be clearly traced in a glacial valley by an obvious *trim line* scratched on the valley wall, with rough, ragged rock above the line, smoothly polished rock below.

Where a tributary glacier once entered the course of a main glacier from the side, it may have left a *hanging valley*. While glaciation is still active, the upper surfaces of main and tributary glaciers will be approximately level. But the tributary will not have the weight to carve as deeply as the main glacier, and its valley will be much shallower. When both are melted away, the higher valley bottom of the adjoining tributary will be revealed to be chopped off by the deeper main valley wall. Quite frequently there will be a spectacular waterfall plunging down from the hanging valley into the deeper valley below. Bridal Veil (620 feet high) and Yosemite Falls (2,425 feet, in two leaps) are perfect examples. Eventually the stream that forms the waterfall will cut its own V-shaped notch in the U-shaped valley bottom from which it now descends.

The upper end of a valley glacier—its beginning point—will be marked by a *cirque*. The glacier originates below a headwall, where eddy currents in the mountain winds cause blowing snow to collect and settle. This accumulation turns to solid ice through nivation, and freezes to the mountain surface. Freeze–thaw cycles and the pull of gravity on the accumulating mass draw the incipient glacier away from the headwall at the uphill end, forming a *bergschrund* ("mountain cleft") between ice and rock. The pulling away plucks rock from the headwall; the rock then becomes part of the load carried down the valley by the glacier. This plucking action is the first step in formation of a cirque (in Scotland, a *corrie;* in Wales, a *cwm;* in Germany, a *Kar*)—the amphitheaterlike mountain bowl that makes one of alpine country's most spectacular features.

Throughout the development of the cirque, the alternate freezing and plucking goes on not only between ice and headwall but also between glacier sides and the valley walls. Headwall and valley sides are radically steepened by the process. So long as the glacier maintains its size, the cirque continues to carve its way uphill, working its way toward the summit of the mountain much as a waterfall does. At the same time, the glacier is carving out the bottom of the bowl and building up a large wall of material as a lip at the bottom downhill edge of the bowl—over which the glacier will eventually spill in a massive icefall, then continue carving its way on down the valley.

Most of the mountain cirques in evidence today started forming in the early stages of the Ice Age, and their glaciers were maintained at full size long enough to accomplish considerable carving. Inevitably, however, in our recent ten-thousand-year warming trend, shrinkage has set in. Once a glacier starts shrinking, the cirque is exposed to ordinary erosive action, which reduces the steepness of its sides, softening the contour of the cirque. This softened cirque may or may not still have a glacier descending from its downhill end. If the glacier is gone, there frequently remains a cirque *tarn,* or lake, its bed the scooped-out bottom dammed up by the lip of glacier-deposited rock. Sometimes the glacier will repeat this process as it works its way down the valley, leaving the string-of-beads effect known as *paternoster lakes.*

Outside the specifically alpine regions, glaciation is still one of the prime molders of landforms, even if it does not there produce the cirques and tarns and hanging valleys that we associate with alpine splendor. Glaciation's usual contribution to the landscape, particularly in North America, is simply to bulldoze it flat—a process that doesn't have much to do with mountains. But viewed in detail, the particular contributions of glacial action not only have a great deal to do with the shape of the landscape, they also demonstrate mechanisms and formations that make the larger mountains more understandable.

The great ice sheets made four major advances and subsequent retreats, the last ending only some ten to fifteen thousand years ago. At the stage of maximum coverage, ice extended over most of North America north of the Ohio and Missouri Rivers, in Europe over the Scandinavian countries and down through central Germany. During the time of advance, glacial action was also going on in the high mountain regions, each with its own discrete ice cap. In North America particularly, the ice sheet's last stage had a flat and featureless landscape to work on for the most part, and therefore the changes left by the last retreat are almost purely the product of the ice sheet's actions. It is these features which have taught scientists how glaciation works on the land.

When an ice sheet is developing, it flows toward its own edges, polishing rock faces beneath its surface, dragging chunks of rock to leave scratches or even chatter marks on those faces. When a glacier moves over a bedrock knob, it polishes, grooves, striates the side of the knob it reaches first, and then, after it passes over and polishes the peak, it plucks rock out of the lee side, leaving a rough and broken surface. Such knobs, polished and rounded on one side, broken up and much steeper on the other, are called *roches moutonnées,* "mutton rocks," not from anything sheeplike in their appearance, but from an imagined resemblance to wigs of the colonial period, which were smeared with mutton fat as a hair dressing!

Where glacial excavation took place—usually where there was a preexisting stream or river valley which had made the first cut through the bedrock layer—the great ice sheets scooped out the familiar U-shaped valleys. Inland, the result was finger lakes, as in New York State; where such action met the sea, the glacier left a *fjord.* Fjords are narrow estuaries, often hundreds of feet deep but with a quite shallow neck, the shallowness caused by the glacier's terminal deposit of rock debris. Upon meeting the sea, the glacier that carved the fjord began calving, and dumped its rock load, unsorted by size, at its point of melting and breakup. In the early stage of development, the fjord was quite likely above sea level; when the great ice sheets melted, rising sea levels then drowned the fjord valley. Much of the fjord country of the world—particularly in Scandinavia—is now being uplifted, which means that those fjords were once even deeper than they are now. The classic fjord–finger lake combination is the Great Glen of Scotland, where a severe transverse fault line completely across the British Isles was later carved out by the British ice cap. At one end of the Great Glen is the Firth of Inverness, at the other the Firth of Lorne (*firth* is a fjord in Scotland). In between there is a series of finger lakes, the largest and deepest of which is Loch Ness.

A specific deposit left by a glacier is called a *moraine;* there are various types, such as terminal (at the end), lateral (along the sides), and medial (down the middle, as below a nunatak). The more general classification of deposits left by the ice sheets includes *drift* (generally the small stuff—clay, sand, gravel—left by meltwater), and *till* (rock of various sizes and textures left in place by retreating ice rather than running water). Old glacial valleys may be flat-bottomed from deposits of drift; younger valleys will have retained more of the concave U-shape, but may have scattered piles of till. In really ancient glacial valleys—quite flat-bottomed now—drift may have accumulated to depths of several hundred feet.

The ice sheets advanced in a series of convex curves, or lobes; at the point of maximum advance, each of these lobes left a similarly curved terminal moraine, which in the Great Lakes region of North America made *moraine belts:* low, running hills arranged in looping concentric curves. Sometimes an ice sheet would leave till in veritable sheets when it retreated; it would also leave large blocks of ice embedded in such till sheets. Subsequent melting then left depressions, or *kettles,* producing the kettle moraine country of Wisconsin: knobby terrain interspersed with small lakes.

When an ice sheet stopped moving and began to retreat, the melting did not necessarily proceed at an even pace. Often streams would issue from well back beneath the ice pack, melting long tunnels to the edge of the ice lobe. The roof and walls of such a tunnel would be solid ice; the stream would deposit sand and gravel down its length, building up a level of deposits higher than the surrounding ground level. When the ice sheet was entirely gone, the stream path would remain as a sinuous raised ridge of sand and gravel known as an *esker.*

In places where the ice sheet was so loaded with till that it had to begin dumping debris before it reached its eventual terminal moraine, it would deposit the material in a low oval hill, called a *drumlin,* composed of successive layers of till laid down under the ice, always in an elongated shape pointing in the direction of movement of the ice sheet. Drumlins—Bunker Hill is one of them—are usually found in groups, indicating a kind of regional development in the history of the ice sheets which still is not fully understood.

Where advancing lobes of the ice sheet met higher ground, then began receding, glacial lakes were often formed between the edge of the ice sheet and the rising land. Streams would flow into those lakes from the surface of the ice as well as from the surrounding high ground, forming deltas of drift material. Streams would also flow alongside the ice margins, building their beds up above the bottom level of the ice sheet. Once the ice sheet had completely withdrawn, those streambeds formed what are known as *kame terraces,* and their deltas made *kame deltas.* Kames are formed of drift, rather than till; they are glacial features, but they are sometimes hard to distinguish from other alluvial deposits left long after all of the ice was gone.

While the great ice sheets were creating all these little local landscape features, the high mountain regions had ice caps of their own—not thick enough to cover the uppermost peaks but sufficient to engulf, to interglaciate, everything in between. For those areas, the ice ages aren't over. There are still twelve hundred glaciers in the Alps. Hubbard Glacier in Alaska and Canada is seventy-two miles long and contains more ice than all the glaciers in Switzerland. Malaspina Glacier in Alaska is larger than Rhode Island; after a long period of recession, it seems to be showing signs of renewed growth. There is evidence of glacial action as far south as Sierra Blanca (12,003 feet) in southern New Mexico. Even Kilimanjaro in East Africa has three active glaciers on it.

The high mountain ice caps have withdrawn sufficiently, however, to reveal the exquisite surgery they have performed on the mountains that they interglaciate. The creation of the most rugged mountain topography of all is the product of an oversupply of cirques. When two adjoining cirques work toward each other, spectacular things happen to the mountain they are on. If the glaciers that formed them are well receded, erosion—on its way to softening and reducing the steepness of the cirques—will finally cut through the wall that separates them to form a high saddle, or *col,* one form of mountain pass. But if the cirque is still growing with glacial steepness, it will join its neighbor in an *arête*—a thin, knife-edged ridge that looks absolutely impassable but that in fact offers climbers the safest and surest route of ascent.

It is when three or more cirques join forces to cut away at several sides of the same peak that you get the final and most spectacular product of glaciation, the *horn peak.* There are several splendid horn peaks in the Tetons. The Canadian Rockies are full of them. But nowhere does one surpass the Alps' perfect mountain, the Matterhorn. Each side of the horn is the headwall of an ancient cirque; glaciers still descend from them. The Matterhorn is mountain-making's finest hour. The spectacular part was all done by ice.

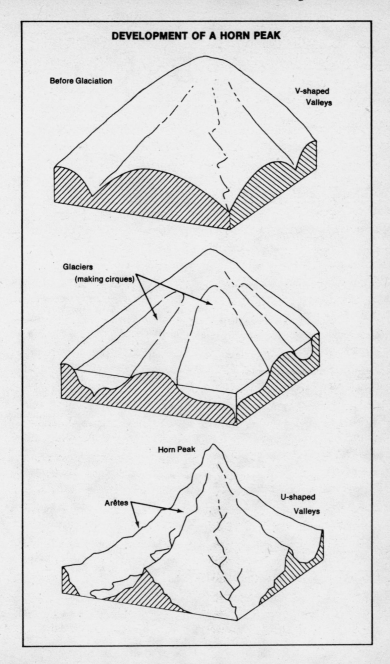

DEVELOPMENT OF A HORN PEAK

Before Glaciation

V-shaped Valleys

Glaciers (making cirques)

Horn Peak

Arêtes

U-shaped Valleys

Book Two

Going There

I heard one startled exclamation from Croz, then saw him and Mr. Hadow flying downwards; in another moment Hudson was dragged from his steps, and Lord F. Douglas immediately after him. All this was the work of a moment. Immediately we heard Croz's exclamation, old Peter and I planted ourselves as firmly as the rocks would permit: the rope was taut between us, and the jerk came on us both as on one man. We held; but the rope broke midway between Taugwalder and Lord Francis Douglas.

—EDWARD WHYMPER, *Scrambles Amongst the Alps*

Chapter 9

The Hard Men

Our stroll up Mount Kinsman was a walk, a hike, not a climb. Let there be no confusion about such things: climbing is quite another matter.

Envision a human form striding across level ground. Now, introduce a little gradient into the vision; the act of walking changes into something closer to the climbing of stairs. (Almost all of our time on Kinsman was spent in that mode of travel.) Add enough steepness, and the walker-climber's attitude changes to that of a crawler—the hands become involved as well as the feet. Increase the steepness still further, to the vertical: the climber-crawler continues, pressed closer to the mountain, hanging by fingers and toes. Still he goes up. (Increase the envisioned steepness beyond the vertical and surely the climber must stop—or fall off? No, not in modern technical climbing, not even if the surface is horizontal, with the climber on the underside.)

Excuse the plodding oversimplification, but in the wash of

romance that surrounds mountain climbing, that singular figure—the human form wearily working its way up a gradient—
tends to get lost. A little more reductionism: more effort is
expended walking up an incline than is needed to walk on
level ground (as demonstrated in our aching thigh muscles on
Kinsman), but the rewards of walking up an incline are
greater than for remaining on level ground. Please excuse also
that whiff of behaviorist psychology—effort versus reward,
pain versus pleasure, and all that—but it contains the kernel of
the mountain climbing experience. It is in the definition of the
rewards that the picture gets muddied. Nonclimbers start call-
ing climbers masochistic mystics with overweening death
wishes; climbers maintain that nonclimbers simply cannot
understand. It is not that the truth lies somewhere in between
these irreconcilable viewpoints; it is that the truth is unavail-
able. Generalizations about mountain climbing are fated to fall
flat on their faces. I will now make some. I am a nonclimber.

Mountain climbing began as an outgrowth of the Age of
Exploration and quickly became a sport, although it has traditionally camouflaged its purposes under the guise of science.
(Two Englishmen named Frederick Slade and Yeats Brown
scandalized the continent in 1827 when they announced that
their attempt to scale the Jungfrau was simply for the fun of
it; the complete lack of any scientific justification for the expedition was considered somehow dishonorable.) Most of what
we have come to know, scientifically, about mountains and
about human adaptation to them has indeed been learned
through mountain climbing. But most of the exploits of mountain climbing have not been achieved for scientific purposes.
The annals of exploration are full of heroic human accomplishment, whether in desert, Arctic waste, jungle, or sea. It is part
of the definition of exploration that one launches expeditions
before one has the information or equipment to deal with the
conditions that will obtain. Mountaineering is no different, and
certainly the major exploits of that sport have involved epic
human struggles against the most forbidding conditions that
exist on earth.

But it is a sport. Among Europeans it is commonly referred to as "Alpinism," and its development in the Alps offers an interesting progression. At first the goal was simply ascent, the "conquest" of all the available peaks. Once they had all been climbed by the easiest way that could be found, which meant via the more or less gentle ridges, Alpinism entered a second stage. The climbers began deliberately selecting the more difficult, steeper routes between the ridges: the faces. After routes had been found by which it was possible to ascend the major mountain faces, *direttissima* became the new enthusiasm: direct routes, straight up, no obstacle permitted to interfere. The deliberate choice of the most difficult route possible up the mountain is a development that leads to some interesting speculation about the motivations of mountain climbers. Once the major faces had all been dissected by straight vertical lines, as they inevitably were, Alpinists were left with nothing to accomplish—in the Alps—but what some cynics regard as stunts: speed records, solo assaults, winter climbs, self-imposed restrictions on amount and type of equipment, and other strange twists on the basic human capacity to haul oneself up onto high places.

Meanwhile, of course, the rest of the unclimbed mountains of the world were being attacked (although no one speaks of "Andeanism" or "Himalayanism"). Mount Elbrus in the USSR, at 18,468 feet the highest peak on the European continent, was climbed by the British in 1868. Kilimanjaro, Africa's highest at 19,340, "fell" to Germans in 1889. Aconcagua, South America's highest at 22,834, was surmounted by British climbers in 1897. Mount McKinley—20,320 feet—went to Americans in 1913. The Himalayas saw various expeditions, most of them British, in the 1920's, including three or four abortive attempts at Everest, the last marred by the tragic disappearance of George Leigh-Mallory and Andrew Irvine, "going strong for the top" at well above 28,000 feet, but much too late in the day to make a safe descent. World War II stopped mountain climbing temporarily but also brought technological developments, notably in lightweight oxygen systems, that led to the golden age of mountaineering, the 1950's. That decade saw the ascent of the first eight-thousand-meter mountain, Annapurna (26,502 feet), by a French team, and, subsequently, thirteen other first ascents of mountains of over twenty-three thousand feet. Including, of course, Mount Everest—*Chomolungma*, "Goddess-mother." Mount Everest's last unclimbed face, the southwest, was scaled by a British team in 1975. *Direttissima*, here we come.

Mountain climbing has been embroiled in controversy since that moment when Whymper's rope broke. Queen Victoria, among others, proposed that mountain climbing be banned altogether. "Why," thundered the *London Times*, "is this best blood of England to waste itself scaling hitherto inaccessible peaks?" The sport needs nothing so dramatic as death to stimulate acrimony, however. Technology reared its fascinating head at that moment in 1786 when Saussure discovered his parasol to be inadequate protection against snow blindness, and its application to the sport has never stopped. It reached something of a premature peak in the early 1920's, in the discussion over the use of oxygen bottles on Mallory's expeditions to Mount Everest. (He was opposed to their use.) Realists, judging from the experiences of other Himalayan expeditions, maintained that the risks from physical debilitation and cloudy judgment during exertion at very high altitudes mandated what the Sherpa natives laughingly called "English air." Romantics held that any success won with such artificial aids would somehow be tainted. Realists won out, but it took high-mountain deaths, including Mallory's, to secure their case.

(Technology can run aground on sheer economics, too. A few years ago the Italians wanted to supply a Himalayan expedition of theirs with helicopters. The affected local governments banned the whirlybirds because their use would be taking food from the mouths of the large and otherwise unemployed porter populations.)

The hardware question continues to rage. Nowadays, mountaineers sometimes are so loaded with mechanical equipment to help them up otherwise unclimbable rock and ice that they clank when they walk: pitons, carabiners, ice screws, wedges, and nuts and "bongs" and "rurps." (The last is the acronym for the "realized ultimate reality piton," whatever that means.) A natural division has sprung up between "free" climbers and "technical" climbers as the technological attainments of the sport have advanced. The latter accuse the former of taking unnecessary risks; the former accuse the latter of merely nailing themselves up the mountain. Artists versus engineers.

A more recent version of this controversy is directly related to a tremendous upsurge of interest and participation in climbing. The sport has grown so popular that climbing accidents in the Alps alone result in a hundred deaths per season, and the costs of mountain rescue missions have nearly bankrupted local rescue organizations. (A good season sees three thousand "climbers" a week on the Matterhorn summit, with as many as ninety people on top at once in good weather.) A less dramatic result of the new popularity has been some overused rock faces festooned with hardware left from previous assaults. In a curious offshoot of the drive for environmental purity—very popular among recreational visitors to mountains—some of the better climbers have begun campaigning for "clean" climbing, in which one removes all of one's own hardware as one goes, restoring the rock face to its original, unclimbed state—and monumentally complicating the climbing job in the process. Less idealistic climbers point out that part of the concern of the experts might just stem from the fact that all the hardware left up there makes easy some of the hitherto difficult climbs, destroying the exclusivity on which the sport's superexperts have established reputations. Nevertheless, clean-climbing enthusiasts have made some difficult climbs for the sole purpose of housecleaning the rock face, clearing out all the old hardware and forcing neophytes to start over from scratch.

Strange sport. It really began as the province of English gentlemen, one more activity for wealthy sportsmen, with its own severe notions of sportsmanship. "In the event of default

[default, that is, in the realms of courage and character, rather than those of finance] the defaulter was ostracized and expelled from the circle of Alpinists," says Showell Styles, biographer of Everest victim Mallory. Mountaineering acquired its own peasant class, Swiss mountain guides at first, then Italians, Frenchmen, Austrians, Germans, Sherpas. The gentlemen accepted peasant participation in their sport with hearty British democracy, once they realized that without the experience, strength, and intelligence of the natives they just wouldn't be able to pull off major climbs. The peasants proceeded immediately to surpass the most noteworthy accomplishments of the toffs. The toffs continued to accept the plaudits: after all, they'd financed the expeditions, hadn't they?

There was a nasty strain of nationalism throughout the sport's early history, back when mountains still "fell" to climbers, "conquered" by their "assaults." English jingoism was demonstrated less by British ballyhoo for their own accomplishments than in their well-bred horror at growing Nazi influence in climbing in the 1930's. In that decade young German fanatics began falling to their deaths—and now and then accomplishing remarkable new feats of mountaineering—all over the Alps, for the glory of their Fuehrer. *Uber alles* took on new meaning in the Alps in the 1930's.

The nationalistic fervor in climbing was presumed to be muted after World War II, but it was not without significance that news of Hillary and Tensing and their successful expedition up Everest in 1953 reached England on the eve of Queen Elizabeth's coronation. The expedition was organized, financed, and led by Britishers. Edmund Hillary was a New Zealander, but of course a loyal British subject; Tensing Norkay was a Sherpa, one of mountaineering's newest peasant class. Queen Elizabeth democratically knighted Hillary—and expedition leader Colonel John Hunt.

If after the war the Sherpas became the new peasant class of mountaineering—and the Swiss, the Austrians, even such newcomers to climbing as the Russians and Japanese, became the new gentlemen—nevertheless a classless society was forming in the sport. In Himalayan expeditions of the 1950's, when a Sherpa would distinguish himself by overachieving for the boss, usually by carrying heavy loads to extremely high altitudes, he was dubbed a "tiger." The sobriquet spread through the sport, coming to be applied to any of the oversupply of heroes in mountain climbing, whatever their nationality. Now, the tigers are gone; in their place are the new classless mountaineering elite known as the hard men.

The hard men are not just highly skilled or courageous mountain climbers, but something else in the bargain. Something indefinable: they may be most clearly characterized by their resistance to characterization. The hard men come from the traditional alpine nations, but also from anywhere else— Scotland, Wales, Canada, Belgium, anywhere. Some are mountain guides, but many are more or less unemployed itinerant laborers and small-scale entrepreneurs interested in employment or profit only as a means to stake the next climb. They have a distinct tendency toward anarchy, even—according to their own folklore—to a kind of romantic outlawry. Some are ex-flower children, dopesters, hippies, mountain bums; I have no doubt that some are also brain surgeons and nuclear physicists. Unclassifiable. They are, by their own mystique, scruffy, hairy, long-armed and horny-handed, lean and dirty. I'm sure there are also short, fat men among their number, even perfectly groomed ones—at least while they are down off the mountain.

They share, in addition to an obsessive love of climbing, a hyperrealistic if rueful sense of the physical toll of the sport. Of the discomfort and pain that accompany even the most successful and routine high-mountain efforts, of that very effort that introduction of an incline into one's route necessarily entails. That is precisely what they are "hard" about. Between climbs some of them regularly ski without gloves to accustom their hands to the bitter cold they will have to endure higher on the mountains. The hard men are fond of rivaling the Sherpas at load-carrying ability at altitude, not out of economic or other necessity, but from sheer physical pride —and as a conditioning device. They train, regularly, by simply running up and down minor mountains as preparation for the kind of physical expenditure they'll have to make on more serious outings. Some of them are virtual alchemists in the areas of nutrition and metabolic balance. They are men (and women—there are women among them) who get very serious about the physics and physiology of mountain climbing. They get serious about nothing else in their lives: about everything else, including their own legends, they are as utterly romantic as the most star-struck, moony-eyed thirteen-year-olds.

As in the case of John Harlin and his obsessive relationship with the north face of the Eiger. John Elvis Harlin II, something of a college athlete and then a jet pilot for the United States Air Force, but first and foremost a mountain climber, was the prototypical hard man; there was even a mountain climber's folk song about him, sung (by others) in mountain huts and bars during Harlin's own lifetime. Harlin began climbing in California, made his way to the Alps, and quickly established himself as one of the bright young stars of mountaineering in the late 1950's. It was only natural that he would become fascinated with the Eiger.

The Jungfrau (13,642), the Mönch (13,448), and the Eiger (13,025)—the Virgin, the Monk, and the Ogre—form a huge mountain wall overlooking the tiny railway station and hotel of Kleine Scheidegg in the Bernese Oberland. The Jungfrau and the Mönch are spectacular mountains but hardly challenging—a railway line was opened to the summit of the Jungfrau in 1912. The Eiger would likewise represent no particular mountaineering obstacle were it not for its northern face. But that face is the biggest and most difficult piece of real estate in Europe. The Germans refer to it as the *Mordwand* (murder wall) as well as the *Nordwand* (north wall). It is six thousand vertical feet of sheer rock and ice. A six-thousand-foot cliff. And as the northernmost peak of the group, it is also a magnet for every storm in the vicinity.

The Eiger Wall was first attempted in 1935, the year of John Harlin's birth. Germans Karl Mehringer and Max Seldmayer were caught on the face by a wicked storm, bivouacked for two days, and then Mehringer went for help. Seldmayer's body was found at the spot known forever afterward as the Death Bivouac; Mehringer's body was not found until twenty-seven years later, on the second ice field which is slightly to the right of center and two-thirds of the way up the Wall. The next year saw the Eiger's worst single disaster, when a four-man German team was wiped out. One member was injured by falling rock, and the disaster took place during the attempted retreat. Andreas Hinterstoisser made it across what is still known as the Hinterstoisser Traverse—two thousand feet up, a hundred-and-thirty-foot traverse without handholds, generally considered the gateway to the "real climbing"—only to fall to his death. The remainder of the party perished on the wall. The Eiger's reputation was secure, although it was successfully climbed by a German team two years later, in 1938.

By the summer of 1962, when John Harlin prepared his attempt, the Eiger Wall had been climbed twenty-seven times —and had claimed twenty-two lives in the process. (Two had already died in the summer of 1962 before Harlin started out.) Harlin teamed up with Konrad Kirch and set out on what he later described as the most rotten and dangerous rock he'd ever encountered. Rockfalls represent the Eiger's first line of defense: Harlin estimated that fully half the climbers on the wall are eventually hit by falling rock, and 5 percent of the fatalities are caused by rockfalls. The ice fields are solid ice walls pitched at fifty-five degrees or more, with a surface "like burnished steel," according to Harlin. Each section of the wall, he said, seemed like a complete climb on a lesser mountain. One section known as the White Spider turned out to be a snowfield in continual avalanche, which Harlin characterized as more like swimming than climbing.

On the first night of their climb, Harlin and Kirch were forced to bivouac on a ledge that didn't even offer room to sit down; they roped and spiked themselves to the wall, their legs dangling off into space, and passed the night that way. In the process they dropped an ice axe, their tea supply, and their miniature stove, so they had no more hot food for the remainder of their climb. Despite this and a later goof that forced them to spend a third night on the wall standing up and holding on by hand, they made it to the top.

They had done so in one of the longest spells of decent summer weather ever recorded on the Eiger, and they had had company. On the night of August 20, 1962—the night they dropped their stove—there were fourteen other climbers bivouacked on the Eiger. Ten of them also completed the climb. (Only Kirch escaped with neither injury nor frostbite.) John Harlin was the first American to climb the Eiger's north face, but in the continuing good weather of that splendid summer, fourteen groups totaling forty-four climbers made it to the top. There were also five fatalities.

Harlin seems to have decided upon reflection that his accomplishment was somehow tainted by the crowds of climbers who made the same climb. And so, of course, he decided to do it over again. *Direttissima*. In winter.

(In 1963 the Eiger saw its first solo climb; in 1964 it was climbed by a woman; in 1965 it got its first suicide, a Japanese climber who was injured high on the peak. Half a dozen direct-route attempts had already been made, but none had gone higher than the second ice field.)

In 1966 Harlin planned a ten-day siege of the wall, teaming up with three other proven hard men: Dougal Haston, Chris Bonington, and Layton Kor. While the Harlin team was waiting for the weather to break in February, however, a German team of eight men started up the Eiger, also *direttissima*, so Harlin and crew rushed into action. The Germans were prepared to spend as many as eighteen days on the mountain if necessary, in a Himalayan-style assault using supply camps and fixed ropes for shuttling men and supplies up and down the mountain. Once the Harlin group gained familiarity with the fickle winter weather of the Eiger, they recognized that they would be forced to employ the same tactics, yo-yoing up and down the mountain to supply two substantial bivouacs. The Harlin team started up the Eiger on February 20. Various members would come down from time to time, and would even rest overnight in the Scheidegg Hotel, but the expedition that started up the mountain on February 20 would be finished with the mountain no fewer than thirty-four days later, on March 25.

From February 20 to March 1, the team made preliminary assaults, fixed some ropes, hauled supplies, and were regularly beaten back by bad weather. The first big push was not launched until March 2, when the team climbed high enough to necessitate an overnight bivouac on the mountain face. They continued climbing steadily until March 5, when a storm forced a twenty-four-hour bivouac. On March 7 the weather cleared and the team climbed again, reaching Death Bivouac on March 10. There Harlin and Haston were forced to remain, immobilized by weather, until March 16. Those two then came wearily down from six maddening days at Death Bivouac showing the first signs of failing health; Bonington and Kor took their places. A weather break on March 18 led to another big push on March 19. On that day the German team, which had run into severe difficulties and was virtually stalled, joined forces with the Harlin team.

On March 20 the weather cleared again, and it was obvious to the combined expeditions that the time was upon them to push quickly and directly for the summit, as another long delay would so debilitate the overextended climbers that they risked serious trouble. Yet after brief gains on the twentieth another storm came in, a product of the Eiger's own freakish mini-climate, and the team was forced to retreat once again to Death Bivouac. March 21 dawned fine, however, and the assault team started again for the top. As they left Death Bivouac, John Harlin was climbing toward them from below. He'd stayed down at Scheidegg for a few days to recoup his energies, and had left the hotel at 1:00 A.M. on the twenty-first to climb to Death Bivouac. The weather held, and on March 22, after overnighting one more time at Death Bivouac, Harlin set out to join the assault team, to add his strength and experience to theirs. He was climbing alone, according to biographer James Ramsey Ullman, "moving strongly, surely, toward that one supreme goal he had sought in his life."* Despite the fact that he and his companions had either been climbing or bivouacking in winter conditions at high altitude on the side of a cliff for most of the previous thirty days, Harlin was still relatively fresh from his recent rest. He was "prusiking," using a friction device to climb directly up a seven-millimeter rope dangling from an overhang. *Direttissima.* The rope broke, and Harlin fell four thousand feet to his death. His was the twenty-seventh recorded fatality on the Ogre of the Alps.

There seemed to be no "cause" of the accident; as well as could be determined, Harlin was not hit by falling rock. All fixed ropes were immediately reexamined. Some were found to be bad, so all climbers who were below the site of the accident returned to Scheidegg, then climbed around the face, up the relatively easy side of the mountain, to provide support from above. Those above the accident site continued their climb. The John Harlin Direct Route was finished on March 25, 1966, by Dougal Haston, Jörg Lehne, Günter Strobel, Siegried Hupfauer, and Roland Votteler. It is marked on the postcards sold in Kleine Scheidegg, traced straight up the color photos of the Nordwand.

John Harlin seems to have been a strange and quirky man, capable of eliciting the strongest emotions—positive as well as negative—in his fellow climbers. His legend, among mountain climbing people, has grown tangled since his death. Two of his Eiger companions of 1966, Dougal Haston and Chris Bonington, helped lead the successful ascent of the southwest face of Mount Everest in 1975, nearly ten years after their Eiger adventures with John Harlin. Both are still climbing. They are hard men.†

---

* *Straight Up* (New York: Doubleday, 1968), p. 272.
† Shortly before this book went to press, Dougal Haston was killed in an avalanche while skiing in the Alps.

I have been struggling to keep a certain sourness of tone from creeping into this hip-shot overview of mountain climbing; I'm not sure I've succeeded. The sourness comes because I am simultaneously too close to and too far from the subject. I am too close to keep in perspective the truly heroic nature of those courageous achievements that are mountaineering's successes (although my eyes go round with wonder every time I hear of another). I find myself unavoidably balancing them off against the fatalities and crippling injuries, some of which have occurred to friends of mine, that mark mountaineering's failures. It is easier to honor heroism at a distance. When it gets close enough to expose the distortions that so often accompany it, I turn squeamish. If in the process I do disservice to the memories of great men, I apologize for it.

But I am also too far from the pure joy of the experience to do it justice. That, too, seems a strange turn. Since my childhood I've been attracted to cliffs and rock faces as a moth to flame, and for most of my years I have just naturally assumed that the very existence of those large vertical surfaces was mostly for my private sport. My first extended experience with mountains culminated with an automobile ride to the top of Pikes Peak, which was fine by me—I was seventeen—but the *real* pleasure and excitement came not at the top of that mountain but at the bottom, where I discovered Garden of the Gods, that neat little park that contains the great, warm, red, soft sandstone hogbacks that mark the eastern edge of the Rocky Mountains.

We pulled into the park at about dusk to camp overnight. I scrambled to the top of the nearest hogback—the Gateway Rock, on the right as you drive in from the east, 350 feet high—before my companions could get a campfire going, and skipped blithely down again in near darkness. I spent an impatient night waiting for light so I could go back up, and not long after dawn that's where I went. I spent most of the rest of the day on that rock, managing at one time to get myself into such a fix that it took me hours to decipher a way down again. I must have crawled the vertical height of the rock half a dozen times, tracing down every crack and fissure as if my sole intent was to memorize its soft contours.

Now climbing that rock is no big deal, don't get me wrong. That is not "climbing," and real rock-climbers must scoff at the mention of it. There are well-trod pathways over much of its surface, and just when I thought I'd pulled off some remarkable piece of agility, I would invariably come across the deeply scratched initials of some rock-climbing vandal—if not his beer cans and sandwich wrappers. But mostly I didn't think of any of that, didn't even think whether or not I was getting to difficult places. I just went there. It was me, sneakers, and fingertips: I was guide, climbing equipment, and appreciative tourist all in one. I had the time of my life. I was never afraid, seldom even slightly nervous, although I was regularly inching my way along over sixty- and eighty-foot drop-offs.

That's the point: no courage was required. Specifically so. At every point where courage was required, I found another route. I didn't want those questions intruding on the fun I was having, didn't want to hang in indecision while I pondered whether or not I could get away with the next step. Whether or not I would fall. None of this was conscious, of course, not then or throughout much of the similar scrambling I did in ensuing years. When courage came to be required—primarily because after long layoffs I would come back each time a little more afraid of heights, and it would take longer to get over *that* simple, elemental fear—I finally quit. I am a nonclimber.

My climbing friends explain to me that with the proper progression—a little guidance, the introduction of equipment, the gradual accrual of finer skills, ropes, pitons, and all the rest—that point at which courage came to be required could have been moved back almost indefinitely. Safe climbing is absolutely possible—assuming no rockfalls and avalanches, no equipment failure or human misjudgment—and the courage in major climbs comes into play in summoning up the will to continue when conditions turn terrible. Or when, for whatever purpose, the precepts of safe climbing must deliberately be ignored. Sometimes I regret never undertaking the progression, but not often. I am a nonclimber. No apologies, no defenses. It doesn't seem to reduce my love of mountains.

But I would bring your attention back to that Colorado summer day I spent swooping and sprinting over every inch of that dead-easy rock face. That's what my sour recital of the sometimes scandalous history of the sport has most seriously missed. That's what keeps mountain climbing sweet for the mountain climbers; the joyous purity of that experience cannot be gainsaid. I can project the development of it for a more serious devotee. From scrambling over dead-easy rocks, to climbs that require equipment if not courage, to the desire to get to more and more difficult places, to the honing of one's courage and character in the face of real difficulties, to the expansion of the experience to include snow and ice climbs as well as mere rock scrambling. To the perfectly understandable, if somewhat irrational, desire to get on top of taller and taller physical structures. To the mountains of expeditions. For all my sourness, at heart I can question no mountain climber's motives.

In the end, the hard man is something of a mythological beast. (No climber worthy of the term would dare apply it to himself.) Whatever it is that stimulates men to work toward achieving whatever degree of hardness must somehow be implied in the progression above. Philosophy, I think, would come later. Yet it is difficult not to be fond of at least the idea of the hard man. I like to imagine the perfect accomplishment for the archetypical hard man. He would pick an unclimbed—preferably "unclimbable"—peak somewhere. He would hitchhike, flat broke but adequately equipped with climbing gear, to the vicinity. He would take a pickup laboring job to earn enough to pay for his provisioning, and when he had that sum, he would quit. He would then go off and climb the unclimbable, alone, preferably in winter, very likely spending an overnight bivouac or two or three roped in a more or less sitting or lying position to the rock face. He would succeed and come down again; if you asked him where he had been, he would respond, "Climbing." And then would proceed to hitchhike to the next mountain.

See, I am as susceptible to the romanticism of the sport as the next person. There *are* these mystics wandering about all our mountains. Not too many of them. It is very likely that a few get themselves killed off in any given year. They don't make big headlines when they do, because nobody but a few other hard men know who they are or how they die. It is a strange sport.

The mountain winds, like the dew and rain, sunshine and snow, are measured and bestowed with love on the forests to develop their strength and beauty. However restricted the scope of other forest influences, that of the winds is universal . . . now whispering and cooing through the branches like a sleepy child, now roaring like the ocean; the winds blessing the forests, the forests the winds, with ineffable beauty and harmony as the sure result.
—JOHN MUIR, *The Mountains of California*

Chapter **10**

The Weather Makers

Mountain climbing's principal danger is not the height but the weather that surrounds those heights. Mountain weather is awful. If there is a redeeming feature to it, it is that the weather is often awful in the literal sense of the term: awe-full. Awesome. Fine weather in the mountains can be finer than it ever is anywhere else—hot, bright days and cool, clear nights. But when it turns bad, as it does rather more often than anywhere else, it can do so in ways that are positively alarming. It has the capacity to strike terror into the hearts of its observers. Whatever else it may be, mountain weather is not boring.

The only dependable result of this awesomeness, particularly for people whose time in the mountains is limited, is frustration. On the simplest level it means that people who go to the mountains to see them are often disappointed. You go for the visual glories and find you can't see anything but gloomy valleys and lowering cloudbanks. On a more serious scale it means that mountain activities that require visibility or even human habitability can become positively dangerous. People have died of exposure on New England's Mount Washington—at six thousand feet or lower—in August. (That the people who do so make gross errors in judgment—T-shirts and walking shorts on a mountain that can get snow in any month of the year—is more than a little contributory.)

At its benign and glorious best, mountain weather is still extremely variable, with striking contrast between the air temperature in sun and in shade, with blasts of gusty, changeable wind, and the ever-present possibility of rain or snow squalls from any quarter, dissolving as quickly as they form. When mountain weather is not being benign, of course, it is usually being horrifying. The highest winds ever recorded on the earth's surface—231 miles per hour—were measured on that same Mount Washington, and it's quite likely that that record has not been broken only because higher mountains are such inhospitable places on which to maintain weather stations. More outlandish weather extremes have been observed, for example, in the Antarctic—in its mountainous portions. Mountains *make* weather.

There are perfectly sensible, predictable reasons for this; the reasons don't make the experience of mountain weather any less frustrating, but they do help explain why it is so consistently inconsistent. Knowing something about the mechanisms behind mountain weather can at least give you something to mull over while you're waiting for it to clear up.

Altitude itself helps power mountain weather, but only by roundabout means. Altitude reduces atmospheric pressure, which in turn influences wind, which has a great deal to do with variations in air temperature and moisture content—and it is the last two variables which are the primary influences on the weather. Atmospheric pressure decreases by about one-thirtieth of its total for every nine-hundred-foot rise in altitude. For animal life the effect can be severe. Above about 10,000 feet, the thinning of the air is sufficient to bring on mountain sickness in human beings: weakness, nausea, headache, disturbed sleep. Mountain sickness usually cures itself within a few days if the victim avoids exertion, but it can be a debilitating introduction to the mountains for the flatlander. At 17,500 feet, atmospheric pressure is roughly half what it is at sea level, and oxygen starvation begins to become a serious consideration. Chilean tin miners—natives—sometimes work at 19,000 feet, but go back down to 17,500 feet to sleep. Sherpas in Tibet regularly pasture their yaks at 18,000 feet, but not themselves. One of Sir Edmund Hillary's Himalayan expeditions spent a winter at 19,000 feet; they found the experience seriously debilitating. Few people anywhere in the world live full-time at more than 14,000 feet.

The lessened pressure at high altitude has a subtler effect on the weather. The little roadside plaques in Rocky Mountain National Park tell us how every thousand feet of altitude is the same as a journey of three hundred miles or so toward the poles, and so above-timberline tundra in the high mountains corresponds in many ways to Arctic tundra. It's a handy analogy but in one sense inaccurate: the Arctic tundra lies under a full complement of atmosphere; mountain slopes don't.

At high altitudes the thinner air has less carbon dioxide, less water vapor, and less dust, as well as less oxygen than at sea level. There is much greater *insolation*—the amount of the sun's energy absorbed by the ground—at altitude. The thinner air reflects less of the sun's heat back into space and absorbs less in the form of raised air temperature; the ground surface gets a great deal more of that energy and therefore heats up more rapidly and intensely than at lower levels. When the sun goes down, the ground cools again just as rapidly and intensely, without a thick blanket of atmosphere to insulate it. On a normal bright day at altitude, exposed ground surface may vary by as much as fifty degrees Fahrenheit between sun and shade. Sizable, rapid variations in temperature make for weather instability.

(While 75 percent of the radiant energy from the sun penetrates the earth's atmosphere to 6,000 feet, only about 50 percent makes it to sea level. The intensity of that radiation on Mont Blanc is estimated to be 26 percent greater than that which reaches Paris, four hundred miles away—and 15,500 feet lower. There are some other interesting effects besides broad temperature ranges from the more intense radiation. High altitude sun is also richer in the ultraviolet end of the spectrum, and often falls on mountainsides tilted at angles so they receive the rays of the sun as directly as does the equator. One result of this is phenomenal if sporadic growth of plants in summer; another is excruciating sunburns on careless skiers in winter.)

Because mountain air heats up rapidly in daytime and cools rapidly at night, mountain atmosphere is required to carry on an eternal balancing act, flowing from cold to hot, from high pressure to low. (It's the same balancing act that goes on everywhere else, but intensified by the mountains.) All that rushing about makes wind—and weather. The temperature imbalance is exaggerated by a general decrease in air temperature with altitude. Rising air does cool off, simply because the decreasing pressure allows the molecules of air to spread out and therefore to bounce off each other less frequently. (Air temperature is primarily a product of this friction; severe cold is simply a lack of kinetic energy in the air.)

It's traditional to credit altitude with a standard rate of cooling, usually given as two degrees per thousand feet of altitude. That figure—a fairly conservative one—is good enough for general purposes, but it combines several different standard rates, and can vary wildly. For example, if air is rising but no condensation is occurring, the cooling will be at 5.5 degrees Fahrenheit per thousand feet (called the *dry adiabatic rate*). If condensation is occurring, the rate drops back to 3.2 degrees per thousand feet (the *saturation adiabatic rate*). Condensation releases heat into the air; evaporation absorbs it. But the dew point, at which condensation occurs, also declines as the air rises, at a rate of one degree for every thousand feet. It's very confusing; suffice it that the higher you go, the colder you get.

Add a fairly high variation in ambient temperature between mountain peak and valley to the already sharply varied sun-versus-shade and day-versus-night temperatures, and the result is going to be weather. Wind, for starters; precipitation as the inevitable follow-up.

When the exposed upper slopes of a mountain are heated in daytime, the air over those slopes gets warmer than air at the same altitude over nearby valleys. The result is a convection current, in which air is propelled up the mountain in a *thermal upslope wind* during the daytime. The upslope wind starts with the first heating of the peak at daybreak, gradually increases in intensity during the day, and dies down to calm at sunset. Then it reverses direction and turns into a downslope wind for the night, as the cooling, heavier air heads for the valley. Hang-glider pilots rely on those upslope winds to get them airborne; it can be assumed that there are no night flyers among the mountain hang-gliders.

This entire process is much like the predictable onshore and offshore sea breezes that switch direction between day and night, powered by the different cooling rates of land and sea. Upslope winds are stronger on south-facing slopes where there is more heating by the sun. Similarly, valley winds blow toward the mountains during the day, and away from the mountains at night. Local residents become so familiar with these conditions that if the regular winds don't appear on time, they know a storm is brewing: local systems have been overcome by larger atmospheric conditions.

Gravity itself creates another kind of mountain wind. Mountain regions, particularly those marked by high plateaus or networks of high mountain valleys, can accumulate caps of cold, dense air; this air then finds its way through wind gaps or over low divides to spill out onto the plains below. The result is a fierce downslope wind. The phenomenon, properly called a *katabatic wind,* is most pronounced on the major ice caps such as Greenland and Antarctica, which have high-altitude interiors and coastal valleys that become veritable wind tunnels when cold air begins draining through them. Gravity-induced winds there often exceed one hundred miles per hour. But any area near a mountain region can experience the same effect, as in the bitter local winds known by such names as the *mistral* in southern France, the *bora* on the Yugoslavian coast, and the *Santa Ana* in southern California.

Characteristic local winds build up their own folklore. That 231-mile-per-hour wind on Mount Washington may have been a bit of a freak circumstance, but it occurred in a most likely spot: that mountain will get winds of over 75 miles per hour—hurricane force—on an average of more than a hundred days a year. Mount Washington is so windy because of the Bernoulli effect, in which air masses whipping along a storm track become squeezed between rising mountain slopes and a cold, dense, upper layer of air well above the peak and are accelerated by this compression. It can happen on any mountain, but Mount Washington happens to lie in a productive storm track and pokes up to an unusual height above surrounding terrain, thus achieving more compression and acceleration of the rising air.

Mount Washington's great winds have to start somewhere, and often enough the starting point seems to be the valley where I live. The height of land to the south in our valley marks a point where a broad wind gap west of Mount Moosilauke joins with another wind tunnel of a tributary of the Connecticut River Valley. The nearby road intersection is known as Bungay Corner (pronounced BUNG-ee, with a hard g), for reasons that nobody seems to be able to recall. When the wind starts blowing up the valley—headed for the Bernoulli effect on Mount Washington, thirty miles away—it builds up a strange periodicity, with eerie calms in between the sharp jolts and blasts of howling wind. Locals call the wind the "Bungay Jarrer," or "Bungay Jar."

Or simply "Bungay"—as when the valley bottom is relatively calm but great winds can be heard roaring up on the sides of

Kinsman; then, a local will say, you can hear Bungay talking. Weird stories are told of the wind's capacity to disturb men's minds, of misery and domestic strife stimulated by its bizarre psychological effect. Of old-timers found stalking through nearby Franconia Notch in dead of night, communing with the Bungay. Not to mention tales of barn doors blown miles down the valley and cattle driven deep into the woods by its blasts. The Bungay Jar is a local hero. Or demon. Nearly every valley in New England has its own equivalent local wind.

There's another form of local mountain wind; it's called the *foehn* in Europe, a *chinook* in North America, although it, too, can occur almost anywhere. The foehn is a warm, dry wind blowing downslope on the lee side of a mountain range. But the circumstances that produce it are better understood in terms of what is happening over the mountain, on the upwind side. The foehn is a rain-shadow wind. It's best to consider the rain before we look at the shadow.

Precipitation happens when a mass of air cools below the dew point—the point at which water vapor starts forming into clouds. Radiation cooling, as on a still, clear night, can generate low fog, but it can't make rain. The only dependable way to get rain is to get an air mass moving upward. There are three common types of such ascension: convectional, cyclonic, and orographic.

Convectional precipitation occurs when a bubble of warm air—generated by a freshly plowed field, a parking lot, a factory, or any other heat source—rises high enough to form a nice, fluffy cumulus cloud, cools further, and dumps a rain or snow shower. If the air in the bubble has a heavy load of humidity, it can grow into a thunderhead, a cumulonimbus cloud, and the shower that may be produced can be quite heavy, if brief. Interestingly enough, the life-span of a thunderstorm averages about fifty-five minutes, and by satellite observation it has been determined that at any given moment there are between twenty-one hundred and twenty-three hundred thunderstorms in existence within the earth's atmosphere.

It is a total that for some reason seems to be maintained with remarkable consistency, whatever the season. Some of those thunderstorms are quite likely to be occurring in mountain regions, but convectional precipitation is not in any significant way linked to mountains.

Neither is *cyclonic* precipitation, the kind that results from those highs and lows on the weather map. To a weatherman a cyclone is simply a low pressure area, whatever its strength as a storm. When low pressure cells and high pressure cells meet, or even when cold and warm air masses meet, there is a lifting of air masses, cooling, and, usually, precipitation as a result. Cyclonic precipitation is the world's major weather maker. The cyclonic-frontal systems occur with particular power in the middle latitudes, where equatorial and polar air engage in a worldwide shoving match. Those middle latitudes contain many of the mountainous regions of the world, but while mountains in the path of cyclonic-frontal systems may serve to intensify or modify their effect, the mountains themselves have little to do with the formation of these weather systems.

Orographic—mountain-related—precipitation is another matter. It results when prevailing winds force an air mass upward along the rising slope of a mountain, cooling it sufficiently to condense the moisture out of it as rain or snow. Thus mountains do "rake" or "sweep" rainfall out of passing clouds, just as the folklore would have it.

Water vapor tends to gather largely in the lower layers of the atmosphere. Pushing those layers against mountains, forcing their ascent, makes for heavy rainfall. Highland areas almost always have greater annual precipitation than surrounding lowlands. Orographic precipitation is responsible for all greenery on the occasional isolated mountain in the midst of barren desert. More commonly it makes the windward side of a mountain range much more heavily vegetated than the lee. That's what's responsible for the great forests on the western slopes of the Cascades of the Pacific Northwest, where prevailing winds pick up great quantities of moisture from the nearby ocean, then dump it on the mountains as they sweep east. Similar conditions prevail along Madagascar's east coast and India's west coast; mountain-generated upslope winds provide a boost to normal seashore wind conditions in both places. A miniaturized fresh-water version occurs in Vermont's Green Mountains, where prevailing winds sweep across Lake Champlain before being bounced upward to unload their moisture in the hills.

Mountain regions collect precipitation by other means than this forced ascent. When lower air conditions are unstable, contact with even a minor slope can trigger condensation; thereafter the added heat released by that condensation sets up a convection cell, which generates rain on its own. The very turbulence associated with mountain air (where vegetationless peaks have little ground friction to help damp out gusts) can cause otherwise layered air masses to mix and grow unstable. Mountains also function as weather barriers, delaying the passage of cyclonic systems—which means that those systems have more time to dump precipitation on the mountains before they move on.

Hence the frustration to mountain visitors. Early mornings can often be clear and fine, but once the mountain weather phenomena go into operation, cloudiness and rain develop quickly. Even when the general mountain weather stays clear, the peaks themselves gather clouds more often than not. Upslope winds can put a cumulus cloud right over the peak, in what one writer calls "the visible tops of invisible ascending air currents." Peaks collect *banner clouds* that stream away downwind like a flag from a staff—"continuously gaining new substance as valley air, riding up a mountainside on the wind's back, condenses near the crest—continuously evaporating old substance at its tattered flagtail end perhaps a mile to leeward as the air mixes with drier air or subsides to a warmer level. Thus the wind blows right through the banner cloud instead of carrying it along—just as if it were a flag of cloth."[*]

[*] Guy Murchie, *Song of the Sky* (Boston, Houghton Mifflin, 1954), p. 193.

The problem with orographic precipitation is that what goes up must come down, and in the case of moving masses of air the phenomenon reverses itself. After passing a mountain summit the air mass expands rapidly down the lee slope, drying out and heating up in the process. (The dry adiabatic rate of 5.5 degrees per thousand feet holds for descending air as well, heating it up instead of cooling it off.) A mountain range with a consistent prevailing wind will have a *rain shadow* extending—sometimes for hundreds of miles—from its down-wind side: an area of extremely sparse rainfall, often desert-like. California's Sierra Nevada gets fifty or more inches of precipitation per year. *Nevada* means snow-covered, and winter storms there dump snowfalls that can literally be measured in feet of accumulation per hour; Death Valley, tucked immediately against the eastern edge of the Sierra and thus well within its rain shadow, gets only about four inches of rain per year. The high, dry plains of eastern Oregon and Washington, similarly shadowed by the Cascade Range, suffer from a climate produced by the same natural mechanism.

Occasionally that warm, dry downslope wind—the foehn or chinook—becomes pronounced and distinctive. In its most vigorous form the foehn wind is intensified by a passing cyclonic system. Denver and Boulder, in Colorado, have in recent years been victimized by tornadolike downslope winds coming off the Rockies to the immediate west. In those cases the foehn winds were pulled to freak velocities by the attraction of massive low pressure areas over the high plains to the east, which grossly intensified normal foehn conditions.

A drop of five thousand to six thousand feet—well within the available relief of the eastern slope of the Rockies—can bring about a jump in air temperature of thirty degrees, and foehn winds with temperatures of seventy degrees Fahrenheit in winter are not impossible. The foehn will often have a relative humidity on the order of 15 percent, which means that its drying capacity is prodigious—locals tell of foehns that vaporize the ice from ponds without melting it. (The process is known as sublimation.) The onset of a foehn is usually quite sudden; one Montana town registered a temperature rise of thirty-one degrees in three minutes. In many winters such chinook winds are the saviors of livestock, melting snow cover rapidly and rescuing herds of cattle from impending starvation. Foehn valleys in the Alps can become springlike oases in the midst of winter, and enjoy measurably longer growing seasons than neighboring, nonfoehn areas.

But the foehn is not regarded as an unmixed blessing, for all its capacity to alleviate temporarily the rigors of winter. It blasts away snow like a hot knife, reducing the water-holding capacity of the mountains and generating winter floods and summer droughts. (And playing hob with ski resort reservations and profits.) It bakes moisture out of the soil and may threaten the health of spring crops and winter wheat. It so severely increases fire danger that in Swiss villages, where most of the buildings are constructed of wood, specially appointed officials go through the town to make sure all domestic fires are extinguished, and smoking is forbidden during the foehn.

The foehn also does things to people's heads. Just as the full moon is reputed to stimulate domestic discord and crimes of violence in the cities, so is the foehn credited with bringing on surliness and irritability among the mountain folk. It is usually preceded by transparently clear but extremely oppressive atmospheric conditions which most people find enervating. "It renders the brain torpid, robs a person of his appetite, and seems to bloat up the entire body," one French observer recorded in 1684. Pressure fluctuations cause a general nervous jumpiness: cats get twitchy, plants wilt, cattle go off their feed. The foehn is blamed for suicides, murders, quarrels, sexual irregularities. Swiss mountain valleys may get forty to fifty days of foehn over a winter and spring, and the fortunate among the populace tend to abandon their mountains for less windy climes until the foehn is over.

Some Europeans say the depressive effect has to do with too

many ions in the atmosphere—I forget whether it is the negative ones or the positive ones that are supposed to do the psychological dirty work. It could well be that the effect is as much environmental as it is psychological. A hot, dry wind blowing the tattered scraps of last fall's detritus through the village streets, exposing the mud and grime that the snows had otherwise so beautifully camouflaged, doesn't do much for anyone's spirits. Add to that the fairly certain knowledge that soon enough the foehn is going to stop and winter is going to return—that you're going to be plunged back into the locked-up, snowbound, icy grip of the dark season for yet another month or two—and it's not too difficult to imagine becoming depressed by the foehn. The Swiss call it *Schneefresser*—the snow-eater.

Not an appealing picture, this climate of rain and snow and cloudbanks tacked permanently onto the peaks above. Yet most of the world's population regards the mountain climate as so salubrious that that's where they've chosen to locate their health spas, vacation resorts, and research centers. The choice of location has often been skewed by romantic preconceptions of what the climate is really going to be like, but there are reasons for those preconceptions, too.

Quito, in Ecuador, is often used as the typical example of just what a mountain climate is supposed to be. It is a reasonably large city (half a million), it's located almost squarely on the equator, and it is well above nine thousand feet. Quito is remarkable for the evenness of its climate: although daily maximum and minimum temperatures may vary by twenty-five degrees or so, thanks to the rapid heating and cooling of thin mountain air, the year-round range between the warmest and coldest months is less than one degree. It is a city of hot sun and very cool shade, in the mountain tradition. Residents report that the fine air is marvelous to breathe, but that you are never quite warm unless you're in direct sunlight.

That's a small price to pay near the equator. Most of the

major cities in equatorial parts of the world are located at relatively high altitudes, the sites chosen specifically for relief from otherwise unbearable climates. Venezuela, Ecuador, Bolivia, Colombia, Mexico, Guatemala, El Salvador, Honduras—all locate their capitals and population centers at high altitudes. The principal characteristic of the equatorial climate is lack of variation from season to season; high altitude climate is marked by the wide variation between daytime and nighttime temperatures. Thus, a year-round succession of warm days and cool nights, a perfectly delightful climate that violates everyone's notion of what the tropics are like. Temperate zone visitors to these tropic capitals usually characterize the climate as one of permanent springtime. India, it used to be said, was governed from above twenty-one hundred meters (sixty-nine hundred feet)—the hill stations, where the colonial governments escaped the heat.

Mountain regions also enjoy frequent temperature inversions, which can make the rigors of winter seem no more than a delightful stimulant. Downslope winds at night drain the colder air from the peaks into the valleys below. The sun reaches into those valleys for much briefer periods during the day than it shines on the surrounding highlands. The valleys can capture and hold pockets of cold, dank air, often fog-laden, while the peaks and shoulders nearby bask in glorious winter sunshine. I once spent a February week in Banff, in the Canadian Rockies, enjoying springlike temperatures of twenty-five to thirty degrees at about eight thousand feet of altitude. The nearest radio station was in Calgary, ninety miles away and four thousand feet lower. It was broadcasting incomprehensible weather reports of below-zero readings. I kept bracing myself for the onslaught of cold that never came. When the weather did break, Banff didn't get colder; Calgary warmed up, thanks to a chinook from the Banff area.

Not to be discounted in any consideration of mountain weather and climate is the quality of the air itself. If mountain air seems to hold more snow, rain, fog, and sheer, miserable coldness, it also holds fewer pollutants, fewer unpleasant smells, fewer of all the characteristics that give postindustrial air a bad name. The air quality indices published daily in the cities are in effect measurements of how un-mountainlike their air is. For all the possible measurements taken by scientific gadgetry in the mountains, and for all the respiratory rehabilitation centers located there, I suspect that one's response to mountain air must remain purely subjective. It feels better. It smells and tastes better than the low-altitude stuff. Language fails in the face of its sensual qualities. Breathing it is like drinking from a crystalline, tumbling, bedrock mountain brook. I know it is subjective, and I can't prove any of this, but here's my advice. It is worthwhile, in the high mountains, to spend some time simply sitting still, breathing the air, paying attention to it. Feeling it flow in and out. (If you've exerted yourself at altitude, you won't have to search out the opportunity, believe me.) It silver-plates your lungs. It carbonates your blood. Don't give me any of that guff about the fickle miseries of mountain weather. Altitude is its own reward.

"In skiing, turning is what it's all about. Everything else is persiflage."—MARTIN LURAY

Chapter 11

Mountain Playgrounds

If you need an alibi for seeking the rewards of high altitude, skiing is as good as any. Originally skiing didn't have anything to do with mountains. Relic skis that predate recorded history have been found in the Scandinavian countries. There, as a means of transportation, skiing was faster and less effortful than snowshoeing. It was a smooth and efficient way to go overland on snow, to get from point A to point B, for the proficient user, so long as no underbrush got in the way and the woods weren't too thick. As a means of transport it was perhaps a bit silly-looking—boards strapped to the feet and all that—but it worked. It was even fun, particularly once you'd climbed a small hill and then could slide down the other side.

It was the sliding down that led to everything else, and took skiing away to the mountains, of course. A few daredevils got so carried away with the fun that they began launching themselves into the air during the downhill portion of their progress, inventing ski jumping. Others, less daredevilish, more masochistic, or perhaps simply more competitive, began racing each other over long distances on skis. Before the Scandinavians had quite realized it, two new sports had been invented: ski jumping and cross-country ski racing (the latter abbreviated, now, by the cognoscenti as X-C racing). Those two sports retain their popularity (in infinitely more complex forms than they had when invented), but neither of them has much to do with the huge, multibillion-dollar recreation industry which has spread giant resorts over the mountains of the world. Neither of them has anything to do with mountains, really.

Philosophers toy with redefinitions of mankind into *Homo faber,* the tool-making animal, and *Homo ludens,* the animal that plays. It was both of these irrepressible human characteristics that were responsible for moving skiing into the mountains. Give the human animal an enjoyable activity, and he will practice it to distraction. Skiing was enough fun (even on *small* hills) that folks just wouldn't leave it alone, despite some serious drawbacks. For example, except for a select and highly skilled few, most would-be skiers just couldn't deal with the degree and rate of motion given to downhill progress by real mountains. (A lot of early ski jumping may have been wholly inadvertent.) Skiers essaying a downhill course had to learn to control those clumsy boards, to save their limbs if not their lives, and in the early days management of skis was an art not lightly acquired. To put the simplest possible face on it, the early skis were almost impossible to turn. Yet a few intense and acrobatic individuals did learn to turn them, and the result was such swooping, soaring flight down the hillsides, so much obvious fun, that the public wanted in on it. Gradually, the ski itself was so refined that management of it became relatively easy. Skiers built themselves a better tool. Mass participation became possible.

Skiing is a sport susceptible to massive overcomplication, but every bit of the complication issues from this simple truth: turning is everything. Without the capability of turning, a downhill ski run is only a trust-to-luck toboggan ride in a miserably exposed position on totally unsuited equipment. With the ability to turn, it becomes that swooping and soaring flight over the snow. The ability to turn the skis leads to everything else—control of speed, ability to stop, avoidance of obstacles, instantaneous choice of ever-changing routes, in the best of instances an ecstatic dance down the mountain.

Skis that could be turned and skiers who could turn them moved skiing into the mountains. Better venues were sought: higher hills with longer, steeper runs than were available in the modest Scandinavian highlands. What greater terrain could there be than in the huge "civilized" mountains of the Alps, already virtually a British resort colony? Skiing split into two disciplines: Nordic, which includes cross-country touring and racing, and ski jumping; and Alpine, which became the picture-postcard, resort-based version that is downhill skiing, now totally served by ski lifts. Both sports remain alive and healthy; each is represented enthusiastically in competitive versions in the Winter Olympics. But it is the latter that has made such tremendous inroads, that has brought so many millions of people and dollars into the mountains.

(Nordic skiing has begun to move into the mountains also, and a peculiar crossbred sport of ski mountaineering—cross-country ski touring in the high mountains, with some winter climbing thrown in just to burn off extra energy—has grown moderately popular. But while millions of Scandinavians glide about their own hills and dales on touring skis, and sales of Nordic ski equipment have shown a sizable increase in the past decade in both the United States and Europe, the gross numbers involved still don't approach those involved in downhill skiing. And there are probably more pure climbers than there are ski mountaineers. The equipment for what are now three entirely separate sports—cross-country skiing, downhill skiing, and ski jumping—has grown so specialized that each is now unusable for the other two.)

Skiing crossed the Atlantic with hardly a pause in the late 1920's and early 1930's, getting established in the Canadian Laurentians and New England, and then spreading rapidly to the Rockies and other U.S. snow-belt mountain areas. (There was some skiing in the American West in the nineteenth century, mostly by transplanted Scandinavian miners.) Now there are ski resorts in Iran, Russia, and Czechoslovakia, as well as throughout Europe and North America. Japan has a well-developed skiing industry (with more active customers than the United States). The Andes, Australia, and New Zealand—with seasons the reverse of ours—now make year-round, big-resort skiing possible. India is investigating the construction of ski facilities in the Himalayan foothills. In short, wherever there is a slope that gets snow, some entrepreneur will soon string a ski lift up it. China may be the temporary exception, but once that country takes a serious look at tourist dollars, a Chinese ski facility is almost sure to follow. Displaced skiers hike to the top of Mauna Loa, in the Hawaiian Islands, and do their sliding on the eternal snows there, bereft of energy-conserving ski lifts. Korea has entered skiers in the Winter Olympics; the Philippine Islands, incredibly enough, hold a voting membership in the International Ski Federation.

Six million affluent Americans participate regularly in the sport, spending over a hundred million dollars a year on equipment alone, and well over fifty dollars each per day, exclusive of travel costs, for their time at the ski resort. One supremely popular Vermont resort claims to process twelve thousand patrons per day on peak weekends, and there are over a thousand ski resorts in North America (although only perhaps a hundred of them can be dignified as "major," and for most of them five thousand skiers per day is a capacity crowd). Walt Disney Enterprises set aside thirty-five million dollars for construction of a single California ski resort in the early 1960's, knocking the rest of the industry on its ear by their boldness and lavish plans. Environmental pressures have stalled that construction ever since, and fulfillment of the original plan may now be beyond the resources of even the Disney people. Never mind; Vail now plans to build an adjunct in the next ten years that will cost *$148 million,* in 1976 dollars.

The equipment and fashion facets of the "sport" of skiing have now discovered planned obsolescence and pump out model changes as regularly as did Detroit in the glory days of the automobile industry. Ski resorts, seldom hugely profitable when they restrict their services to providing ski facilities to transient customers, became the bellwether of the condominium and second-home boom of the late 1960's. That boom has since gone bust, while ski resorts sit on an oversupply of unsold housing, but their ancillary real estate business shows signs of coming back. Skiing, in short, snatches its fair share of the forty billion dollars that Americans spend each year on sport. It may be even bigger business in Europe and Japan.

All this from skis that will turn? Yes. More. People changing their lives, uprooting homes and families, swapping livelihoods, simply to make skiing more available. Thousands of marginal service-industry employees—ski instructors, ski patrolmen, ski lift operators, maintenance crews, busboys, chambermaids, waiters, bartenders—putting up with ridiculously low wages and otherwise intolerable living and working conditions, just to hang on by their fingernails in the midst of the affluence of ski country, in order to go out and get their fill of sliding around on those skis that will turn. Ski bumming— college dropouts, stockbrokers gone native, wistful romantics who have given up on the straight life, in numbers that totally eclipse those of their brothers-under-the-skin who have chosen the beaches and tennis courts and country clubs in search of the "soft" and sybaritic life. Skiing is a certifiable addiction. On skis that turn.

I have suffered that addiction. If I have cast a dyspeptic eye on mountain climbing without ever having done much of the

Real Thing—and I freely admit that that's just what I've done—no such disclaimers are required with regard to skiing. I've been there. I can't say the monkey is yet off my back, although in recent years I've found myself skiing less and enjoying the mountains more. In fact, between skiing and me there is something of a love–hate relationship. It is my misfortune, I'm sure, but it certainly adds to the intensity of the experience.

The Hate Part

Here are some of the things about skiing that keep our relationship a mixed affair. When I became editor of *Skiing* magazine in 1966, good-quality ski boots cost seventy-five dollars, bindings—the hardware that attaches boot to ski—twenty dollars, the best skis a little over one hundred dollars. Now, top-quality boots cost over two hundred dollars, bindings just under one hundred, and skis from two hundred to two hundred fifty dollars. It is not difficult, with fashionable ski clothes, to stroll out onto the slopes sporting a thousand-dollar investment. Dynamic obsolescence in ski boots, God help us all.

The technology is admittedly fascinating, and many ski buffs become as absorbed by its fine points as racing car engineers. Boots, for instance, used to be sturdy leather shoes with notched soles that would accept early-day ski bindings but which could also be used, off-season, for hiking and climbing. Now they are rigid plastic encasements so specialized that not only can they be used only for downhill skiing, they also make standing upright—in a nonskiing position—downright painful. The goal in ski boot development has always been maximum stiffness, the better to translate the subtlest muscular twitch anywhere below the knee into instant response at the ski. Modern boots are mere plastic shells, albeit festooned with mechanical buckles, hinges, Vernier-grade adjustments, and external stiffeners. The human foot does not like life in a plastic shell, particularly a totally rigid one. (There was even a magnesium-shelled boot on the market for a short time.) Therefore, the boot interior is padded and custom-fitted with any of an assortment of plastic pads, foams, and gels—and at least one model has an internal air bladder, complete with its own tiny hand pump for readjusting pressure. For a while it was all the rage to fit boots by means of a rubberized bladder into which a plastic foaming agent was introduced while the boot buyer stood in a quasi-skiing position in the ski shop, trying to hold the pose until the plastic set up in a perfect custom fit. (Every ski shop was thus forced to invest thousands in expensive foaming equipment and training of personnel to operate it; the costs were of course passed on to the customer.) Problems with this massive technological overkill have just about done away with the custom foam job, and new plastic materials have supplanted it, but, for a couple of busy years, going to have your boots foamed was the foot fetishist's ultimate thrill.

As with boots, so with bindings. During its infancy skiing suffered a scandalous accident rate of just about six injuries for every thousand skier-days. The extra leverage those long boards—attached as they were to fragile limbs—imparted to the force of a fall made every spill an invitation to the orthopedist. What was needed was some means of attaching the skis securely so long as the skier needed them, but allowing them to cast loose in the event of a serious tumble. The mechanical ingenuity that has gone into meeting that need has been immense. Skiers seem to have infinite capacities for inventing new ways to fall, and the binding engineers have set it as their duty to provide releasable ski bindings—so-called "safety" bindings—for every conceivable falling motion.

The engineers have done pretty well in recent years, since they finally recognized the problems inherent in attaching rigid boots to flexible skis acting under loads that can shift instantaneously in any direction, with friction quotients that vary more significantly than does the physical loading. Expensive modern bindings, properly installed, adjusted, checked, and maintained, are really pretty safe. Unfortunately the percentage of those millions of skiers who are willing to bother with all that expense, time, and care remains small. The injury rate has gone down somewhat in recent years, but skiers still fall and break their bones a lot. (One side effect of modern equipment has been to move the injury sites to new places on the body. The traditional skiing injury used to be the "boot-top fracture," just at or above the ankle, with the old soft boots. Modern high boots move the strain up to the calf or knee—and with the improvements in both boots and bindings, skiers now suffer nearly as many shoulder and arm injuries as they used to broken ankles.)

Skis—the improved tool that allows turning—have shown the most spectacular technological advances. The "perfection" of a metal ski (actually an aluminum-plywood sandwich) by an aircraft engineer named Howard Head was the breakthrough that made skis easy to turn. It also assured that the all-wood ski would go the way of the dinosaur as far as downhill skiing was concerned. The first Head skis were so easy to turn that the pros dubbed them "cheaters." Along with the earlier invention of metal ski edges (giving a positive "bite" for turning on hard snow) Head skis were responsible for the explosion of skiing into a mass sport. Anyone could do it: skiing became almost as easy to learn as ice skating, and the exponential growth of the sport was the immediate result.

Too easy, in fact: for the strong, skilled skier, the new cheaters were wiggly, unstable, inadequate for higher speeds. With the development of a practical metal ski, ski design leaped from a woodcarver's art to a science, complete, inevitably, with computer analysis of the effect of variations in sidecut, bottom camber, torsional stiffness, and running surface. Exotic materials overwhelmed and displaced the aluminum-plywood sandwich, and skis began to get neoprene antishock layers, foam plastic cores, fiber-reinforced plastic wet-wrapped bodies, and other such space-age complexities. It became theoretically possible to build a ski with just about any degree of flexibility, strength, and response that a skier could dream up. Unfortunately, skiers' wants can't be similarly objectified, and every skier wants something different: the variables in skier weight, skill, and strength, in snow consistency and such minutiae as response time and the degree to which the resort has groomed its slopes will always keep the picture confused.

The identification of more and more variables has led to confusion rather than simplification, and it is still—perhaps more than ever—impossible to design a single ski model that suits every skier and all conditions. While the prices continue to rise, the industry now finds itself approaching the ridiculous position of trying to convince the skier to purchase different pairs of skis for different conditions. An ice ski, a powder snow ski, an Eastern ski, and a Western ski. One gets the vision of the skier carrying something like a golf bag full of skis as he goes, a kind of quiver, and stopping at each variation in the mountain's pitch to select a proper design to handle the change.

In other words, scientific as the technology of skiing has become, there is still a generous dollop of black magic in the mix. There's more than a hint of pure psychology involved, in the sense that a skier's confidence in his equipment has as much to do with securing satisfactory performance from that equipment as does any inherent technological advantage. New skis can be the feather in Dumbo's trunk: if you believe in them, they make you fly. Keep the faith. Meanwhile many of the fine points of technological trickery in modern equipment can make a difference to an Olympic racer; but for you and me, they remain just about what brought our attention to them in the first place: advertising copy.

No, that's too cynical. The improvement of ski equipment has made a tremendous difference in the ease with which the sport is learned and in the proficiency with which most people now practice it. I can't deny it. But what that technical sophistication has also done is create an affluent elite in the sport who can in effect buy the performance that their own athletic skills could not otherwise secure for them. There is perhaps nothing wrong with that—the elite are going to find a way to express their eliteness in any human sphere, I suppose—but the status competition that goes on just in the sphere of ski equipment leads to some ugly excesses in what used to seem a clean white sport.

(Skiing is of course "white" in another sense also. By its very expense, it suffers from de facto segregation. There are black skiers, even black ski clubs, instructors, ski patrolmen, racers—but they are still comparatively rare. Sympathetic well-wishers occasionally launch programs to give ghetto kids, of any color, a chance to experience skiing. The intent is wonderful, and the kids always seem to have a good time. But the programs invariably founder on the huge expense involved, even when many of the elements of the expense—transportation, food, housing, ski equipment, access to the slopes, instruction—are more or less donated.)

The same energy explosion that led to all that technical development in skiing also led to a lot more. The invention of stretch fabrics and their adaptation to ski pants in the mid-1950's made ski clothing look so good that the "ski look" swept through all sportswear, and the Beautiful People started going skiing just for the opportunity to wear all the neat clothes. They became skiers, the sport spurted ahead as the very In-est of In things to do, and European resorts began to host Brigitte Bardot and Aly Khan and John Kenneth Galbraith and the Kennedys. Vail—President Gerald Ford's favorite pleasure dome—started off as a high mountain cow pasture in the early 1960's and blossomed into skiing's first New Town, completely designed around and devoted to the notion of lift-served downhill skiing. Nobody knows how many billions have been invested there by now, but it has become a city, with real estate prices that are positively Manhattan Islandish. Vail now threatens to be crushed by its own success and is expanding down the length of its own valley and onto surrounding mountains as rapidly as environmental restrictions will allow.

There are other New Towns in American skiing—Snowmass (Colorado), Snowbird (Utah), Jackson Hole (Wyoming), and Big Sky (Montana)—built primarily by millionaires or giant financial combines, seldom with a prayer of turning a profit in the foreseeable future, existing now as monuments to the developers' egos (and offering superb skiing, if in strange locations and at uncomfortable prices). None except Vail holds a candle to the *old* ski towns: in Europe, Davos, Kitzbühel, Gstaad, and Cortina; in the United States, Stowe, Aspen, and Sun Valley.

Stowe was a sleepy Vermont town that was adopted by some New York superrich in the 1930's, who proceeded to finance ski development primarily for their own amusement. The development and the town caught on with the skiing masses, to the distress of the New Yorkers (and many of the Stowe-ites). Some of the New Yorkers moved on, but Stowe continued to prosper, with a wickedly challenging mountain and good if ultraconservative skiing management. It remains the dowager queen of American skiing, with what is usually the finest skiing available in the East and an overlay of snobbishness that can cause frostbite. Underneath the social chill, however, there's a warm, hospitable town, if you can escape the tourist label and get into it. It's where the best skiers in the eastern United States tend to congregate.

Aspen is a reclaimed silver mining town in central Colorado, almost totally dormant before World War II, developed immediately after the war into a mountain resort with its own unique flavor. An American millionaire named Walter Paepcke and a transplanted European ski expert, Friedl Pfeifer, had in mind a Shangri-la-ish cultural center, and it did, haltingly, become that. But while Paepcke's back was turned, Pfeifer gathered some ski people and built it into a ski town. There was this magnificent skiing mountain, Ajax, hanging over the town, just begging to be put to proper use, which Aspen proceeded to do. Now Aspen has four different mountains developed for skiing—one of them is a truly great one—and some of the most consistent snow conditions anywhere in the world.

It has become—given the town, the facilities, the hotbed of ski culture that it represents—the best place in the world to go skiing.

But not the best ski mountain. That's in Sun Valley. Back in the 1930's the Union Pacific Railroad had this track stretching out into the midst of nowhere in Idaho and no passenger traffic on it. Passenger traffic was important in those days. Chairman Averell Harriman—already a dedicated skier—told his men to put something out there that passengers would want to ride to even in the dismal months of winter. Sun Valley was the result. It too had a European ski expert behind it, who found the mountain known as Baldy overlooking the tiny town of Ketchum and talked Union Pacific into building their resort there. Early on, Sun Valley became a playground for socialites from Hollywood and New York: not only was there a lot of Union Pacific luxury laid on for celebrities, but Idaho also had divorce laws very similar to Nevada's. For purposes of marital fission, the bus trade went to Reno, the carriage trade to Sun Valley. Harriman designed it that way.

The glory days came and went for Sun Valley, and Union Pacific came to regard it as just as much a white elephant as the distressing requirement that the railway continue to provide passenger rail service in the jet age. In the early 1960's a Los Angeles millionaire named Bill Janss, who had been a top-flight ski racer just before World War II, bought Sun Valley. He turned it back into a skier's mountain, and if the resort hasn't been a great money-maker—despite some condominium development and other profit-minded local desecrations—it has remained the sentimental favorite, the single best-loved mountain among skiers in the land.

The Love Part

What makes Mount Baldy in Sun Valley such a remarkable ski mountain is not easy to identify. It juts up abruptly in the southeastern fringe of Idaho's Sawtooth Range, seemingly well separated from the rather low foothills—and that makes for spectacular views from almost any spot on the mountain. It is not terribly high by Rocky Mountain standards, at ninety-two hundred feet, but thirty-four hundred of those feet are skiable, which insures nice long runs—still, not so long as those of many European ski areas. Baldy is also not remarkably steep sided, for a ski mountain. There is a point of no return in ski slope steepness, beyond which the mountain can't hold snow and remain skiable; Baldy offers its fair share of slopes that teeter on the brink of that quality. Perhaps there are more *long* steep runs than on most mountains, but in that restricted category, Baldy is still not the champ. (In the United States, Jackson Hole holds that title.)

Yet Baldy is somehow just right. The combination works. It has the ridge-and-gulch skiing familiar to the Rockies: gentle trails run the length of both the shoulders of the ridges and the bottoms of the gulches in between; breathtakingly steep faces connect ridge and gulch, take your choice. It has broad open-slope skiing. It has bowls. Oh, my, yes, the bowls. Above-timberline cirques that catch and hold snow in open expanses so broad they defy skiers to cover them with ski tracks. Get to the bowls on Baldy when the snow and the weather are right and you can discover the maximum soaring freedom that skiing ever allows. You gulp once at the top, let your skis run until the speed gets scary, then start throwing wide, carving turns, semicircles of smoothness, turns you can bear down on, lean into, use full weight and strength on. Turns that go on and on until you realize that you have to stop and rest before you fall apart. You pull up and lean, gasping, on your ski poles, wind tears streaming down your face, and try to control your grin. And you are a quarter of the way down the mountain, with all that snow yet to be skied.

That's the love part of my relationship with skiing. The rest of the sport is irritatingly . . . competitive. The skills are elusive, requiring more skiing time than most of us can ever afford; and while there may be endless fascination in the acquisition, there is always someone skiing just ahead of you who does it better. And therefore seems to be having more fun at it than you are, and thus infects you with grim-jawed determination to improve, to do better. There are mystiques and machismo and snobbery and incessant status-scrambling throughout the sport. The politics of skiing—yes, there is even a politics of skiing, as in any big-time, big-money sport—are ludicrous, and the industry that feeds off it sometimes seems composed entirely of rug merchants and bunco artists. Its popularity too often leads to environmental disaster: development for downhill skiing purposes is a hell of an ecological insult to an otherwise innocent mountain, no matter what the ski developers claim about sound design. The weather and the snow are never right, the crowds take all the fun out of it, it takes too long to get to and is too expensive once there, and there is always this sense that the wrong people do it, for all the wrong reasons. As in every other human pastime.

There is also, simply, pleasure in it; in all the competitive struggle and ugliness, one always risks losing sight of that fact. Watch a skier standing in line to ride the lift up the mountain. He will *play* with his skis and the snow. He'll slide the skis back and forth, set his edges and release them, toy with every little hummock and dip in the lift line's path, spank tips and then tails on the snow, pull his skis together to make little vertical ridges, patterns on the snow. He can't leave it alone. Like a child in a sandbox, using his skis instead of pail and shovel, patting and smoothing the conformable, sensual snow, continuing to milk a kind of mindless, infinitesimally small pleasure out of this miniaturized version of what he wants to be doing up on the slope. Making his body and his skis *do* things. Patting the snow as idly as one pets a cat. Sensual pleasure.

As in the valley, so on the mountain: he keeps at it—we all do—in pursuit of one of Those Days—days that can occur anywhere in ski country, east, west, Europe, or Japan. Such a day will dawn cloudless and blue-skied; the temperature will come up in the golden sun to about twenty degrees, and the day will take on the snap of a bite out of a rock-hard green apple. It is a day to be first on the lifts and last off the mountain, and in between you will not be able to get enough skiing, there is not enough skiing available to cram into every second of such a day. You will ski in control and out of it; you will find that your skis *will* turn at the gentlest whim, and by early forenoon you will discover that you have simply become your skis. You will become a temporary physical manifestation of the essence of movement over snow, pure speed and sensation and downhill-plunging kinetic energy. The day will pass in a hyperoxygenated dream of skill and mastery; the end of the day will find you with knees like wet noodles and a fine, vibratory jangling of fatigue throughout your muscular system. In addition to your other aches and pains you'll probably also have a lump in your throat—of gratitude, for mountains, snow, gravity, sunshine, winter, the newfound soundness of your body and the totally unexpected relationship it has suddenly established with your head.

It doesn't happen every time, but it happens often enough to keep us—grumbling, bitching, not at all sure that that's what we want to be doing—going skiing. It could be that skiing still doesn't really have anything to do with mountains. I think it does.

. . . these little jewels, insignia, orders, agraffes . . . an
endless inventiveness governed by the development and
unthinkable differentiation of one and the same basic
scheme, the equilateral, equiangled hexagon.
—THOMAS MANN, *The Magic Mountain*

Chapter 12

The Crystal Lattice

One-fourth of the land area of the earth is "mountainous," or
above three thousand feet in altitude; one-fifth of the surface
of the earth is snow-covered throughout the year. There may
be less overlap than those figures imply. The permanent snow
line lies below the three-thousand-foot mark for all land south
of the fiftieth parallel in the southern hemisphere and for all
land north of the sixty-fifth parallel in the northern hemisphere, so there is considerable snow cover on nonmountain-
ous terrain as well. Nevertheless, snow cover, particularly of
the permanent sort, is as intimately connected with the mountain landscape as it is with the polar regions. A great deal of
the oversupply of precipitation that the mountains collect is in
the form of snow, even in summer.

For that matter, most precipitation spends some part of its
cycle as snow, and since precipitation in the amount of about
124,000 *cubic miles* falls to earth each year, it is perhaps not so
surprising that snow cover is as widespread as it is. Where the

snow is permanent, it is nevertheless a major sculptor of the landscape beneath—silently, invisibly preparing new land-forms and scenic delights for generations yet unborn, for peri-ods when continental alignments and perhaps even polar loca-tions are changed in ways beyond our current imagining. For those areas where the snow advances and recedes with the seasons, it constitutes an often unappreciated resource of im-mense value. Mailmen, highway maintenance crews, construc-tion supervisors, and mayors positively hate the damned slippery stuff. So do old folks, insecure in their tottering mobil-ity. Only kids have the temerity to love it, getting from snow the message that centuries of agricultural wisdom in our bones should transmit to us but seldom do: stop. Stop work for a while. Play. Recreate (interesting word). Rest—as the land does during the snow months.

Snow is more than a signal for a kind of annual sabbath, however. It is also the blanket that keeps the organic world viable through the bitterness of winter. It is a storehouse, more effective than all the dams in history, for the single resource that powers industry, sustains agriculture, maintains our very life—our water supply. And as a bonus, it is not only an aes-thetic boon, a fresh coat of paint to cover our uglier environ-mental disasters, but also a gentle reminder about what it was that made Jack a dull boy. Lovely stuff.

But what *is* snow, really? An accumulation of ice crystals, yes, formed from the water vapor in the air when the tempera-ture is right and precipitated out to fall to earth. Simple as that, but also infinitely variable, infinitely complex in its struc-ture. There was a curious Vermonter named W. A. "Snowflake" Bentley (1881–1935), who devoted his life to the photography of snowflakes—just that, nothing more, no word of explana-tion, just beautiful photographs, brilliant white crystals on a coal-black background. Thanks to him, we've been given to understand that no two snowflakes are alike. Meanwhile meteorologists tell us that there can be ten million snowflakes in a cubic foot of snow and that throughout time enough snow has fallen to cover the entire globe to a depth of something like fifty miles—estimates that make Bentley's claim seem mathematically unlikely, to say the least.

But then, perhaps not: look at the mechanism. Moisture in the atmosphere can be in any of its three physical states—gas, liquid, or solid. When the air is cooled, its capacity to hold that moisture is reduced; the moisture condenses out. If the condensation takes place at above freezing temperatures, droplets of water are formed; if below freezing, crystals of ice are formed. Each droplet or crystal takes as its nucleus a microscopic particle of dust or salt—particles of atmospheric pollution that can range all the way from industrial waste to volcanic eruption to the evaporate of sea water. *Tiny* particles: five to ten million cloud droplets to form a good-sized raindrop; perhaps a million ice crystals to form an ordinary snowflake.

It is possible for moisture to go directly from gas to solid, bypassing the liquid stage entirely. The process is called *sublimation*—the same that allows snowfield ice crystals to grow in size on their way to forming glacial ice. (Sublimation also takes place in the opposite direction, ice to vapor—that's what happens during the hot, drying blast of a foehn wind.) When moisture is sublimated directly from gas to the ice crystal state in the atmosphere—and only when the liquid step is thus omitted—a snowflake is born.

The original crystal will be six-sided. The hexagon is the crystalline structure of ice, whether in snow, hoarfrost, or the cubes in your cocktail. The reason has to do with electrical charges and water molecules and the way they link up in what crystallography calls the crystal lattice. When there is an orderly atomic structure in a solid, the outward form will be bounded by smooth planes, symmetrically arranged. Common table salt forms near-perfect cubes; diamonds form tetrahedrons. The angles between corresponding faces of any two crystals of the same substance are identical. Hexagonal ice crystals are the building blocks for hexagonal snowflakes. This structured regularity would seem to predict a serious challenge to Snowflake Bentley's claims of endlessly repeated originality. But look:

As that crystal sublimates water vapor onto its surfaces, it may grow stubby arms at the points of the hexagon—six rays that give it a distinctly starry appearance. A *stellar*, or *dendritic*, snowflake. Additional hexagonal crystals may grow out from those arms. Several of these stellar snowflakes may clump together during snowstorms, the arms entangled, forming a feathery fluff an inch or more across—although individual dendritic flakes rarely get larger than about half an inch in diameter.

Or, that original crystal may grow arms, then sublimate more moisture to fill in the spaces between the arms, forming a larger hexagonal *plate* snowflake. Plates form because snowflakes have a tendency to develop on horizontal, rather than vertical, planes. A raised design—almost any design at all, so long as it is symmetrical within the hexagon, virtually kaleidoscopic—may etch itself on the surface of the plate. Actually, the design will be formed of microscopic hollow structures enclosed by ice while the plate is growing. The design will usually be repeated on both sides of the plate. Hexagonal plates sometimes then grow rays from their corners, gradually transforming themselves into larger dendritic flakes with plates as their centers.

Or that original crystal may grow into the simplest form of all snowflakes, the hexagonal *column*—usually less than an eighth of an inch long. Hexagonal columns act as prisms to the light; the colored halos you see around the sun or moon are usually formed by light shining through high thin clouds made up of floating snow crystals in the form of hexagonal columns. The hexagonal column may then grow a flat plate on each end, sometimes even adding a third plate midway between, pierced by the column like a wheel on an axle. The plates that form the caps on the two ends of a column will very likely be quite different in structure and size, sometimes so much so that a "collar button" snowflake is formed, with one end much larger than the other. Capped hexagonal columns can also grow in clusters from a single point. They seldom exceed three-sixteenths of an inch in length.

At some point in its development that original crystal may pick up a coating of tiny cloud droplets that freeze directly to the surface. This usually happens when a very cold snowflake, falling from on high, passes through a lower layer of cloud or fog that is at a warmer temperature but contains supercooled droplets of moisture. The process transforms the hexagonal shape of the snowflake into an irregular lumpy mass called *graupel*. These snow pellets—usually frozen hard enough to bounce when they hit any kind of firm surface—will fall in sudden showers over a limited area in the midst of a larger snowstorm. Snowflakes can also grow in the form of *ice needles*, very slender hexagonal columns with sharp points rather than plates on the ends, or as *irregular crystals* growing haphazardly in irregular plates or rods, more or less from a common center but without any discernible organizing pattern. Strangely, however, this kind of disorganized snowflake form is the exception rather than the rule—a tribute to the organizing power of the crystal lattice.

International meteorology has identified ten different general classifications of frozen precipitation, and all but two of them are snow. The other two are *sleet* (in this country, frozen raindrops; the rest of the world uses that term for mixed snow and rain), and *hail* (originally a kind of frozen raindrop, but with added successive coatings of ice it gains as it is recirculated from top to bottom several times in the turbulence of a cumulonimbus cloud). There is no known way of predicting what conditions will produce which kinds of snowflakes.

But infinite changes can be wrought on those ten basic configurations because infinite variations are available in the conditions that form them. The more moisture there is available and the longer distance or time the snowflake falls, the greater its development will be. Snowflakes tumble and strike each

INTERNATIONAL SNOW SYMBOLS

SYMBOL   EXAMPLE

Plates: sometimes in combination of plates.

Dendritic or stellar: often in clumps.

Columns: can group into columnar stars.

Needles: hexagonal like columns, but with points on ends.

Spatial dendrites: stellar combinations not arranged on a single plane.

Capped columns: collar-button shapes, plates on one or both ends.

Irregular crystals: hexagonal particles, but no other organizing scheme.

Graupel: "soft hail", hexagonal shape overwhelmed by frozen droplets.

Sleet: frozen raindrops, ice shell with wet inside.

Hail: layered re-coatings of ice.

other on the way down, and each tiny splinter can form the nucleus for a new flake—in a chain reaction that often helps keep snowstorms growing. Changes in temperature mean changes in the amount of available vapor and in the sublimation rate. The snowflake may fall through layers of air with different wind strengths, which vary the falling time. The types of snowflakes falling in a given storm will vary from hour to hour, and from place to place. Permutations are infinite. Snowflakes which fall short distances *tend* to be small and of the basic rod-and-plate configuration. Flakes that fall great distances, in warm temperatures, tend to be larger and more fully developed into elaborate star shapes or dendrites. But the opposites can occur.

I don't mean to play whimsical games with this question of alikeness or non-alikeness among snowflakes. But the very conceit—for that's what it is—is whimsical. Carry the analysis or examination to a fine enough point, and there are no duplicates. Not in nature, not anywhere else. It all depends on how you want to split the hairs, of course. The surprising thing is not that Snowflake Bentley was right, but that anyone should be surprised at his observation that no two snowflakes are alike.

So long as the snowflake is falling, it is undergoing constant change. Once it reaches the ground, it . . . goes right on changing. It was a separate entity, an isolated unit afloat in an alien sea; now it is a mere particle in the structure of a more or less plastic mass. There are several interesting physical changes possible once the flake becomes part of the snow cover. Some of them lead eventually to glacier ice; others only govern the shape and strength of the snow cover until the spring thaws come along and turn that cover into mountain stream water.

The first change is called *destructive metamorphism*—it might more simply be called "settling," except for the complexity of the process. Dendrites and other elaborate flakes are unstable crystals. Once within the snow cover, the points, spikes, jagged edges, and other high points of the individual flake begin immediately to sublimate into water vapor—each tiny star in its own gassy bubble of air. The moisture is sublimated from the points toward the center and is resublimated there as ice. The stars and plates and prisms change into more rounded granules; the high points disappear. The rounded granules take up less bulk and have less surface area, so the snow cover settles. Perhaps 90 percent of the depth of new-fallen dendritic snow is air; within three days or so destructive metamorphism will reduce this to 70 percent, which means the snow depth will shrink a like amount. The process goes on even if the air temperature remains constant, although temperature variations will affect the rate of change. The settling increases the bonding strength of the snow, as the smaller crystals with their more rounded surfaces have more contact area; and water vapor tends also to be sublimated to those contact points, resublimating and bonding crystals together. That's one reason ski resorts blast new snowfalls with explosive charges—to blow the air out of the snow and reduce it to settled powder, to increase its bonding strength and reduce the danger of avalanches.

Snow consistency is also changed by *constructive metamorphism*. The key to constructive metamorphism is the very variety of the layers of snowpack. Every new layer of snow has different characteristics from the layer laid down before it, because temperature, humidity, and other conditions vary from storm to storm. Even man-made snowpack varies from layer to layer, despite the ostensible control over its production. Different layers of snow have different insulating capacities: new "wild" snow—that stuff that is so loosely packed that it runs off a shovel like dry sugar off a scoop—may be 99 percent air, while old snow may have reduced the volume of air within it to 20 percent or less. Snow near the surface of the pack can be almost any temperature below freezing, depending on the surrounding air, but it warms up rapidly as you go deeper, and at ground level it is always very close to thirty-two degrees Fahrenheit. The lower, warmer layers are in a continuous process of sublimation, giving off water vapor which is carried by the rising of the warmer air to the colder layers above. The lower, warmer crystals shrink (and can be eliminated entirely in the process, reducing the total number of crystals in the pack); the upper, colder crystals resublimate the vapor, growing in size by constructive metamorphism.*

One interesting result of constructive metamorphism is the *cup crystal*, also known as the beaker crystal, or depth hoar. Destructive metamorphism makes snow crystals into rounded granules; during constructive metamorphism these granules grow facets—predictably hexagonal in shape—on their rounded surfaces. As the process continues, the facets develop cupped surfaces, putting up a stepped, pyramidal outer surface, turning the granules into hexagonal cones, or cups. They can grow as large as half an inch in length; further sublimation sometimes fills in the cup with solid ice. Cup crystals don't form unless there is a fair amount of air circulation within the snow, so they are more common on steep, irregular slopes, particularly where there is some undergrowth buried by the snowpack to hold air spaces open.

Cup crystals can be dangerous. They don't bond together and can form something very like a layer of ball bearings under the snow cover, greatly increasing the slope's tendency to slide—already a high risk because of the steepness of the slopes where cup crystals usually form. Cup crystals are usually found in the lower and middle depths of snowpack—invisible down there, inviting disaster—but in very cold weather, particularly on north faces, virtually the entire snow cover can form into this depth hoar. Ski resorts often pack such slopes in an attempt to prevent cup crystal formation, but the process can still go on deep within the snow cover.

* For this explanation of destructive and constructive metamorphism, I'm indebted to Colin Fraser's fine book, *The Avalanche Enigma* (London: John Murray Ltd., 1966). I'll be relying much more heavily on that work in Chapter 13.

The final change that snow crystals undergo is *melt metamorphism,* which turns snow eventually into glacier ice. Melt metamorphism is the growth of ice crystals by constant thawing and refreezing. Near the surface it makes that delightful corn snow; deep within the snowpack it eventually builds the solid bulk of ice that makes a glacier. During the period of nivation into glacier ice, this frozen material eludes the standard categories. The particles of old snow are to some extent joined, so it is not quite snow; but the air interstices are maintained, so it is not quite ice either. At that point in its development, what it really is is extremely rotten ice.

Frost is not, as is often assumed, frozen dew—in the sense of a deposit of liquid dew that then freezes. To form frost, water vapor in the air is sublimated directly onto surfaces that are colder than the ambient air temperature. In its most bounteous state it's called *hoarfrost,* which can take the form of plates, needles, scales, fans, or any of the six-sided structures that develop in snowflakes. Often at lower altitudes these frost structures will all be pointed toward a nearby body of water, since the water vapor that formed them came from that direction. If the frost has a particularly furry look, it is usually made of ice needles, which are hexagonal and often hollow. After a very cold night, *tabular frost* may be formed, as leaflike as the pages of a book. When the snow surface is colder than the air—usually after a still, fairly warm night—*surface hoar* can form on the snow, with flat, leaflike crystals that glisten like tiny armor plating on the surface. Surface hoar will usually sublimate away during the day, but if the weather turns cold enough and a new layer of snow is deposited on top, it can make an extremely unstable layer within the snowpack.

Not all frozen moisture deposited on the mountains takes the form of snow or frost. *Rime ice* is a familiar phenomenon, thickly coating man-made structures at high altitudes. Rime forms when supercooled droplets hit anything solid that is cooled well below freezing—it's a deposit of ice in which the grains are more or less separated by trapped air. Under a magnifying glass it looks like clusters of tiny white pearls. It always builds up to windward, and its weight can be damaging to any structure not braced against just such accumulations.

It is the separation of the grains of ice that distinguishes rime from *glaze,* the latter formed when falling rain hits very cold objects and freezes solid to them in a sheetlike coating. Glaze results when there is a layer of below-freezing air at or very near the ground, with warm clouds above. The same kind of temperature inversion can cause sleet, but in that case the layer of cold air must be several thousand, rather than several hundred, feet thick—to give falling raindrops time enough to freeze solid. The clear ice pellets of sleet are irregular in shape because although they first form as a thin shell of ice around the streamlined raindrop, expansion during freezing then pushes that shell out of shape.

Weird stuff, snow. The average ten-inch snowfall will run over a hundred tons to the acre in weight in low country, usually a little less in the high mountains. Maybe a million billion flakes—per acre—in a ten-hour storm. From fifty feet of sidewalk five feet wide you can shovel about a ton of snow for every fifteen inches that falls; your roof can easily gather twenty thousand pounds of snow per storm. Weathermen equate a foot of snow to an inch of rain, but only as the roughest sort of estimation—the moisture content can vary so that it takes anywhere from five to fifty inches of snow to equal an inch of rain. Besides which, moisture content will vary wildly during the actual snowfall itself, and thus from inch to inch within the snowpack.

Anywhere in snow country you will find locals who will identify snow clouds for you, but in fact snow can fall from any kind of cloud cover—more from some than from others, of course. Locals will also tell you that "it's too cold to snow," a judgment guaranteed to bring wry smiles from polar explorers and mountain climbers, who have seen heavy snowfalls in every below-freezing temperature ever recorded. Nevertheless, the heaviest snowfalls in the United States do occur at between twenty-four and thirty degrees Fahrenheit. The heaviest average annual snowfall in this country is recorded at the Paradise Ranger Station on Mount Rainier (the mountain is 14,410 feet—I'm not sure of the altitude of the station), at over 575 inches per year; that station also recorded the highest single-year accumulation of over one thousand inches. Again, measurement is always a bit dodgy: many snowstorms blow so hard that an accumulating gauge would be more effective mounted horizontally than in the accepted vertical fashion.

Weird stuff indeed. Snow is a plastic medium once it has fallen, but every layer has a different plasticity, and different conditions can radically change the bonding strength that holds it together. That squeaking crunch you hear underfoot as you walk through snow—old-time radio sound-effects men used to squeeze boxes of cornstarch to simulate it—is caused by the breaking of snow crystals under pressure. It is more extreme in very cold weather, and as the temperature climbs the pitch of the squeak deepens and then disappears. The same more or less knowledgeable locals will estimate the temperature from the sound, which would be fine if only there weren't all those variables in humidity, crystal structure, amount of air in the pack, and so forth. If only nature would hold still for a moment. The sound goes away at warm temperatures because the crystals can then bend without breaking, thereby making the snow plastic. The bonding comes about by the interlocking of crystal points and branches in newer snow, by capillary action and refreezing in older stuff; again, every layer develops a different strength.

Certain conditions add greatly to that strength. *Crust* is just what the name says: any hard snow surface lying on a softer layer; it can be formed by the heat of the sun (melting), rain (freezing), or wind (destruction of crystal structure, resulting in closer bonding of surface layers). It can range from a thin layer only sufficient to keep snow from blowing about to a structural integrity that allows you to walk over it without breaking through. Back-country mayhem can develop when snow sets up a crust strong enough to support pursuing dogs but not solid enough to support fleeing deer. Such a condition is more common than most of us realize.

Wind pack—vicious stuff familiar to Everest expeditions—is presumed to be formed when water vapor is driven into the snow cover, where it sublimates and is frozen onto the crystals at or near the surface, binding them together. But wind pack is often solid to considerable depth, and the physical damage done to the crystals as they are driven about by the wind may ultimately have more to do with creating wind pack than the refreezing of surface snow. Wind damage breaks up the crystals into ever smaller units, allowing more surface contact crystal to crystal, which allows the pack to set up a stiff crust more rapidly. The perfect example is plowed snow—particularly that blown through a rotary plow, which sets up very quickly into snow that is very hard, very heavy. Many's the motorist who has had a rude shock from what looks like a soft, forgiving snowbank beside the road but which turns out upon impact to be much closer to concrete in consistency.

That's why man-made snow is so dense by comparison to the natural stuff. Ski resorts in marginal snow areas have long been using compressed-air guns plus water to manufacture snowpack. It is difficult to make large snowflakes with a snow gun—the flakes don't fall far enough, don't have enough time to accumulate all that lacy filigree that makes big, dendritic flakes. Add the destructive force of the gun itself, in which compressed air is pumped through a tiny nozzle to atomize the water. Add the fact that most snow-making is done in marginal areas, where violent freeze–thaw cycles are common. Freeze–thaw cycles speed up metamorphism, with its various settling, compacting, and ice-making effects. Snow-makers talk a lot about producing good powder, but nature is not inclined to cooperate.

Snow creeps, of course—down ski slopes as well as other

mountainsides, off over the edges of roof eaves and cliff faces, anywhere it can get gravity to take it. Destructive metamorphism is the culprit, leading to the settling of individual snow crystals—settling, that is, with the eternal downhill bias. Because of creep and the plasticity of snow, slopes with a convex curve to them are in a state of shear, concave slopes under compression—tensions that are crucial in the triggering of avalanches. Creeping happens within the snow cover itself, crystal to crystal; snow can also "glide," but that's when the body of snow moves over the ground as a mass, in one form of avalanche. (Avalanches, as we shall see, don't always scour away the entire snowpack down to the ground.)

Wind sculptures snow into fabulous shapes. Down on the surface of undisturbed snow cover, the wind can build ripple marks, corrugations of the surface exactly like those formed by gentle water currents in a sandy creekbed. If you've ever flown over desert dunes, you know that those same patterns are repeated on a gigantic scale in the larger dunes, or *barchans*— U-shaped drifts with the points aimed downwind. Snow barchans are also common, formed by exactly the same process. The wind also builds *sastrugi*—sharp, irregular ridges parallel to the prevailing wind pattern, formed by erosion and deposition of the snow.

Where snow builds up on a high ridge in great quantities, wind, plus the tendency of snow to wind-pack, can create the most exquisite piece of snow sculpture of all, the *cornice*. The prevailing wind pulls snow over the top of the ridge and packs it in a concave curve to match the eddy current; the result is a curling lip of snow very like a wave of frozen surf held immobile just at the moment of breaking into a comber. Below the lip is a sharp reverse curve, almost forming a transverse snow cave along the ridge line. Underneath that, snow accumulates in a thicker mass called the *scarp*. Avalanche patrolmen regularly kick loose whatever cornices they can get to, to prevent the mass of snow held poised above the slope from breaking loose later; if they don't, skiers or climbers may venture out onto the cantilevered projection of the cornice, which will hold them up—for a while. Then the cornice will let go, and add human bodies to the load of destruction it carries down the mountainside. (Actually, as dangerous as the cornice looks poised above the slopes, there's a greater snow load, and thus more capacity for destructive avalanche, in the scarp beneath the cornice. And it can let go without disturbing the delicate curvature that hangs above it.)

It should also be remarked at this point that snow isn't white. It is clear. That is, it is made up of billions of tiny, clear prisms, each of which breaks up all light that strikes it into the entire spectrum. All the colors. The befuddled eye, unable to handle that kind of sensory overload—unable to make all those fine distinctions—turns it back into whiteness. Perceives it as white. This diffusion is what causes the dreaded *white-out*, a weather condition that can cause anyone in snow country to become totally disoriented. When there is blowing snow under an overcast sky, the daylight is so diffused by the multiplicity of reflecting surfaces that all contrast vanishes—along with the horizon and any sense of what is up, down, or sideways. The effect can be so befuddling that you have difficulty even standing up, particularly when the wind is strong. Skiers in a whiteout often think they are standing still on their skis, waiting for visibility to improve, and discover only when they crash into something that the slope they thought was level was in fact tilted and that they were moving when they thought they were standing pat.

Just as the snow can effectively damp out all color by, in a sense, overwhelming it, it can also reverse the process. Catch the sunlight right on the surface of the snow, and the prismatic effect will come clear in all its multicolored visual splendor, in dazzling glints of color. Occasionally in high country one gets a sighting of "diamond dust," the smallest form of snowflake of all. Look for it on sunny, cold mornings, when there is thin fog down low and clear skies above. Rising vapor sublimates into airborne ice crystals that don't really coalesce into snowflakes at all but hang as suspended prisms, shattering the sunlight into a kind of dry rainbow. Breathtaking.

So: snow. In our imaginations it would lock up the higher mountains against our intrusion, but in fact—with care—it can be an aid to accessibility rather than a barrier. We climb over it and ski on and in it—and radically change its structure when we do, compressing, packing, breaking down the crystal lattice. Pushing it always in the direction of solid ice. In some conditions we melt it with our ski bottoms as we go, just as the blade of an ice skate does, and we glide on a film of water, the snow refreezing as we pass. In other conditions—fresh powder, "wild snow" to the avalanche people—we ski so deeply within it that it threatens suffocation. Always we mold it, disrupt it, mess it up; it comes back with yet another coat and erases our piddling messes as a mother wipes up after sloppy children.

Snow is ice, but more than ice. Ice plus air? You can't really understand snow in terms of physics after all, states of matter and all that stuff. Solid, liquid, and gas just won't do the job. Ah, but think of it this way. Picture a triangle. Label the first point "Ice" (the solid state). Label the second point "Water" (liquid). Label the third "Air" (gas). Now look at all that space within the triangle. That's snow. All that space, representing the infinitely variable possibilities. All of them can be found up there on the mountains.

Like the weather, forest fires, and the inner city, avalanches
are a powerful stronghold against empirical analysis, not
because they yield no measurable information, but because
they yield so overwhelmingly much.
—GEORGE SIBLEY, "Part of a Winter," *Mountain Gazette*

Chapter **13**

Avalanches

At one time in my squandered youth I taught school in the
rimrock country of west Texas. For off-hours sport another
teacher and I used to go out regularly to the farther reaches of
that desolate landscape, climb up to the top of the cap rock,
and roll boulders down the canyon sides.

We would hike along the upper ledge in search of the
largest rocks we could dislodge. When we found one we
would grunt and strain to pry it loose, dodging the scorpions
and centipedes disturbed by our labors, and tip it over the
edge. It would . . . roll. Gaining speed slowly, it would
tumble and lurch and finally pick up enough momentum to
take an occasional ponderous leap. It would knock down a
small mesquite tree here and there, but mostly it would only
mash cactus and knock splinters off other rocks en route. Often
as not it would catch a flat spot—on itself or on the canyon
wall—and simply slide to a disappointing stop, sometimes
within ten feet or so of its launch site. But that would be

counterbalanced by the next one, which might roll all the way to the bottom, leap the dry creekbed there, and work its way a few shuddering yards up the opposite slope—eliciting, I suppose, a weak cheer from the two of us as we watched: that, somehow, was the object of the silly game.

For a few months this became our obsessive pastime, which tells you as much about the availability of recreation as it does of the mental state of west Texas schoolteachers. We would walk for miles in search of just the right boulder and began carrying along a six-foot steel pinch bar—twenty or thirty sweaty pounds' worth—just to help us pry loose the really big ones. Inevitably we found our ultimate rock, a monster nearly as tall as we were, poised so delicately on the rim that we could actually make it teeter slightly where we found it. Still, it took most of a Saturday morning of hard physical labor to break it free. I seem to recall that we actually considered walking the three or four miles back to the car and driving home for pick and shovel to make the job easier. But we succeeded without the extra tools.

There is no real punch line to this story. We tipped it over the edge and were instantly frightened by the enormity of what we had accomplished. We both sat down as if stunned before it had rolled twenty feet. It went all the way, thundering and thrashing and shaking the very earth, setting off a minor rock avalanche in the scree slope beneath the rimrock. It took out at least one good-sized mesquite and leaped completely over another one, with however many thousand pounds of accumulated momentum; it cleared the creek bottom, rolled up the other side for a bit, poised uncertainly for a moment, and rolled back down again to come to rest in the creekbed, where it undoubtedly still lies twenty years later. But it was truly scary while it rolled, and without talking about it my friend and I simply turned—once it had finally shuddered to a stop—and headed back for the car. We never went rock rolling again.

It was mindless, small-boy vandalism, and it bothers me

now that we did it, and did it with such glee—although even now, in a new age of sensitivity to natural processes, I can't see that we were doing much more than speeding up erosion. The memory reminds me of Thoreau enthusiastically arching firebrands into Walden Pond at night and exulting in the beauty of the sight. Or Wallace Stegner, not too many years before my west Texas adventures, rhapsodizing about tossing burning tire carcasses into the Grand Canyon. All our heads have been changed since then. That doesn't excuse or ameliorate the earlier insensitivity.

The only point in bringing up such a senseless activity in a chapter about avalanches is to recognize that there is a certain fascination—in all of us, I think—with massive physical occurrences. Whether it is small-boy vandalism or not is moot: I could no more talk about mountains and snow and then ignore avalanches than I could speak of volcanoes without mentioning Krakatoa's spectacular fireworks. Avalanches are amazing. In one sense they are a metaphor for what is always going on in the mountains anyway at a much slower pace: a kind of erosional equivalent of time-lapse photography, compressing eons' worth of erosion into instants of real time, seeming to pull down the mountains at a frightening rate. Yet in most cases, where slide paths are comfortably established and no man-made structures intrude, the great snowfields can slide away to their hearts' content all winter long, and the next summer's visitors may find no more evidence of avalanching than an occasional twisted sapling. Does the avalanche that slides in the hidden mountain vastness make a roar?

The avalanches we know about, however, do affect man. Avalanches are amazing because their destructive power is so much greater than their physical dimensions would seem to warrant. One researcher, working before the improved communications of the twentieth century, recorded nearly 17,500 avalanches in the Swiss Alps in one year alone. The snow avalanche is an utterly common occurrence. Yet like tornadoes —with which in fact they have a lot in common—each avalanche is a freak of nature. A major avalanche, swooping down on a hapless village, will mow down a line of houses, then inexplicably hop over a single house, only to smash the next to matchsticks. Fatalities have resulted from avalanches twenty yards wide and a hundred yards long, the bodies dug from a pile of snow at the end only two or three feet deep. And of course human beings have been swept up in an avalanche, carried a mile or so downslope over vertical distances in the thousands of feet, and—you guessed it—spit out uninjured. Stories of tornadolike whimsicality have been thoroughly documented: the avalanche smashes house and barn, wipes out family and livestock, leaves not a stick standing—and three hundred yards up the opposite slope someone finds an intact china closet where it was swept from the house, not a single dish chipped.

That whimsicality has led to a great deal of superstition and hysteria surrounding avalanches, much of it among not so primitive people. What seems like sheer capriciousness in the behavior of an avalanche usually turns out to be only the working of physical laws and properties that are on the second or third order of observability. Avalanche research aimed at sifting out those laws and properties, in hopes of predicting avalanche action and preventing or reducing the destruction therefrom, has been going on since the 1930's, primarily in research operations above Davos, Switzerland, and around Alta, Utah, the latter under the supervision of the United States Forest Service. The research is always underfunded and working against incredible obstacles; if the Swiss are ahead of the United States in it, that is because they had the object lesson of World War I as a stimulus. Out of approximately eighty thousand Austrian and Italian troops serving in the Tyrol, almost half were lost to avalanches. "The mountains in winter," said skiing pioneer Matthias Zdarsky, who had been put to work teaching mountaineering to the Austrian troops, "were more dangerous than the Italians."

(Zdarsky, incidentally, was caught in an avalanche himself in 1916, during rescue work aimed at uncovering soldiers buried by a previous slide. He suffered no fewer than eighty separate fractures and dislocations during the few minutes of the experience—during all of which he was fully conscious—before finding himself lying uncovered on the surface of the snow. Rehabilitation took eleven years, but Zdarsky lived to ski again.)

Avalanche research has made considerable headway in understanding the mechanisms at work in forming and releasing the great gouts of snow that wreak so much destruction. In the process, in science's methodical way, various classifications and categories of avalanche phenomena have been proposed. The classifications are somewhat inexact, and every large avalanche has aspects of several different types. But it is only through such classification that a beginning has been made in understanding the avalanche's terrible destructiveness.

Local mountain folk have long divided avalanches into two basic categories: the airborne, blowing-snow avalanche—*Staublawine* in Switzerland—and the ground avalanche, or *Grundlawine*. The former are the most explosively destructive, perhaps largely as a result of their tremendous speed. The Great Glärnisch slide in 1898 happened to be timed from start to finish. A large cornice gave way near the summit of Vorderglärnisch at 11:20 A.M. and poured over the village of Glarus —four and a third miles away and 5,750 feet lower—in a little over one minute. (The billowing cloud of snow that accompanied it didn't settle for another six minutes.) The avalanche thus reached a speed of somewhere between 225 and 250 miles per hour. It can perhaps be assumed that witnesses in 1898 did not have stopwatches in hand, but modern measurements with deliberately started avalanches have shown that speeds of over 220 miles per hour are not out of the question for a large airborne avalanche, and 180–190 mile per hour winds are common.

The forces generated by winds of that velocity alone are sufficient to accomplish much of the freak damage that airborne powder avalanches regularly cause. Skiers have been sucked into them from *above* the slide's starting point. Trees that manage to remain standing have their limbs stripped off—but more frequently the trees themselves are snapped off at ground level before the body of the avalanche reaches them, from the force of the snow-free air blast running ahead of the slide itself.

The physical process that creates such forces has been likened to that which governs gas flowing through a pipe—and there's even a curious resemblance to the behavior of glaciers. When particles in suspension are flowing through the atmosphere, they drag air along with them by friction. The air is almost a passive stream being dragged along by particles under the force of gravity; thus the energy of the particles is spread to a much larger mass. As with gas in a pipe (and glaciers), friction along the edges slows down the outer layers of this "tube" of air flowing down the slope, and pressure then causes the inner, central mass to accelerate. Hence the resemblance to such curious behavior as fire storms: once the mass is set in motion, it is self-accelerating.

New particles are constantly being sucked in from the sides, and extreme turbulence is set up in the outer layers of moving air. The greater the speed, the greater the turbulence; irregularities in the path—cliffs, trees, gulleys—also increase the turbulence. These swirling turbulences generate speeds perhaps twice as fast as those of the slide itself, creating rapid, intermittent blasts—lasting about a tenth of a second each—at sharp angles to the main thrust of the avalanche. There are vertical swirls as well as horizontal ones, of course, which helps explain some of the freak effects of airborne avalanches.

The extremely turbulent air seems to do more damage than either the main blast of air or the snow load. A house struck by those short, sharp blasts will simply disintegrate as if it had been shelled by artillery. Fragments and debris are frequently left in a circular pattern, giving rise to earlier theories that it is pressure differential—as in tornado destruction—that causes the damage. The oblique blasts, however, are a more consistent explanation. One researcher describes a twelve-inch concrete wall attacked by such gusts: the concrete was simply blasted away from between the metal reinforcing rods, leaving only twisted steel where the wall had stood.

Any ramplike structure—a cliff, rocks in the path, even a building "securely" tucked into the slope—will launch a ground avalanche into the air. But once a critical speed is reached—estimated to be about fifty miles per hour—no ramp is necessary; turbulence along the ground will shove the slide into the air all by itself. It is not necessary for an airborne avalanche to achieve massive size to become destructive, incidentally. In Austria in 1952 a slide only twenty feet wide plucked a bus from a line of vehicles on a small bridge and tumbled it over the side. Eleven out of thirty-five aboard were killed; another bus in front and a car behind were left untouched.

Ground avalanches, particularly those containing wet, loose snow, can cause the same degree of damage, but it is different in kind, generated by the tremendous power of great weights of snow driven inexorably into valley structures. Ground avalanches move much more slowly—often at twenty miles an hour or less—but they set up like concrete when they stop. Using averages from avalanches measured in the past—a sixty-five-hundred-foot descent at twenty-two miles per hour for a million tons of snow and rock—avalanche scientists estimate that a destructive force on the order of twenty million horsepower is not unusual for such slides. The final deposit from that kind of avalanche can be a hundred feet thick, can wipe out roads and railroad tracks, and can dam rivers, causing flooding. When roads and railroads are thus blocked, they are often simply tunneled out under the debris until spring melts the accumulated ice. Rivers will eventually tunnel their own way to release. An avalanche in the French Alps in 1862 dammed the River Isère; the river cut a tunnel beneath the ice, and the ice itself was used as a bridge for seventeen months—through the heat of two summers.

Merely dividing avalanches according to where they *go*—in the air or on the ground—is not a fine enough distinction for research purposes, and scientists have now identified several other crucial characteristics. In 1955 Professor R. Haefli and Dr. M. de Quervain of the Swiss Federal Snow and Avalanche Institute proposed five different criteria for classification of avalanches. It's as clear and concise a method of recognizing the significant features of avalanches as has yet been devised.

The first criterion is the type of breakaway: from a single point on the slope, or along an extended line. *Single-point* avalanches are usually composed of loose snow and are started by the tiniest of disturbances. Avalanches that break away along a line are called *slab* avalanches; they require a fracture across the snow surface, which is usually somewhat wind-packed. Slab avalanches leave an uphill wall, vertical to the snow strata, at their point of origin.

The second criterion is the position of the sliding surface: *full-depth*, when the entire snow depth slides, down to bare ground or rock; and *surface* avalanches, in which only the top layers of snow let go.

The third criterion is humidity: whether the snow is wet or dry. Wet snow is generally characterized as that which will cohere or ball up when a handful is squeezed; dry snow won't pack into a ball in your hands. It's a rough test, but sufficient.

The fourth criterion is the form of the track in cross section. It can be *unconfined*, as when the avalanche occurs on an open slope, or *channeled*, as when the slide runs down a gully, canyon, or other delimiting surface feature.

The fifth criterion—originally the only one—is whether the avalanche is airborne or not. Ground avalanches are referred to as *flowing*, as the laws that govern their behavior are those of hydrodynamics rather than aerodynamics.

Almost any combination can occur, of course. That is, a loose-snow avalanche starting from a single point can be full-depth or surface, wet or dry, unconfined or channeled, airborne or flowing, and so forth. Avalanche danger generally goes up as wind and intensity of snowfall increase, and as temperature drops; high temperatures cause the snow to settle and bond more quickly, reducing the tendency to slide. Wind pack is crucial in setting up slab avalanches. But in seeming contradiction to its name, wind pack sets up more quickly in sheltered spots, where wind-damaged snow crystals can settle. Therefore the danger from slab avalanches is increased in spots sheltered from the wind, such as depressions, gullies, around rock outcroppings, below man-made structures such as ski lift towers.

Wind pack doesn't settle very much, in the sense of shrinking the snow depth. The snow crystals are ordinarily too damaged for destructive metamorphism to be effective. But that destructive metamorphism goes right on in the snow beneath the slab formed by the wind pack. This can leave a slab as a concave arch above a depressed snow body below—a situation that needs very little external force before it all collapses and a violent slide is kicked loose.

Wet-snow slab avalanches are more common in the spring, during warm, sunny periods when meltwater percolates down through the snow until it reaches an impervious layer of rock or ice, then runs off under the slab, providing a lubricated runway. A wet-snow slab often starts to slide with a slow "yawn," as the fracture zone splits ponderously apart. The sliding motion may not immediately carry throughout the downhill length of the slab, so that heaves and folds are thrown up in the apron of snow below the fracture. Occasionally such a slide will stop right there, leaving a kind of wrinkled washcloth effect on the snow surface. Once such a slab gets up headway, it usually breaks up into a wet loose-snow avalanche—then, when it stops, it freezes *really* tight, so that it must be chopped or blasted for removal.

A convex slope, under tension from snow creep, is more likely to slide than a concave one, which is under compression. Thus areas near the tops of gullies and ridges and along exposed shoulders are generally more dangerous than elsewhere. But since depressions and other concave surfaces catch more snow, such areas shouldn't be considered safe refuges. When there is a series of interconnected gullies down the mountainside, a slide in any one of them can trigger slides in all, since the first slide in effect yanks the support out from under the others.

Tree-covered slopes are safest, but the slope must be densely forested to provide effective cover, and even then a slide originating well above timberline—and thus getting up a great deal of snow load and momentum—can carry a long way into the densest of forests. Grassy slopes are dangerous, particularly those left uncut the previous summer: the long grass stems lie pointing downslope under the snow and serve as a runway for full-depth slides. (Shortly cut stubble holds better than uncut grass.) Brush on the slope will hold snow, but it provides enough air space within the snow to speed up formation of dangerous cup crystals; surface avalanches from brushy slopes are common occurrences. Rocks, terraces, animal paths, or any other surface irregularities help stabilize a slope against sliding; but once destructive metamorphism has set in within the snow, most of the irregularities will be filled in with dense snow, and surface avalanches will pass easily over them.

A great deal of rather inconclusive research has been done on the slope angles necessary to produce avalanche conditions. Involved are both the static friction angle (the angle at which granular material will commence to slide), and the kinetic friction angle (the angle at which such material will remain in motion once set in motion). These angles differ for different types of snow, of course, none of which is strictly granular. Any slope between twenty-two and fifty degrees must be considered capable of sliding. Light, dendritic snow won't slide even at ninety degrees as long as its points and spines are intact to interlock; once it gets smashed and pulverized by the wind, it can slide at angles as low as seventeen degrees. Very wet snow can slide at six or seven degrees. Slopes of more than fifty degrees don't usually accumulate snow in sufficient quantities to make for dangerous slides; instead, they dump continuously in small slides during storms, unless very warm conditions set in. And it should be kept in mind by anyone venturing into deep snow areas that that twenty-two- to fifty-degree range applies only to the starting point for avalanches: once the snow gets up some momentum—particularly if it reaches the airborne state—it can carry for miles over much gentler slopes.

And slides are triggered by almost anything—although the folklore about the monster slide triggered by a hiccup or a sneeze is probably an exaggeration. Before it slides, any snow-covered slope is in a state of equilibrium, however precarious: the strength of the snow bond balanced against any stress on that bond. Anything that decreases the strength or increases the stress can precipitate a slide. The strength can be reduced by destructive metamorphism, which reduces the interlocking of dendritic crystals; by rises in temperature; by rain; or by constructive metamorphism, which builds up an unstable layer of cup crystals within the pack. Increases in stress are caused by such things as additional snowfall, with its added weight, or rain. Clearly, many of these effects work in opposite directions. More snow adds to the strength of the snowpack by bonding action but also increases the stress through the added weight. Temperature rises generally tend to cause snow to settle and form a better bond, but if the rise is sufficient it will weaken the cover or even introduce meltwater into the equation.

Obviously, so confusing an array of physical qualities makes the job of prediction a difficult one. The Institute for Arctic and Alpine Research in Boulder, Colorado, has been trying to come up with a computer-based method for forecasting avalanches. For an article in *Mountain Gazette,* George Sibley interviewed Don Bachman, who worked for the Institute:

> To give you an idea of the magnitude of the analysis process, Bachman and the other assembled avalanche people . . . have been collecting data in these four main categories: meteorological—air temperature, wind speed and direction, precipitation, precipita-

tion rates, moisture content, humidity and barometric pressure; terrain—angles of avalanche slopes, directions of paths, geomorphic characters of starting zones and running paths, and exposure to sun and wind; snowpack properties—layering, surface and internal tensions, temperature gradient throughout, snow densities throughout (centimenter by centimeter), rate of heat exchange up through the snowpack, crystal metamorphism and formation; and avalanche history—avalanches that ran normally during the four-year period, and avalanches that were brought down by [State Highway employees] Pete Peterson and Sid Foster.

Stick that in your Computron and smoke it. Or watch it smoke.*

Every avalanche story seems to be a great story. Sibley's collection of them contains a dozen or more. The teasing, whimsical quality of avalanches, the feeling that one is being toyed with by the fates, is never better demonstrated than by his narration, in the same piece, about "the Mother Cline," one of the some thirty major avalanche chutes that descend into Red Mountain Pass between Silverton and Ouray, Colorado:

One day last winter the Mother Cline sort of played around with one of the snowplow drivers. Going up the pass, Jim Campbell found that the Mother had slipped a little snow onto the road. He was blading that off when more snow came down, right on top of the truck, denting in the roof and banging up the flashing blue light. He was able to drive out from under the new snow, and went at it again—only to have the snow slip a third time, this time dumping on the hood and fenders. The plow had depreciated considerably in about ten minutes there, but he got the snow off the road, finally, and moved on up the pass.

But Mother Cline wasn't finished with him. On his return trip the slope unloaded again, for the fourth time in a couple of hours—with enough force this time to completely bury the front of Campbell's plow, breaking out all the glass and packing the cab. The only thing that saved Campbell was his hard-hat, which got jammed over his face by the snow and left him a little breathing room. Fortunately for him, there was a car right behind his plow

* George Sibley, "Part of a Winter, Part Two: Red Mountain Pass," *Mountain Gazette,* No. 39, p. 20.

with a man of quality at the wheel. He jumped out and dug away the snow and glass from Campbell's face so he could breathe. Campbell survived with only face cuts and bruises, but the plow was very nearly totalled. Some joker, Mother Cline.*

So much for jokery; most avalanche records are not so good-humored. In this and the previous chapter I have depended heavily on *The Avalanche Enigma,* Colin Fraser's thorough-going study of snow and its behavior under stress. Mixed in with the science in that book are details of literally hundreds of avalanches, going back well before the disastrous year of 1720, historically the most damaging avalanche year before modern times. Fraser records with particular care Europe's "Winter of Terror" in 1950–51, when extraordinarily heavy snows were augmented by two separate storms in January and February, each of which dumped six feet or more of new snow on the Alps. There were more than eleven hundred avalanches in Switzerland alone that winter. Nobody knows the total toll; 240 people were dead from avalanches by the twenty-second of January, with the second storm still to come.

Fraser also describes ice avalanches, a rather simpler phenomenon caused when glacier movement pushes over a drop-off, breaks off, and falls to the valley below. Simpler, but catastrophic—as when a chunk of the hanging glacier of Têtes Rousses let go in 1892, fell five thousand feet, changed from ice into a muddy, semiliquid substance, rushed another eight miles into the valley below, and killed 150 Frenchmen.

It is a long step from the mindless rock rolling I once indulged in in west Texas canyons to the Têtes Rousses disaster. It is a long step beyond that to Peru, January 10, 1962. Quoting Fraser:

This is the largest single avalanche disaster on record. It killed more than 4,000 people, 10,000 animals and completely destroyed six villages, and partly destroyed three others. A young Peruvian geologist, Benjamin Morales, carried out an investigation nine days after the disaster and presented a fascinating paper on the subject

* *Mountain Gazette,* No. 39, p. 15.

during the Avalanche Symposium in 1965. One's mind boggles when one hears Morales describe this stupendous phenomenon.

North Huascarán, at over 22,000 feet, is the second highest mountain in South America and its summit is covered by an ice cap. The avalanche began at an altitude of about 21,000 feet, when part of the ice cap broke away, and it finished in the Santa Valley at 8,000 feet, so travelling through a vertical height difference of 13,000 feet. The distance it covered was 10 miles and it did this in 15 minutes. (A telephonist in a village not destroyed saw the avalanche start and timed its course.)

A mass estimated at between 2.5 and 3 million cubic metres broke away along a front about half a mile in length, and where the ice cliff at the edge of the cap is about 180 feet high. In the first part of its course the ice plunged more than 3,000 feet down a near-vertical rock face, pulling out immense blocks of rock as it went. The mass landed in the glacier circus below with tremendous impact; the noise was heard for many miles around and an enormous cloud of powdered ice swirled up and blotted out the summit of the mountain. This concussion started a secondary avalanche of about 300,000 cubic metres which followed the main one down. The main avalanche also tore out more ice in the glacier circus, and by the time it reached the glacier tongue its volume had swelled to about 5 million cubic metres of ice and rock. The mass moved down the 35° gradient of the glacier at about 65 m.p.h. and then tore into the twisting channel between the lateral moraines.

At the first bend, it climbed more than 500 feet to the outside rim and deposited a large quantity of material outside the channel. The avalanche took with it, as it went, more and more of the moraine until it formed a rolling mass more than 175 feet thick. At the second bend in the channel part of the avalanche climbed 350 feet onto a small plateau and left blocks of rock measuring up to 50 feet by 25 by 30.

Thereafter, the ravine had a gradient of only 8–10° but the avalanche rushed on, gouging out both slopes of the channel and destroying a village. At a slight curve further down, a branch of the avalanche climbed a hill 275 feet high, left a 6,000-ton boulder on the top, and then rejoined the main stream. The avalanche then swerved into a larger valley, climbed 265 feet up one side and destroyed another village. Further on, where the valley widens and joins the main Santa Valley, the mass began to fan out. It spread to a width of 1½ miles, annihilated four more villages and partly destroyed two others. It reached the Santa River travelling at about 20 m.p.h. and climbed 100 feet up the far bank to destroy part of yet another village. The avalanche had eroded so much rock, soil, and sand during the course of its 10-mile run that its final volume is estimated to have reached the almost unimaginable total of 13 million cubic metres.

Few people in the path of the avalanche were able to escape. One who did was the telephonist in Ranrahirca, the largest of the villages destroyed. She was warned by a colleague in a nearby village who saw the start of the avalanche. But she thought the warning was a joke—and one in poor taste at that—before she took it seriously and fled.

Another survivor was a potato merchant who was waiting for a lorry by the roadside near Ranrahirca. He heard a noise "like many aeroplanes flying over Huascarán" and, looking up, saw the avalanche already well on its way. He began to run for safety and shouted warnings to others as he went. Many people paid no attention, and two women even remarked that "the snow of Huascarán always fell like that." Others ran to their houses or into the churches where, of course, they were killed. The potato merchant was almost exhausted when he saw some horses tethered by the roadside. He hauled himself on to one and galloped away. Looking back, he saw the avalanche cross behind him. At the front of the mass the ice blocks were constantly cracking and breaking up, creating a pall of powdered ice. He saw the village of Ranrahirca engulfed.

The Santa River was dammed but, fortunately, the water soon burst through the debris and the flooding down the valley was not as severe as it might have been. Even so, roads and bridges were destroyed as much as 28 miles away.

Book Three

The Mountain Life

It is the season of perfect works, of hard, tough, ripe twigs, not of tender buds and leaves. The leaves have made their wood, and a myriad new withes stand up all around pointing to the sky, able to survive the cold. It is only the perennial that you see, the iron age of the year.
—HENRY DAVID THOREAU, *Journal*, Nov. 25, 1850.

Chapter **14**

The Green Hills of Earth

That mountains are green instead of a mottled, rocky gray is a tribute to the stubbornness of the growth process. Plant life in the mountains fights ferocious battles: uprooting winds; long periods of killing cold and brief blasts of overstimulating heat; a water supply that varies only from too much to too little; destructive weights of ice and snow; too little atmosphere and too much radiation. Yet the plant life perseveres and covers the mountainsides with forests, softens them with lawnlike meadows, decorates them with brilliant wild flowers. It pushes its microscopic forms into conditions approaching polar severity—and they take hold. In spite of everything that the weather and the atmosphere and the nonliving rock do to make life implausible, green things just will grow. And multiply.

Characterizing conditions in the high mountains as "polar" may not be too farfetched. Imagine the northern and southern hemispheres as, in effect, giant mountains, joined base to base at the equator, with the poles as their peaks. While radiation levels, atmospheric pressure, and atmospheric chemical makeup may not quite match up in this pole-to-peak comparison, climate and growing conditions do: above eleven thousand feet, there is frost every night, even at the equator.

The comparison is also slightly distorted because not that many mountains arise directly from equatorial rain forests, with equatorial vegetation growing on their lower reaches. But start halfway up the hemisphere, in the middle latitudes, and the comparison grows more accurate. The vegetation zones that march up the mountainside will compare directly to those you would encounter if you traveled from the middle latitudes to the pole. Grassland turns into broad-leafed forest, which in turn gives way to needle-leafed forest. This evergreen forest grows more sparse as one goes up the mountain (or poleward): the trees become miniaturized. Finally it dies out completely, replaced by tundra—dwarf species of flowers and grasses, mosses and lichens—which in turn give way to Arctic wastes. Snow and ice. My map of the northernmost peninsula of Quebec is cut by a slashmark denoting the "northern limit of wooded country." The slashmark continues around the northern hemisphere, of course, at just about the point where July temperatures reach no higher than fifty degrees: the timberline of the world (for the northern hemisphere). One degree of latitude on the "mountain" that is the northern hemisphere is roughly equivalent to four hundred feet of altitude on a temperate zone mountain.

Mountains are made of rock; before plants can grow, there must be soil. Disintegrated rock, from frost weathering or whatever process—that fine dust paddied up behind every rootlet on our stroll up Kinsman—isn't classified as soil until it holds rooted plants, which can't root until there is "soil." Never mind the seeming double bind: soil does form. Rock weather-

ing produces the inorganic part, which gives it most of its
weight and bulk. The organic portion is eventually derived
from living and decayed plant and animal matter, bacteria,
fungi, worms, insects, roots, wastes of various kinds. Gar-
deners depend on earthworms to convert all these materials
into rich, loamy soil and aerate it in the process. Earthworms
can't live at mountain altitudes and temperatures. The process
takes place nevertheless, though more slowly. Mountain soil is
never rich; considering the temperatures that vegetation faces
at altitude, soil richness may be the least of its problems.

Still, things grow. Soil *is* formed, at infinitesimal pace, in
microscopic increments. One book describes a typical mini-
cycle:

Kobresia [a common tundra sedge] needs a fine deep humus soil.
In such an environment it flourishes, along with certain cushion
plants. Unfortunately, gophers are very fond of the cushion-plant
roots, and in the course of their excavations one of these small
rodents may throw up onto the surface of the ground several tons
of soil in a year, smothering the individual plants. Strong winds
eventually blow this soil away entirely, and *Kobresia* dies out, for it
can no longer prosper in the gravelly soil that remains. The area
begins to be colonized by a new type of vegetation—the lavender-
clustered sky pilot, the white-flowered yarrow and the blue-flowered
harebell, all of which grow high enough to withstand the piling up
of dirt. But these plants are not to the gopher's taste and it moves
on. Slowly the cushion plants creep back with their long taproots
which can probe deep in the gravel for water. In their dense
clusters they collect dust, and the decay of their bodies adds to the
accumulation of humus soil. Once more *Kobresia* is able to move
in. When it does, it kills off the sky pilots, yarrows, and most
cushion plants, for its shallow, wide-spreading roots catch all the
water that falls, and the cycle is completed.*

That tiny cycle, at mountain altitudes and in mountain conditions, can take a hundred years to complete. My bushwhack-

* Lorus J. and Margery Milne, *The Mountains* (New York: Time-Life
Books, 1962), p. 89.

ing on top of Kinsman, in search of a view to the west, now embarrasses me: as I tromped beyond the prepared path, I was wreaking havoc on delicate hundred-year soil processes going on underfoot.

Mountains simply skew the seasons. There is a summer of three months or so, overlapped at each end by an almost inconsequential spring and fall; the rest is winter. The winter is unrelieved despite the occasional clear, hot, sunlit days—days of such fierce radiation, perfectly angled, that here and there in pockets among the rock faces, microclimates of near-tropical intensity are created. No matter: the nightly frost will remove all that tropicality.

Winter always seems to be the dead spot of the year. Particularly as it strikes the high country, in those eight-month onslaughts, it would seem inevitable that it must kill everything—nature's hammer, smashing out life with its frigid sterility. The sterile appearance is a deception, however, and winter is really not so much a time of extinction as of dormancy, of rest. Growing things not only accommodate themselves to winter, they actually use the period as an important segment in their life cycles. The longer that period lasts, the longer the life form resists going on to the next part of its cycle. Any periodic activity in nature, such as a certain stage in a plant's life cycle, is delayed by about four days per degree of latitude away from the equator; the figure merely reflects the longer winters as one moves away from the sunburned equatorial latitudes. By extrapolating from the latitude–altitude analogy, then, every hundred feet of altitude is also roughly equivalent to another day of winter each year for a given latitude. Life cycles in mountain terrain will be slowed accordingly.

Thus in wintertime, and on mountains, maturation is slowed; so is aging. (That may not explain those youthfully sexy ski instructors of popular legend, but it gives at least a pseudoscientific rationale for James Hilton's invention of age-proof Shangri-la—named for an actual mountain pass, Chan-gri-La, about ten air miles from Mount Everest. It also means that southern girls *do* mature earlier.) Most mountain plants are perennials, taking two or three seasons to bring seeds to maturity. Growth can be very slow, some high-altitude seedlings growing at rates of an inch or less every ten years, putting out two tiny leaves each abbreviated summer. (Lichens are much slower; a patch of lichens a quarter of an inch tall may represent several hundred years' growth.) More evidence of the fragility of high-altitude environments, assuring that henceforth I will stay on the path. Gathering mountain wild flowers can seriously disrupt the reproductive chances of whole species, for example.

The temptation remains great: alpine wild flowers show some of the most brilliant coloring in nature. The marvelous selectivity of evolution has provided this extra attractiveness for a region where insect life is sparse and cross-pollination is therefore a dodgy proposition. Bright as the flowers may be, the leaves tend to be dark, for increased heat absorption. Many of the leaves are thick and waxy, to resist evaporation and wind chill, which affects plants just as it does animals and slows growth. Other mountain plants have fuzzy coatings, such as that of the edelweiss, for the same reasons: insulation. The buds of snow willows show an even more elaborate adaptation. They are covered with a fuzz that appears to be white. The hairs of that fuzz are actually transparent, however, and each has a black core. Light, and therefore heat, penetrate the translucent part each day and are conducted by the black core to the dark bud, where the heat is stored against the coming cold of night.

Specific plant adaptations abound at high altitude. Cushion plants—small aggregates or clusters of matted stems that form into a tiny pillow or dome-shaped mass close to ground level— are particularly adapted to mountain cold. A two-inch plant of this type will commonly put out twelve inches of root structure, to anchor against the wind and search out the unreliable water supply of the barren upper mountain. The low, tightly bunched, above-ground portion of the cushion plant is extremely wind resistant. Each plant colony is a tiny forest of matted stalks, providing its own shelter and an effective heat trap. Temperature within the cushion may be twenty degrees warmer than surrounding air. That warmth attracts insects just as do bright colors, enabling the cushion plants to compete with their brighter cousins for assistance in cross-pollination.

Closeness to the ground is in itself a highly advantageous characteristic in high-mountain plants, helping them resist or escape the incessant winds. As the Milnes point out, this is reflected in what naturalists call "belly plants"—named for the position you have to assume to observe them. Belly plant names reflect the same characteristics: *prostrata* (prostrate); *procumbens* (forward leaning); *caespitosa* (clumped); *acaulis* (stemless); *humilis* (humble).

Evolution undoubtedly provides a genetic stimulus to the development of such low-profile greenery, but mountain conditions themselves effectively prune back existing species. Mountain plants must be supple to survive high winds; very few leggy, woody plants make it in the higher reaches. Some species that make sizable trees in the lowlands—such as the limber pine and many varieties of willow—do well at altitude as flat, low-lying shrubs.

Snow makes all the difference. It is so effective an insulator that many plants grow in normal fashion to the depth of the annual snow cover, but not an inch higher. The snow cover is responsible for the *krummholz* ("crooked wood") forest—that dense, twisted shrubbery around timberline. Balsam fir, black spruce, even white birch and mountain ash may grow in the krummholz, as trees a hundred years old but only two feet tall. Their seedlings sprout in summer and grow through the seasons until they reach the maximum depth of the winter snows. As soon as the plant tries to poke its top above the snow's insulation, the severe wind and cold simply prune it back. The little ends are nipped off; the tree's growth capacity is thwarted, and it is pushed into the twists, turns, and dense matting of the krummholz.

Timberline is never surgically precise anyway—sometimes it is only a matter of definition, really, to decide where trees leave off and tundra begins. Looking up at timberline from the valley below, it may look like a precise division, but it never turns out that way on closer inspection. And sheer altitude is not as significant a determining factor in locating the timberline as are the type and quantity of soil, the local climate, the water supply, even the steepness of the slope.

Cold is more significant than altitude in determining what grows in the mountains, but desiccation is a more serious threat to high-altitude plant life than sheer cold. Many species have developed a waxy, resinous coating for their buds as a protection against this drying effect of the cold mountain winds. Mountain perennials tend to develop a very small cell structure, those cells filled with fluids that remain heavy with dissolved nutrients throughout the winter, providing a trickle of nutrition—and serving as a kind of antifreeze. The nutritional storage is necessary because below about forty degrees soil waters fail to dissolve out the nutrients the plants need. Other forms of antifreeze protection have been developed. Seeds, for example, have very little moisture in them, and don't freeze—some seeds have withstood laboratory temperatures of two hundred degrees below freezing without losing viability. Many varieties actually need a long period of dormancy. Aspen trees need months of below-forty-degree temperatures before they can open their wax-covered buds later in the spring.

Aspen are among the few deciduous trees that do well at high altitudes. Deciduous trees must be safely dormant by the dead of winter, because they have a watery sap that will freeze, expand, and split the tree. (That's the source of that sharp *crack!* you sometimes hear echoing out of the woods on a below-zero night, particularly in the New England mountains; it is a deciduous tree that didn't get its sap shut off early enough. Exploding.) To stop the sap flow, the leaves *must* fall. In order for this to happen, in response not to increased cold but to the lengthening nights of fall, a layer of relatively impervious tissue is formed between the leaf twig and the stem. This cuts off the water and nutrient supply. The chlorophyll is not renewed, and the leaf loses its green color—which exposes the other colors already in the leaf, the glorious spectrum of the fall foliage. Then the cells at the base of the stem give way; the leaf falls; the tree is safely "stored" for winter.

The needle-leafed species that clearly predominate at mountain altitudes have developed other solutions. Evergreens don't go completely dormant. They don't spend food and plant energy leafing out each spring, and therefore are sitting on the mountainside poised, ready to start photosynthesis the moment the temperature and light reach a point that will support the process. One might say that whenever the sun comes out, winter or summer, the evergreens start feeding. The needles of evergreens contain resins that function as antifreeze, and the needles also have the capacity to seal wounds—pines can be pruned year-round with no serious damage to the tree. All trees arrange their leaves to get maximum exposure to the sun; the conifers are no exception and quickly shed needles that are too shaded to perform photosynthesis, so the process of reshaping the tree to accommodate growth goes on continually. Trees with V-shaped forks—elms, poplars, box elders, willows, black locusts, and silver maples—sustain heavy damage from snow and ice loads, and keep to valleys and lowlands. The steeple shape of firs and spruces helps them survive such loads: the limbs are flexible enough to droop under the weight without damage, and spring back when wind or thaw unloads them.

The different species of plant life tend to make horizontal layers across the mountainside. Venturesome individuals may get outside the narrow layer that provides the most agreeable conditions, and if climatic conditions don't kill them off they will simply be overwhelmed by the species for which that layer's conditions are more favorable. But conditions are usually so different on opposite sides of a mountain that those horizontal layers seldom extend around the circumference of the peak. The zone of alpine meadows is wider, the tree line lower, the snow line higher on the driest side of the peak, and vice versa. The snow line is six thousand feet higher on the south side of the Himalayas than it is on the north.

In the American West, ponderosa pines and junipers take over the lower slopes and most of the south-facing slopes, needing more sun and warmth. Englemann and Colorado blue spruce fill in the north slopes; Douglas fir will be intermixed on both north and south slopes, able to survive in both climates. Douglas fir will cover a mountain slope—heavily—to about ninety-five hundred feet, then begin giving way to spruces and subalpine firs. Spruce is darker in color, with spiky needles and cones that hang downward; the firs are lighter, with softer needles, and the cones generally sit upright on the branches. It's easiest to learn to tell them apart when you find them growing side by side, as you occasionally will. The two species display admirable cooperation in establishing forests on difficult mountain slopes. The fir is short-lived but grows rapidly, casting seeds profligately, almost as a first-wave panzer operation to hold soil, stop wind, permit the development of forest cover. Spruce grows more slowly, but is long-lived and stable, in effect nailing down the forest gains the fir have set out for it.

Excuse my anthropomorphisms. When skunk cabbage manages to melt its way to the surface of the snow by running a fever—as much as twenty-five degrees warmer than surrounding air temperatures—it is almost impossible to resist attributing such actions to motivations hitherto arrogated to human beings. Snow buttercups have been found blooming underneath twelve-foot snowbanks, surely as clear a statement of optimistic spunk as ever fell from the lips of any human Molly Brown. Snow buttercups do eventually have to have sunlight to sustain their life cycles. But the plant is so well adapted to the vagaries of mountain weather that it can go a year at a time without ever reaching the sun at all. Metabolic processes produce heat within the plant, enough to trigger the blossoming. When it does get to the sunlight, it produces the various starches and sugars at a furious rate in the root system, and can get enough ahead of the process to store up energies for future sunless seasons.

Adaptation is the name of the mountain survival game, of course. Avalanches not only sweep away all vegetation—at least in the full-depth versions—but also can carry away a great deal of the precious underlying soil, scarring the mountainside for hundreds of years to come. Yet some species of plant life, such as the so-called "avalanche willow," are so well adapted to steep slope conditions that they can withstand all but the most destructive slides. It is as if they are determined to make and hold soil. They cling so tightly to the slope in densely matted clumps, and put up so little growth in forms that would allow snow buildup, that they seem almost to trigger minor avalanches by themselves, shrugging off accumulations of snow before the buildup reaches the danger point.

It is also difficult to avoid anthropomorphizing the evolutionary process itself, with all its endless trial-and-error creativity. Difficult conditions almost seem to put evolution on its mettle, and mountains provide some of the most difficult conditions of all. Much of the variety of mountain plant life is undoubtedly produced by genetic mutation caused by the extremes of cold, heat, chemical imbalance in the atmosphere, and radiation that characterize the natural environment of the high country. In that sense, mountains speed evolution, forcing adaptation at relatively rapid rates, ringing quick changes on the infinite organic possibilities of earthly life.

Yet there is an interesting contrast implied by the similarity between high mountain and Arctic species. Mountains quite frequently contain species that are found only at very high altitudes or very high latitudes. There are species of alpine avens that grow only in the perfectly miserable climate of Mount Washington's Presidential Range and in a limited area of Nova Scotia; a white-flowered version of the alpine bluet grows in the same mountains and on two islands in the Gulf of

Saint Lawrence, and nowhere else in the world.* Evidence makes it clear that the advancing and retreating ice sheets of the ice ages were responsible for carrying plant species and seeds thousands of miles from their natural habitat. That's what must have put the avens and bluets on Mount Washington. But it should also be noted that during those ice ages, most high mountain peaks were not entirely covered by the moving ice sheets, which were not deep enough. Those peaks thus stood as veritable islands of stability, whereon evolution proceeded at its normal, stately pace, while the gross and unusual changes and dislocations of the ice sheets went on about them.

Disaster fans are fond of pointing out that a rise of only a very few degrees in worldwide temperature would melt the ice caps, causing flooding of most of our major seacoast cities. Mountain lovers might take some small comfort from the realization that however disastrous that flooding would be in the short run—removing great quantities of useful land from our inventory—nevertheless, a subsequent development would restore at least some of the damage. A temperature change sufficient to melt the ice caps would also raise the timberline—worldwide—above the heights of the tallest peaks. It would take several hundred years to happen, granted, but the forest would inevitably climb right on up and conquer the same bleak and rocky peaks that the mountain climbers covet so dearly. Better make that several thousand years, to give time for the dawdling millimeter-by-millimeter process of soil building to permit the ascending forest a foothold. That time scale won't do much for the inundated residents of New York and Tokyo, but compared to most mountain processes, it will happen quickly enough to be almost reassuring.

* Peter Randall, *Mount Washington* (Hanover, N.H.: University Press of New England, 1974), p. 117–120.

Up and over the second ridge, and winter's on the dark
side of the hill again. The snow is full of tracks. It makes
one feel blind and deaf not to know what's written plainly
there. Tracks everywhere . . . mink, fox, weasel, possum,
mice—all have left their messages, and I can't read.
—JOSEPHINE W. JOHNSON, *The Inland Island*

Chapter **15**

All the Little Live Things

That the creatures with which we share the planet should
choose the mountains as habitat seems surprising. Mountain
conditions are as inhospitable for animals as for plant life, and
the forbidding terrain creates further dangers in sheer precari-
ousness. Animals do simply fall off cliffs and over ledges—although more rarely than might be imagined—and get caught
in rock slides and snow avalanches. What mountain wildlife
does not have to endure, however, is much interference from
man, and that fact alone makes the mountains a favorable
habitat. Remove our meddlesome presence, the animals seem
to be telling us, and they'll gladly put up with just about
anything else. We do leave the mountains relatively uninhabited, and the high country therefore collects great numbers of
wild creatures. Equally surprising, so does the Arctic, at least

in its subzones, and the altitude–latitude analogy of the preceding chapter is just as applicable to wildlife as it is to plants.

Animals are more affected by air content and atmospheric
pressure than plants are. Oxygen deficiency becomes a serious
handicap for animals as well as human beings above about
eighteen thousand feet, where air pressure is half that of sea
level. The Tibetan yak is the unquestioned altitude champ
among warm-blooded mammals, grazing comfortably near the
twenty-thousand-foot level—challenged for the honor of having the highest rangeland only by the Andean chinchilla. Wild
sheep may range up to nineteen thousand feet in the Himalayas, and are followed there by a select few of their predators,
mostly wolves and foxes—gasping for breath, it might be assumed, as they pursue the sheep. The vicuna, guanaco, alpaca,
and llama—all South American relatives of the camel—have
developed specific blood chemistry that enables them to thrive
in oxygen-poor air, but nevertheless don't range much above
sixteen thousand feet. (That the camel is also well suited for
desert life further demonstrates that genus's remarkable adaptability.)

Birds are understandably more comfortable with high altitudes. Graylag geese migrate from Siberia to India, directly
across, and therefore above, the near thirty-thousand-foot
Himalayas. The alpine chough, a cousin of the crow found
throughout European and Asian mountains, has been seen taking off from snowfields at the twenty-seven-thousand-foot
level on Mount Everest. Just *barely* taking off, after a long
downhill takeoff run in search of airspeed where there is almost no air in which to speed. Bugs, in their pestilential way,
may be hardier yet: spiderlings and springtails have been
found in mini-colonies above the twenty-thousand-foot level,
again in the Himalayas.

Although atmospheric pressure is more critical to animals
than to plants, it is still the sheer cold of the high mountains
that is most limiting to both. For animals, cold and altitude are
closely related. The ability to withstand cold depends heavily

on the rate of metabolism, and the oxygen content of the atmosphere helps determine that rate. The prodigious appetites and rates of oxygen consumption for birds—and the resulting high body temperatures—are well known. As temperature drops, more food and oxygen are required to maintain body heat at survival levels. A hungry hummingbird can go comatose at not much below fifty degrees Fahrenheit. The smallest mammal found at high altitudes, the mountain shrew, has a heart rate of twelve hundred beats a minute, and must eat every waking hour to sustain life.

It is the cold that dictates evolutionary mountain adaptations. Biologists debated for years over the existence of separate high- and low-altitude chinchilla species. In the end they determined that the only real difference was the length of tail: what they took for a high-altitude chinchilla was exactly the same animal as the low-altitude version, except it had evolved a shorter tail in order to have less surface area to keep warmed with body heat. (One can almost envision an animal version of the krummholz effect, the burgeoning little chinchilla tails being nipped back by frost.) Body extremities get smaller as the habitat gets colder. Hares and rabbits demonstrate this phenomenon elegantly. Arizona jackrabbits carry ears like sails, to help them dissipate body heat in desert climes; Arctic hares have ears so short by comparison that they seem almost catlike. You can virtually determine the latitude—and altitude—at which a rabbit lives by the length of its ears.

Small, warm-blooded animals have great problems with cold because of their slight bulk and large surface area, making retention of heat difficult. Small extremities are just the start of the solution; development of an extremely heavy coat, with special adaptations of the very hair structure within the coat, helps even more in reduction of heat loss. It is no accident that chinchilla and mink fur have become symbols of the ultimate in luxury in human apparel. Eons of evolution have given these tiny mammals, active through the winter, the finest coats in the animal kingdom.

Carrying those two cold-weather adaptations—small extremities and heavy coat—to their logical conclusion would result in the most efficient possible shape for heat retention: a fur-covered ball, giving maximum mass with minimum skin area. That's precisely the direction taken by evolution in the small mountain mammals. Even those that have retained a string bean anatomy will curl up at rest into a ball-like shape to conserve heat. When they are pursued, they stretch out to full length as they run, and can therefore quickly dissipate the extra heat generated during exertion. With techniques of heat retention so developed, heat dissipation can in turn become a problem. Arctic lemmings may die of heat prostration when air temperatures reach seventy degrees, and it is common to see any of the small mountain animals—marmots and the like—stretching out to full length on a snowbank, cooling their bellies, on hot, bright mountain days.

Warm-blooded mountain animals cope with cold by migrating, hibernating, or seeking shelter—underground or under snow. The last solution is best suited for the small animals—rabbits, hares, lemmings, voles, ground squirrels, pocket gophers, marmots, pika, various kinds of mice, and such unfamiliar foreign species as the hyrax and the vizcacha—all the small gnawing animals that inhabit the mountains. Some of them do hibernate, more or less, but most simply burrow down to the warmth of the earth, store as much food as possible, and go on as before, eating and breeding with furious intensity. The food supply at high altitudes is always precarious; that fact and the natural presence of predators combine to control population.

Occasionally, however, these controls fail, and a second level of balance mechanisms comes into play, some of which are marvelously intricate. A female vole matures sexually at five weeks and may produce litters of eight young every three weeks throughout the summer. Lemmings, which breed throughout the winter, can produce eighty young per female per year. Overproduction quickly takes care of surplus food, in the rare case where such exists, but reproduction tends to shut down before the food is exhausted. A kind of nervous futility takes over the animal colony. Females get irritable, fighting males and resisting breeding. They may destroy their own litters. Food collection and nest building are neglected. The stress of overpopulation in lemmings can actually cause brain damage.

It may be simple overcrowding, or the exhaustion of some single necessary element in the diet, but now and then something stimulates lemmings to mass migration. They come swarming down out of the mountains, seeking less crowded conditions in the valleys—and insuring their niche in the folklore as mass suicides. The folklore is wrong. Lemmings are good swimmers, but occasionally the pressure to migrate is sufficient to drive them into bodies of water too broad for their own stamina. They are seeking survival, but they appear to be bent on hysterical self-destruction.

Generalizations about mountain adaptation don't adequately represent the fascinating individual accommodations to cold, snow, and life in the high country that some animals have developed. The snowshoe rabbit—which isn't a rabbit, but, properly, a varying hare—is fitted out with high-country accoutrements as if it had shopped for them from the L. L. Bean catalog. It has small ears, a compact shape, and a thick coat for heat retention; it also has very large feet, which would seem to be a contradiction, at least for purposes of warmth. But those huge feet are thickly furred and capable of spreading out for a snowshoe effect, giving it a kind of flotation over the snow. (The snow leopard, the ruffed grouse, and the forest-dwelling marten have also developed special snowgoing footwear.) You may spot a varying hare in wintertime, but you'll have to be quick about it: it will disappear instantly in a shower of snow. Varying hares can do twenty-five miles per hour, in short bursts, over almost any surface.

And the varying hare . . . varies. It changes its brown summer coat for a well-camouflaged white in winter. (So do the ptarmigan and one species of weasel. The latter, when it is in its winter white coat, is the ermine, that other luxury fur, kissing cousin to the mink.) So far as scientists have been able to determine, the change of coat is triggered by changing light values in the fall of the year, which act on the pituitary gland through the animal's eyes. A similar but more mysterious color adaptation is shown by the Himalayan rabbit. It too has a camouflaged white coat, all year round, but its ears, tail, and feet are quite dark, to absorb and retain heat. In the laboratory, if white hair is shaved from the Himalayan rabbit, it will grow back white if the air temperature is kept above sixty-eight degrees Fahrenheit, but dark if the temperature is kept below fifty degrees—no matter what the area of the body. If hair is removed from a dark area, and that area kept warm, the hair will grow back white. Biologists are still shaking their heads over this one.

(These winter adaptations don't hold a candle to one adopted—according to the Eskimos—by the all-white, admittedly nonmountain polar bear. The polar bear is all white except for a shiny black button of a nose—dead giveaway against a snowy background. So when the polar bear goes seal stalking on the ice pack, it will lie flat on the ice and hold one white paw over its black nose to complete the camouflage until it gets close enough to its prey to make a charge. The Eskimos swear to it.)

Birds migrate thousands of miles, in well-established flyways that often leap from continent to continent. But the altitude–latitude analogy is precise enough that some other species—mule deer, elk, bighorn sheep—simply migrate vertically, coming down to lower mountain valleys in winter, climbing back up in the spring. A considerable conservation of energy is thereby achieved, which can be of crucial importance to the animal's survival. Deer in particular operate on a narrow energy budget in winter. They will feed heavily in the fall, storing as much fat as possible on their bodies, and with the coming of the snows they go into deer yards. ("Deer yard" conjures up a corrallike cleared area in the woods, but actually it is simply a maze of narrow, winding, interconnected trails, packed down as the deer move about in single file in search of browse that is not yet snow-covered.)

The deer yard is chosen for a reasonable amount of available forage, usually on a south-facing slope—if an overhanging peak provides additional shelter, so much the better. Once chosen by a herd, the yard becomes at least a semipermanent feature of their home range, as they return to it winter after winter, a habit that helps biologists in their studies. Once the deer have yarded up, their metabolic rate becomes critical. They pass the hard part of the season as close to the pilot light level of metabolic activity as possible, since simple maintenance of life makes a high demand on energy in the extreme cold. The deer move little, deliberately parceling out the available forage. They prefer deciduous buds and shrubs, or white cedar, but will switch to red spruce and balsam fir buds (in the Appalachians and Adirondacks) or Douglas fir buds (in the Rockies and other western ranges) when necessary.

The danger to deer from marauding dogs or other predators—or mountain visitors, particularly cross-country skiers, whose movement is silent—is that when the deer are startled into flight, they expend energy beyond the amounts they can easily make up at winter forage levels. Thus, even if they escape the predator, they may eventually starve from the exertion. Mountain village dogs on the loose are particular offenders in this regard. And unarmed and even well-intentioned snowmobilers wreak more havoc on deer populations than do any other human group except hunters.

The problem is compounded by the deer's anatomy. Deer don't have the teeth for much chewing, so they pull their food off the stem—you can recognize areas where deer have been browsing by the distinctively ragged, stripped-down shrub ends. To utilize this very rough roughage, deer have a complex arrangement of stomachs, and for digestion to take place certain bacteria, called *commensals,* must be present in their systems. The commensals are specific to certain plants. Once a deer starts to starve, it may lose the commensal relationship. Once that happens it does no good to provide the deer with alfalfa or other rich foods: the deer will starve to death with a full stomach if it doesn't have the commensals specific to the new diet. Deer must eat all year—they can neither hibernate nor store much food. They do get a heavier coat in winter, with increased numbers of hollow hairs for improved insulation. And then they drift downslope to where the snow isn't so deep and become very quiet. And wait.

The pika—so close a cousin to hares and rabbits that it might best be considered a true mountain rabbit—has an even stranger dietary habit. Pikas winter under the snow, living primarily on dry grass fodder that has been carefully gathered all summer long. This limited diet is augmented by *refection*—consumption of fecal material which contains essential vitamins. The pika leaves dry, green droppings during the day, but its night droppings are covered by a layer of mucus that keeps them moist. While these night droppings are exposed to air, bacteria in them forms the necessary vitamins. The pika then swallows them, to mix them with fresh food in a redigestion process. It's a nutritional form that may offend the weak of stomach, but without the vitamins formed thereby the pika would be dead in about three weeks.

The line between true hibernation (literally, "wintering"; the much rarer summer form is called "estivation") and other kinds of grossly reduced winter metabolism and activity is a little hard to draw. There are fewer true hibernators than we generally assume, and the process itself is still somewhat mysterious, even to biologists. The bear, for example, is virtually a symbol of hibernation, but most bears are not true hibernators. Hibernation may be triggered by accumulations of fat stored for winter, or by glandular changes wrought by seasonal variation. The sex glands and organs of hibernators are underdeveloped in the fall, overdeveloped in the spring. During hibernation, body temperature can drop to forty degrees Fahrenheit or less, and the hibernating animal may breathe only once every ten to fifteen minutes. Carp spend the winter half-buried in mud in the stream bottom, their metabolism cued to the temperature around them. At thirty-eight degrees the carp breathes about thirty times a minute; below thirty-two it does not breathe at all. But it is not dead; it is in a state of suspended animation, and can survive that way for up to twenty-nine days. (Other species can survive as long as a year.) Even if frozen into a solid block of ice, so long as the tissues are not frozen, the fish can revive.

By contrast, the respiration and heartbeat rates of "hibernating" black bears stay about the same as in the nonhibernating state. Body temperatures drop ten degrees or less. Bears accumulate layers of fat up to four inches in thickness in the fall, and their coats become extremely dense and glossy. Their stomachs contract and refuse food. The huge Kodiak Island brown bears—which are closer to true hibernators than black bears—actually cram themselves with cranberries as a laxative to flush out their systems before going down for their winter sleep.

Most bears, from the giant panda (related to the raccoon) to the common black bear, are mountain animals. The black bear, found throughout both eastern and western mountains in the United States, eats roots, pine needles, hair, and other indigestibles in the late fall; these form the *tappen*, an intestinal plug that stops digestive action for the duration of the bear's reduced winter activity. Hikers may find expelled tappens in the springtime woods; the size of the tappen can indicate how long the bear slept the previous winter. Once the tappen is formed, the bear spends the winter drowsing, waking, stirring, drowsing again—but not eating. Females may not go to sleep until shortly before giving birth to a litter, and can be easily aroused at any time in the winter, particularly to defend the cubs. The cubs are acutely helpless at birth but spend their early lives in the shelter of the den, with a warm and plentiful food supply from the napping mother. With the spring thaws the bear becomes active again, but can't resume normal habits —and gets very cranky—until the tappen is passed. Springtime bears are to be avoided.

Many of the small gnawing animals—and other warm-blooded creatures of the mountains that are not so specifically linked to the heights, such as skunks, raccoons, badgers—may sleep for days or weeks at a time, but still are not true hibernators, their bodily functions remaining near normal. Raccoons will come out of their dens to hunt food during January thaws; their mating season is in late January or February, and they will usually be active by that time, as will skunks. The small animals you see at roadside at night in late winter are usually on the sexual prowl.

Skunks exhibit this behavior, and it is part of an interesting relationship with the great horned owl. After several days of below-fifty-degree weather in the fall, skunks go underground, denning up, sometimes in groups to conserve heat. Depending on the severity of the winter—or the altitude of the den—skunks may sleep anywhere from two to twelve weeks. Then the males wake, in early February, even as early as late January, and are ready to mate. They come above ground and range up to five miles or more in search of a den containing receptive females. These males won't be driven in, even by extreme cold.

Meanwhile the great horned owl, a shy and retiring bird, chooses to nest deep within the woods in dead of winter—a seemingly inhospitable time to try to hatch and rear young. But for great horned owls, skunk is a nutritional staple, and along about February, when the owls need more food for their broods, the woods just happen to be full of these equally nocturnal, extremely randy, male skunks. It all works out. The female skunks, usually impregnated by this time, stay underground longer, avoiding owls and providing safe gestation for the next generation of skunks. And newly hatched owlets feast on skunk fathers, developing a taste, one supposes, that assures the continuation of the relationship.

There is, of course, a lion of the mountains: the puma, or cougar, a distinctly western-hemisphere cat that ranges from the Canadian Northwest all the way down to the tip of South America. The cougar adapts readily to forest or desert, but it is in the mountains, on the loose scree slopes and rocky ledges, that it comes into its own. Up to eight feet long (including tail), weighing up to 250 pounds, it is a powerful and devastating predator, favoring deer but known to kill and eat everything from rabbits to twelve-hundred-pound elk. It is also unjustifiably feared by man, although the only known occasion of the killing and eating of a human being by a cougar occurred in 1924. The bad reputation may come from the cougar's high level of curiosity, as it will often follow a man encroaching on its territory—even a man on horseback—for miles, for no discernible purpose other than to watch. Unfortunately, that bad reputation has brought the cougar to the verge of extinction by man.

Similarly, the snow leopard, even more specifically adapted to high mountain life, has been hunted nearly to extinction—in this case not so much out of fear as out of greed. The snow leopard has the misfortune to possess one of the most beautiful coats of any furred animal. Its coat is white or bluish gray with black rosettes, with a thick, wooly undercoat. The remarkable beauty of the coat caused the furriers to bid the price so high that hunters nearly destroyed the snow leopard population years ago, throughout their native Central Asian haunts. The mature cat grows to about seven feet in length, of which three feet is thick, furry, well-insulated tail—a necessary counterpoise for balance on slick and icy mountain terrain. It has tiny ears, in keeping with cold-weather adaptation, but huge, spreading paws, also heavily furred, like those of the snowshoe rabbit. The snow leopard ranges upwards of thirteen thousand feet in summer, comes back down to about six thousand feet in winter, and does its best to avoid contact with man. Nevertheless, we've now reduced the total number of snow leopards so that it is estimated that there may be no more than four hundred of them still extant.

The only other cat of extensive mountain habitat is the wildcat, or bobcat, which inhabits backwoods regions in the mountains of North America and Europe, but is wily enough rarely to be seen. The wildcat is a larger, stockier, bobtailed version of the domestic house cat—in fact some biologists still argue that there is little difference between wildcats and common house cats gone feral. Wildcats seldom exceed a couple of feet in length, feed on small rodents and rabbits, and often become exceptionally skillful bird hunters. They may develop such a taste for fowl that they switch to domestic poultry, which results in a bounty being placed on their heads. Most farmers would prefer to see the species simply wiped out, but so far the wildcat has escaped that fate.

Mountain cats and other predators feast on upland game birds—grouse, partridge, pheasant, and the like—but don't make a dent in overall mountain birdlife. The extreme mobility of birds has led them to seek the remote and otherwise inaccessible mountain reaches for safe nesting. A great part of the mountain bird population consists of "l.g.b.'s"—bird watcher slang for the "little gray birds" whose multitudes of species, differentiated sometimes by the tiniest of distinctions, drive those bird watchers to distraction. But the mountains are also home to the big birds, the majestic soaring species and predators, the giants among the earth's flying creatures. Eagles, hawks, falcons all seek the safety of high, craggy cliffs not only for nesting but also to survey vast territories, which they then restlessly patrol. Condors and vultures likewise ride soaring currents mountainward at day's end, conserving energy. (Some giant condors cannot get airborne in still air on level ground, particularly after a full meal. They must pick roosting points that provide either a stiff prevailing breeze, or enough of a drop-off to give them a head start in picking up airspeed. Caught on level ground, they must wait—in total vulnerability—for sufficient wind to allow them to fly.)

All of the large birds are more or less threatened in modern times. Pesticides and other chemical pollutants in the food chain cause them to lay eggs that are infertile to start with, or too weak-shelled to last through incubation. Because of their high visibility, the predators are blamed for a great deal of livestock depredation—on the flimsiest of evidence—leading to such obscenities as the shotgunning of eagles from light planes in the American West. (Somehow it is more than that: we simply can't resist shooting at big birds, for some reason, and enforcement of protective laws is virtually impossible.) Large birds need large territories—fifteen to twenty-five square miles for a pair of nesting eagles. (Eagles do not, like many birds, fly for the pleasure of it; most of the soaring they do is aimed at maintaining their territories.) All of these threats to their safety have served to drive them deeper and deeper into the mountain wilderness. Sightings of the larger birds—with the exception of the profligate vultures and buzzards—become progressively rarer. It is our loss. Meanwhile, back in the mountains, the big birds hang on to a tenuous existence.

Specific mountain adaptations in the bird world are everywhere. That alpine chough seen fluttering painfully into the air at twenty-seven thousand feet on Everest can breed at up to nineteen thousand feet, and the chough is seen scavenging around most high alpine stations in all seasons. Like most mountain birds, the chough is a highly skillful flyer, seeming to take great joy in toying with the tricky currents that play around the cliffs and ravines of the treeless upper reaches. The raven, a cousin of the chough, is perhaps as skillful a flyer but is even more adaptable; it nests at fourteen thousand feet or more, but unlike the chough, which sticks to the highlands, the raven ranges everywhere, even, in bad weather, in the cities.

Two mountain birds, the torrent duck and the dipper, feed primarily underwater, the former mostly in Andean rivers, the latter almost anywhere in the world where there are mountain streams. The dipper, a tiny, undistinguished, wrenlike bird, has very heavy oil glands at the base of its feathers—natural waterproofing—and skin flaps that close its nostrils. It swims skillfully underwater by flapping its wings, and can fly into or out of water without changing its line of motion. It turns up bottom mud in search of small insects, larvae, and fish, diving sometimes as deep as twenty feet.

L.g.b.'s—finches, nuthatches, siskins, redpolls, twites, crag martins, wall creepers—love the mountains. Some have beaks peculiarly adapted to feeding on the seeds from coniferous trees; others thrive on high country grasses and above-timber-line vegetation. Wall creepers and crag martins prefer cliff faces, feeding on insects that have also mastered the heights. Rock thrushes and accentors prefer above-timberline terrain also, the latter nesting to 18,500 feet in the Himalayas. The ring ouzel is presumed to have been a high mountain bird that was forced downslope by the severe conditions of the ice ages, and now prefers below-timberline but still mountainous country. There is never a shortage of birds in the mountains.

Because of their enormous surface area and very slight mass, birds are excellent radiators (which suits them for the tropics) and terrible heat sinks (which unsuits them for the mountains). To survive in cold country, they have developed a body covering that is the most efficient thermal insulation known to man. It is no accident that the warmest mountain climbing clothing is stuffed with down, and all of our "miracle fiber" technology has produced no better protection against the cold than this form of feathers. Still, birds remain vulnerable. While great numbers of their species flee the mountains in winter, dozens more flee *to* them, from farther north. The great joy of birding is its seasonal variety, with summer birds, winter birds, and what might be called trans-seasonal birds—just passing through. As in achingly beautiful geese and duck flights which punctuate the temperate zone seasons. Mountains not only skew the seasons, they also accentuate them, intensifying their contrast. Mountains also force their human inhabitants into a closer, more observant relationship with the natural world. It is almost impossible to live in the mountains without falling in love with birdlife. Look around any high alpine station or ski resort, and you'll see well-stocked feeders, oftentimes serviced regularly by the burliest of mountain guides and avalanche patrolmen.

Insects, whose breathing apparatus consists of tubes leading from various spots spread over their external skeletons, are relatively unaffected by the lowered air pressure of high altitudes; some of them, such as the springtail, are even capable of extracting oxygen from the moisture that collects on their skin and thus in effect need no air at all. Springtails are among the most primitive insects known, and are distributed everywhere throughout the world, including above six thousand feet in the Antarctic, as well as the twenty-two-thousand-foot levels in the Himalayas. The name comes from the method of locomotion: the spike of a tail is folded underneath the abdomen, held in place with a ratchetlike latch of horny material. When the latch releases, the tail springs downward and flings the springtail through the air. (The tiny particle of muscle material that powers the tail is the strongest yet discovered.) Springtails feed on decayed plant material where available, and, it is presumed, microscopic wind-blown materials in the otherwise almost sterile high mountain altitudes. They are in turn eaten by various jumping spiders, including the species found—in immature form—at the same Himalayan altitudes, thus forming what one writer has characterized as an "aeolian" —wind-produced—food chain. Centipedes and various tiny flies and midges have been found at slightly lower altitudes.

As altitude is not critical in limiting the range of insects, neither is temperature—a surprising fact for species that have no body temperature of their own, and are therefore totally at the mercy of ambient heat levels. Insects do need quite a bit of external heat to pursue an active life, but when the heat isn't available, the insect simply goes dormant until it returns. As bumblebees will be discovered crawling groggily over the ground on nippy late summer mornings, so do the various mountain insects reduce their mobility during much of the mountain year. Below about sixteen thousand feet, insect life is not much different from that of sea level, as far as the number of species and their types are concerned. Butterflies, moths, and flies do as well in the mountains as anywhere else. But their life cycles may be strung out over two or three years on high, whereas at sea level they can sometimes squeeze a couple of generations into a single summer. They remain longer in the larval and pupal stages too; extended periods may be spent in total dormancy, simply waiting for the short bursts of fecundity of mountain summertime to continue the inexorable life processes.

The ultimate restriction on insect viability is lack of water, which can indeed be a problem in regions of permanent snow. Even there, however, protruding rock will absorb more heat than the surrounding snow, and thereby manage to melt small pockets of accumulated moisture. (Without the excess of heat radiating from rock or other dark surfaces, the snow will sublimate directly into vapor.) These pockets of meltwater, usually in niches in or under the rock, support small insect communities. They also tend to trap pollen and other windborne organic materials, which become part of the local food chain. We tend to think of insects as constant voracious feeders—judging in part from those occasions when insects feed on us in the mosquito and black fly seasons—and indeed they will feed that way when conditions permit. But in marginal circumstances they can go without feeding for long periods of dormancy, exhibiting an incredible degree of what might be characterized as a kind of stupefied patience. Eventually the very variety of mountain weather will produce favorable conditions and bring them back around.

Birds and insects do fine, in their ingenious adaptability, but the absolute masters of the high country are the true mountaineers: the various goat, sheep, and antelope species that thrive in the most inaccessibly rugged terrain the mountains can produce. The bighorn sheep of the American and Canadian Rockies, and the chamois and ibex of the Alps are the most familiar, but there are many more. Most of them are related fairly closely to the domestic goat, long a favorite of mountain dwellers for its hardy self-reliance and its ability to wring a living out of the poorest of soils and sparsest of vegetations. In the wilder versions of these species, those characteristics are even more highly developed.

It is in their climbing ability that these creatures excel over all others. The chamois regularly makes standing leaps up vertical distances of twelve feet or more, and shows no hesitation at broad-jumping twenty-foot gaps and chasms. One of the more dumbfounding spectacles of mountain country is the sight of mountain goats grazing casually on what would appear to be vertical cliff faces, springing nimbly from invisible hoofhold to invisible hoofhold, seemingly oblivious to thousand-foot drop-offs that yawn below.

They can do so because they have developed the best climbing footgear in the animal kingdom: split-toed hooves that can grip the slipperiest bare rock, thanks to the hard-rubber texture of the hoof material and cup-shaped depressions in the soles of the hooves themselves. With the tiniest of purchases, the hoof can support the weight of the entire animal; a built-in afterclaw helps prevent sliding when necessary. The animals that survive develop great skill at placing these specialized hooves and coordinating their movements, needless to say. They've also developed muscle, tendon, and bone structure that is not only strong enough to launch the tremendous leaps, but also shock-absorbent enough to cushion the landings. A normal-sized mountain goat will often drop twenty feet or more to a pinpoint ledge landing—never mind the consequences of a miss—and go on grazing on the wisps and sprigs of greenery there as casually as if it had only stepped off a curb.

The mountain sheep and goats (and related antelope) have developed digestive systems to match the ruggedness of their favorite terrain. They are able to live on the extremely limited vegetable matter of the rocky high mountains because they have sufficient patience—augmented by special grinding molars and four-part stomachs—to extract every calorie of food energy from the little sustenance available to them. Their tongues are long, muscular, with very rough surfaces, to function as an additional food pulverizing and chewing organ, and to support their indefatigable jaw muscles. They must eat almost continually, and the search for food is interrupted only for mating. The bighorn sheep of the Rockies husband their food so carefully that during the first snowfalls of the year they eat only the grass tops and seed heads that project above the snow, making no effort to get at the rich supply below. As the snow starts getting deeper, the bighorn does dig down through it to the grass supply. During the desperate deep-snow months, all the rams of the same relative size and status within the herd—ordinarily standoffish in the extreme—will line up side by side in the snow to dig feeding trenches for the rest of the herd.

The bighorns have headgear to suit their names, of course, massive curled horns which serve a defensive purpose but are put to more poignant use during the mating season. Then, competing rams choose off and hold butting contests, mighty duels that fill the hills and valleys with the reverberations of their clashing horns. The loser, usually the younger and smaller animal, goes his dazed and addlepated way, his fatherhood postponed until he gains another year's growth. The victor, equally dazed and addlepated from all those head-on collisions, proceeds to impregnate his harem.

(There's an interesting relationship between the bighorn sheep and their mountains. The bighorn's worst enemy is a parasitic worm that settles in lung tissue. Part of that parasite's life cycle is spent in a small mountain snail which must have limestone to live. Therefore bighorns that live in granitic mountains are ordinarily healthy, but when their range includes mountains of limestone and marble, as in the Dolomites of Italy, they have difficulty surviving the worm infestations.)

Even more spectacular headgear, used for precisely the

same purpose in a quite similar ritual, characterizes the ibex: great, towering, prominently ridged horns, scimitar-shaped, sometimes three feet in length. The horns were once prized for their supposed medicinal value, and by the mid–nineteenth century the ibex was almost wiped out in the Alps. Victor Emmanuel II of Italy then began a campaign to protect and restore the herd. A group of five was reintroduced to the Swiss Alps in 1911 and has grown, with protection, to more than two thousand animals. The ibex now ranges from the Pyrenees to the Caucasus, with closely related species throughout Asian mountains. There's still some confusion about just how many species of ibex there actually are.

The chamois, along with such exotic animals as the takin, the serow, the goral, and the klipspringer (Afrikaans for "rock jumper"), is a member of a species related to both goats and antelopes. (So is the Rocky Mountain goat.) Chamois are famous among Americans principally for the soft, lint-free, water-absorbent hide used to polish automobiles and silverware. Europeans know the graceful creature as one of nature's best climbers, a shy, wary beast with such acute hearing and eyesight that hunting it is an exercise in exasperation. With a long-haired coat with thick underfur, the chamois is well protected against mountain cold and keeps to its preferred range—five thousand to seven thousand feet—in the rockiest, steepest possible terrain winter and summer. Folklore would have it that the ten-inch horns, hooked slightly to the rear at the upper end, are shock absorbers, saving the chamois's neck in an occasional head-first fall. (Bighorn sheep do have shock absorbent structures at the base of their skulls, which allow them to avoid injury during the mating rituals.) Chamois fall so seldom that it's a little difficult to check out the folklore, but rockfalls and avalanches do catch an occasional chamois, and in those circumstances the delicate horns are little help.

One more mountain animal must be acknowledged: the yeti. A large mountain ape, five and a half to six feet tall, weighing perhaps two hundred pounds, "covered with short, coarse hair, reddish brown to black in color, sometimes with white patches on the chest," according to a compendium of descriptions gathered by zoologist Edward W. Cronin, Jr., writing in the November, 1975, issue of *Atlantic Monthly*. "The hair is longest on the shoulders. The face is hairless and rather flat. The jaw is robust, the teeth are quite large, though fangs are not present, and the mouth is wide. The head is conically shaped, and comes to a pointed crown. The arms are long, reaching almost to the knees. The shoulders are heavy and hunched. There is no tail." Native only to the Himalayan highlands.

In other words, the Abominable Snowman. Along with such imagination-stimulating mysteries as the Loch Ness monster and Sasquatch, the big-footed giant of the American North-west, a curious mixture of real evidence and hysterical report-ings. Subject of innumerable sightings (although not too many by Westerners) and not a few hoaxes, including some discred-ited scalps stored in Himalayan monasteries. Obviously an-other figment of the overworked (and underoxygenated) imaginations of Himalayan mountaineers. Yes, of course.

And yet, and yet. Cronin makes an excellent case. Mountain apes are not unknown, including some gorillas in Africa—whose existence was scoffed at by Western scientists for gen-erations, despite consistent reports by the local populations—that live at up to 12,800 feet. ("The kouprey, a large wild bison, was not discovered by Western Science until 1936," Cronin points out, "when the first specimen was identified inside the Paris zoo.") Fossil remains of a very similar ancient ape, *Gigantopithecus,* have been found in Himalayan foothills, and have been carbon-dated at as little as 500,000 years of age. The extremely rugged topography of the Himalayas could easily hide such a large primate; there are areas therein which still have not been penetrated by Western scientists, and very likely won't be during the foreseeable political future of the region. That the animal is most probably nocturnal only adds to its elusiveness. In those climes the nights are not conducive to biological observation. It is very likely not a *high* mountain ape, not a creature of the snows after all, but one most comfortable in the comparatively lush valleys among the mountains. It just happens occasionally to traverse the higher ridges in journeying from one valley to the next. Scaring the wits out of the mountaineers as it traverses.

The sightings and evidence are very good. Many natives of the area automatically include the yeti in any list of local fauna, and undocumented sightings of the beast itself are common among the locals. Analysis of what were reputed to be yeti scalps and footprints have been largely bungled—scientists have been forced to try to untangle local politics, religion, and folklore along with the physical evidence. Cronin himself was "convinced" when, after camping overnight at about twelve thousand feet on a Himalayan ridge, he awoke to find otherwise inexplicable footprints in the snow, crossing the ridge near his tent. Photographs of the footprints, taken under exacting scientific conditions, compared almost exactly with similar shots taken many miles away by Eric Shipton and Michael Ward twenty-one years earlier.

Cronin believes. He also hopes—an interesting stance for a zoologist—that the yeti, if it does exist, is never "discovered":

If it were to be found and captured, studied and confined, we might well slay our nightmares. But the mystery and imagination it evokes would also be slain. If the yeti is an old form that we have driven into the mountains, now we would be driving it into the zoos. We would gain another possession, another ragged exhibit in the concrete world of the zoological park, another Latin name to enter on our scientific ledgers. But what about the wild creature that now roams free of man in the forests of the Himalayas? Every time man asserts his mastery over nature, he gains something in knowledge, but loses something in spirit.

"These aren't hills, Lionell, and you know it. These are mountains, boy. I've seen them in the East and once is enough. These are outcroppings of the goddamned innards of the earth, by God, and I'm not going over them! You can let me out right here!"—LARRY WOIWODE, *Beyond the Bedroom Wall*

Chapter *16*

The Hard Life

Using mountains, for what might be called real-world purposes, is too much trouble: there is always that nagging, debilitating gradient to deal with. Sporting uses such as climbing and skiing are only fringe phenomena, growing out of a frivolous oversupply of time and money. Such fringe uses are always introduced by short-term visitors. The permanent residents of the mountains seldom have the energy left over, after dealing with the gradient, to invent new games.

It is a painfully unromantic fact, but for those real-world uses only the hard-pressed elements of society will put up with mountains for long, and only as a desperate measure, in the face of sheer lack of space elsewhere. No other reason is powerful enough to keep them there. Only a few minor agricultural specialties, for example, can be considered to thrive in the mountains—tea in the foothills of the Himalayas, coffee in the foothills of the Andes. (Neither, interestingly enough, is particularly nutritious; both are stimulating enough that many cultures lump them with drugs.) There is a fair amount of mountain pasturage of sheep, cattle, and other livestock, but again, only out of necessity. All those animals would thrive more securely in flat country, if only there were room for them.

So would people. Mountains are hard places, and they produce hard people. Mining, lumbering, and the heavy construction for harnessing water power are the only industries that pull substantial numbers of new people into the mountains, or provide any kind of steady employment for the sparse populations already there. Mining, lumbering, and construction are hard jobs (harder in the mountains), demanding hard people. Distressing as the stereotype may be, it is true: any people driven to remain in such inhospitable regions take on a different character from that of their brethren in the flatlands. From the tigerish Sherpa to the massive-lunged Andean, from the stolid Swiss to our own hillbilly mountain men, the traditional character of mountain people is a cut apart. Our frontier literature has consistently romanticized this character as somehow nobler than that of other men. Such moral judgment may be skewed by the scenery. The character and the lives of mountain people are simply different. Harder.

When the first New England mountain folk gave up and fled to Ohio, after lifetimes of dealing with their home terrain (and, oh dear, their home weather), they wrote home of a land of milk and honey they had found out there west of the Mohawk Valley. All they really meant was that the topsoil could be measured in feet rather than in tentative inches, and the fields did not actually grow stones, as any White or Green Mountain pasture in their experience had always done. The news of such agricultural richness siphoned off the more opportunistic of the hardscrabble farmers of New Hampshire and Vermont. "Ohio Fever," it was called. Going to farm in Ohio after a decade or two of the New England experience was, to those careworn pioneers, very like retiring.

The lure of the rich soil did not sway everyone, however.

The farmers who stayed to fight—and it was a fight, uninterrupted warfare against ice, acid soil, growing seasons brief as an eyeblink—may have done so out of conservatism and fear of change, but, to judge from their descendants, a stronger force was behind their apparent commitment to the mountain colonies: pure stubbornness.

As in any farming operation, flatland or otherwise, there is among New England mountain farmers a strong, almost poetic relationship with nature, a natural product of the tempering of impatience by the inexorable tides and rhythms of the outdoor world. There is also, among those New Englanders, an underground vein of barely controlled rage. No matter how much patience is applied, mountain life seems unfair: every step, every act, every plan is that extra bit harder, requiring, in addition to its own intrinsic physical demands, the juggling act between gravity and gradient. Every step takes that much more effort, whether the required energy is supplied by fuel for man, animal, or machine. Mountain life is, literally, an uphill battle—and the downhill portions aren't all that much easier. Mountain terrain is responsible for the invention of the earliest and most rudimentary braking systems, whether in the form of leg muscles, improved footwear, or complex mechanical contrivance. Braking takes energy too. Fists get shaken at the mountains in New England.

If this litany of painful effort and bad temper makes the mountains sound like a dreadful place and discourages you from going there, that's perfectly all right with the New Englanders. The mountain people are not looking for company. (It is the people in the leisure phenomena who are looking for population growth. What they want to do is *sell* you the mountains—and then, often as not, get out themselves.) After ten years of residence in Easton, New Hampshire, population one hundred, I am still regarded as a transient, as I will be for another fifty years or so. Then I'll become a local, if I've outlived enough of the truly native, Easton-born residents, and can therefore tell older stories, from before my neighbors' memories. And if I don't in the meantime start demonstrating egregiously nonlocal behavior.

Stubborn maintenance of isolation, innate conservatism (usually of the nonideological variety—Europe's oldest self-governing community developed in the mountains, in Switzerland), fierce loyalty to place, even a deep pride in being able to survive in so obviously difficult conditions—these are all characteristics that fit the mountain stereotype, anywhere from New Hampshire to Nepal. Add to that a sense of independence (see self-government, above) and self-reliance that can seem to border on the pathological. Generations of mountain isolation have developed the tradition of competence at all the subsistence skills, no matter how crude that competence. It is no accident that the nonindustrial, freelance, usually illegal distillation of whiskey has remained a time-honored highland art, whether in Scotland or Tennessee. Or that collection of whiskey taxes from those mountain distilleries has always been so difficult. The New England adage, "Use it up, wear it out, make it do, or do without," is quite a serviceable mountain ethic, particularly when it, whatever it is, must be replaced out of the slender fruits of a mountain economy—and then hauled up from the flatlands before it can be put into service.

Many of the traditional nonagricultural occupations of mountain folk, particularly in Europe, are specific responses to snow: the long winters, the enforced idleness and lack of easy transportation. In previous centuries, cottage industries have been the result: woodcarving, clock making, the manufacture of optical and scientific instruments, weaving, embroidery, the production of lace. The long indoor winters have had other, less positive results. Tight, fetid houses, lack of exercise, extremely limited mental and physical stimulation have led to high rates of mental disturbance and alcoholism. Tavern life often became very important to a mountain community as the only social intercourse available.

The mountain life has advantages as well as disadvantages as far as health is concerned. But historically the isolated mountain community, with limited health care and a startling degree of inbreeding, has betrayed its primitive state. You still see a lot of physical deformity—harelips, crossed eyes, humpbacks, dwarfism—in the mountain backwaters. The limps, gimps, canes, and crutches of insufficiently treated injuries abound. Insanity and imbecility are not uncommon. Mountain life may not seem healthful at all, from the evidence of the native inhabitants.

I claim to live in the mountains, but my home is at eleven hundred feet and the surrounding peaks, if they can be so dignified, top out at less than a mile in height. Therefore, if I go directly to elevations of over eight thousand feet, often as not I will develop mountain sickness. It is a miserable affliction, striking me with persistent headache, nausea, minor dizziness, and interrupted sleep. It lasts about three days, all else being equal. (If I put in some cardiovascular training beforehand, I suffer little altitude effect but the disturbed sleep. A couple of weeks of running, even at home altitudes, will make me relatively immune—for up to perhaps twelve thousand feet.) Mountain sickness—*puna, soroche, chuno, mal de montagne, Bergkrankheit*—can be very serious, turning overnight from mere discomfort into such ailments as pulmonary edema. It strikes vacationing skiers with particular viciousness when they rush from low to high altitudes, without acclimatization time, trying to get the maximum number of days on the slopes. At very high altitudes, as on Himalayan expeditions, it can even knock down well-trained Alpinists who have done everything possible to prepare for its effects.

Our blood is normally 100 percent saturated with oxygen at sea level; most of us are exhausted if the blood saturation drops to 65 percent, unconscious if it reaches 55 percent. Acclimatization is the process of getting used to the effects of lower and lower saturation levels. Chris Bonington reports that climbers acclimatized to nineteen thousand feet have been discovered functioning well, performing hard exercise, with blood saturation levels as low as 45 percent. Acclimatization of mountain climbers is usually organized to provide two days of adjustment and rest for each rise above ten thousand feet, with each stage of the upward advance limited to under three thousand feet. But above twenty-four thousand feet, oxygen deficiency begins to cause degeneration of body tissue—damage to the liver and other organs—faster than acclimatization can accommodate it. It is a rule of thumb that a climber can climb above twenty-six thousand feet only once a year, and needs a full year thereafter to recover. In any case, once mountain sickness sets in, it is best to descend; and the lower you can go the better you'll be, the quicker you'll recover.

Despite all this, Bolivian tin miners regularly do hard physical labor at above eighteen thousand feet. That is, pride, stubbornness, and independence are psychological attributes, or perhaps cultural acquisitions; but physical adaptation to mountain life is another, quite measurable matter. There are mountain populations that have remained at high altitudes long enough—over centuries—to have acquired physical characteristics to fit the locale. Andean and Himalayan residents live comfortably at fifteen thousand feet and work at much higher altitudes, although they usually return to the lower levels to sleep.

The natives of the high Andes and Himalayas are short and stocky by Western standards, with characteristic barrel chests and massive lung capacity. In addition, their alveoli—the tiny pockets in the lung tissue where exchange of oxygen for carbon dioxide takes place—are permanently expanded, further increasing lung capacity, to help them extract every useful molecule of oxygen from the air. Tests on Andean Indians have shown that their hearts are as much as 20 percent larger than the hearts of individuals of comparable size and weight who live at lower altitudes. The Andeans also have about 20 percent more blood, by volume, for equal body weight. The blood itself is composed differently, much richer in red corpuscles, as much as 60 percent higher by weight in the hemoglobin that actually absorbs oxygen from the air into the blood stream. (Accelerated production of hemoglobin is one of the body's earliest adaptations in the acclimatization process. After seven weeks at altitude, you'll have 50 percent more blood cells than you would have produced at low altitude.)

Along with the larger heart, high-altitude residents tend to have a slower, more efficient heart rate—at low altitude usually the sign of a superbly conditioned athlete such as a distance runner or a cross-country ski racer. (The latter are considered by physiologists to be among the best-conditioned athletes in the world, incidentally. For you and me, a "normal" resting heart rate is somewhere in the neighborhood of seventy to seventy-five beats per minute; in a cross-country skier in good shape, a rate of forty beats per minute is not uncommon.) A high red cell count means thicker, more viscous blood; that, combined with a slow heart rate, leads to a seeming contradiction. One of the reasons frostbite is a constant danger to mountain climbers is that at high altitudes the blood actually thickens and slows in the veins, no matter how hard the overworked heart pumps away. Small arteries in the fingers and toes can go into spasms. Slowed circulation means diminished body heat to the extremities. It is a rare Himalayan mountain expedition in which no non-Himalayan member loses some toes or fingers to frostbite.

The native's thick, hemoglobin-rich blood and slow heart rate would seem to invite a similar disaster. Yet every Himalayan expedition returns with wondrous tales of Sherpa bearers who carry heavy loads barefoot across the snowfields on the way to the mountain with no ill effect. Andean Indians perform similar feats. The accommodation that prevents frostbite in such circumstances is complex. A slow heart rate does not mean sluggish circulation, but rather the opposite: more blood pumped with each heartbeat, greater heart efficiency. Moreover, it is lack of oxygen that thickens the blood of the short-term visitor to high altitude, and the highlanders have developed the capacity to keep their oxygen level high, their blood flowing fast despite its richness. They have also evolved short, chunky bodies, stumpy arms and legs, and comparatively huge hands and feet. Within their compact bodies, the circuit time for a given particle of blood is brief, as the circuit itself is not so long as in a taller person; the blood returns quickly to the well-heated body core for rewarming. Finally, the high-altitude residents have developed a more extensive capillary system, with larger, more direct linkups between artery and vein, particularly in those well-developed hands and feet. More and bigger capillaries speed up circulation.

The Himalayans and the Andeans are both of Mongoloid origin, the Andeans descended from emigrants who crossed the land bridge from Asia a third of a million years ago and founded the Inca civilization. Like the Eskimo—also a former Asian—they have developed such cold-resistant characteristics as broad, flat faces well-insulated with fat, and epicanthic folds over the eyes. (Eyes need protection. Recent research has shown that skiers who don't wear goggles risk freezing the very surface of the eyeball when running downhill at high speeds, even in fairly moderate temperatures.) In this adaptation to both cold and high altitude the Andeans did have one advantage in a naturally occurring product of their adopted land: coca—yet another mountain stimulant that grows at up to six thousand feet on the east side of the Andes. Ancient Inca messengers chewed coca leaves while performing feats of incredible endurance, and Andeans still measure distance—on foot across the mountains—in terms of cuds of coca leaf required to reach the destination. Coca's role in high-altitude adaptation is not fully understood, but the drug does provide a powerful stimulant:

After eating a simple breakfast of ground corn porridge, they would start with their heavy packs, weighing from seventy-five to more than one hundred pounds, strapped to their backs. All day long they traveled at a rapid gait over the steep mountain spurs and across mucky swamps at an altitude that to us, without any load whatsoever, was most exhausting. On these trips the Indians neither rested anywhere nor ate at noon, but sucked their wad of coca throughout the entire day. These Indians we found very pleasant, always cheerful, happy, and good natured, in spite of the fact that their daily toil subjected them to the severest hardships and the most frugal fare.*

The poor Himalayans, by contrast, had to make do with booze: *chung,* a beer made by pouring boiling water over grain, or *rakshi,* a "distillate of chung, toadstools, rotting wood, and anything else fermentable or distillable," according to *Mountain Gazette* contributor Robert Schulteis. "It is volatile stuff, producing temporary dementia, migraine headaches and hallucinations, and turning mild-mannered kulis into kukri-wielding homicidal maniacs. And it tastes awful—on a par with French gin or Kachina peach brandy." Poor Himalayans. But then, they didn't have that long walk from Asia to South America before settling down to the task of adapting to high altitude.

Tibet, Peru, and Mexico each supported high mountain civilizations for thousands of years, but those three enclaves have been exceptions among the mountains of the world. In Peru and Mexico the mountains served as sanctuaries, and when the mountains were breached by outsiders, the civilizations therein quickly fell. Tibet remains mysteriously unchanging, although its takeover by the Chinese bodes ill for the future of its carefully preserved isolation. Elsewhere in the world, mountains have served more often as barriers than as sanctuaries. Political history for the most part weaves its way around, rather than through, the mountains. Civilization prefers to spread along the flatlands, the river valleys and coastal plains, and leaves the mountain interiors and their people alone—a perfectly agreeable arrangement for both parties, at least in the early stages. The mountain "primitives" tend to

* J. T. Lloyd, *A Treatise on Coca* (Cincinnati, Ohio: Lloyd Brothers, 1913).

regard the city folk as lost souls steeped in sin and corruption in their pursuit of the soft life; the urban populations consider the mountain peasants a negligible concern, socially retarded, of no moment in the course of empire. Until they begin wanting what the peasants have, as, inevitably, they will.

While mountains and their people may be too much trouble, the passageways through the mountains are another matter. Trade routes seek out the mountain passes, develop them, make them into minor-grade political entities. Cultures clash via the passes. Military significance is never far behind. There is no denying the military importance of high ground, no matter how slight; the great tacticians have always depended heavily on contour maps in planning their campaigns. Mountain passes exaggerate this military truth. They can ordinarily be held with small forces, and their secure possession can paralyze the movements of the enemy.

Thus mountain passes have often been tied directly to the triumphs and disasters of military history. Many of the greatest triumphs have resulted when existing passes were ignored, as when Alexander the Great bypassed the heavily defended Khyber Pass between Afghanistan and India, and swept through the Hindu Kush in 327 B.C. Or when new passes were found where none were known before, as in Hannibal's daring adventure in the Alps that brought him into Italy from the undefended—"impregnable"—north, in 218 B.C. The Alps were long an undigested political lump in the middle of Europe, and the Saint Bernard Pass (8,110 feet) between France and Italy, the Saint Gotthard (6,292 feet) between Switzerland and Italy, the Brenner (4,495 feet) between Austria and Italy were the routes that brought the digestive juices of commerce—not to mention military devastation—to assimilate the mountain wilderness. Roncesvalles Pass (3,900 feet, in the Pyrenees between Spain and France), Thermopylae (sea level, between Thessaly and Greece), and the Khyber (3,500 feet) were all sites of crucial battles that changed Western history.

American history is so intimately tied to westward movement that dodging or outwitting mountain ranges was almost a national obsession. In New England the "notches" let the earliest settlers work their way from lush valley to lush valley, penetrating ever inland: Franconia, Crawford, Smuggler's notches. The first major encouragement to mass movement westward was provided by the "gaps" through the Appalachians, of which the Cumberland was the most heavily traveled of all. After the rolling midwestern agricultural bonanzas and the oceanic prairies, the Rocky Mountains threw up so formidable a barrier that many of the forty-niners on their way to California opted for the sea route clear around Cape Horn. Overland emigrants had to deal with the historic South Pass (7,550 feet) on the Oregon Trail, Raton Pass (7,834 feet) on the Santa Fe Trail, and, much later, lofty Loveland Pass (11,992 feet) to get over the Rockies. Perhaps the most notorious American pass of all was the Donner (7,135 feet), through the last barrier of the Sierra Nevada. The military activity associated with these passes was limited mostly to defense of pioneer expeditions from marauding American Indians resisting further encroachment on their lands. Such campaigns were not extensive, and the heroism demonstrated in the American mountain passes was not so much military as it was simply human. Epic struggles for sheer survival were almost routine, as might be expected: the pioneers seldom recognized at the outset that what they were attempting were in effect mountain climbing expeditions encumbered with Conestoga wagons loaded with complete families who had no mountain experience at all. Such tragedies as befell the Donner Party—forty out of eighty-seven dead in the devastating snows of the winter of 1846–47, the remainder surviving in part through cannibalism—were only to be expected.

(Cannibalism would return to the mountains, to impinge upon the consciousness of us all, with the Chilean air crash in 1972 in the Andes, when sixteen members of a Uruguayan soccer team survived seventy days in the high mountains with the help of that same grisly solution. Mountains do make hard terms—and produce hard survivors.)

What keeps mountain life different from that of the lowland cities is the enforced isolation; the basic cause of that isolation, simply enough, is the difficulty and expense of providing transportation and communication within the mountain country. The long-term effect of this isolation on the lives of mountain people has been demonstrated in the Balkans and in the Scottish Highlands, but nowhere more eloquently than in the quite similar Southern Appalachians. All three of these areas are famous for the longevity and bitterness of their interclan battles. All three of these areas are what the geologists term "maturely dissected uplands." The point can be made that maturely dissected uplands produce feuds.

In the Appalachians, the various Anglo–Saxon immigrants, finding the coastal lowlands already snatched up by prior arrivals, pushed on into the mountains. (Mountains have historically been populated by overflow from the plains that surround them. So many overrun, outmaneuvered, or defeated groups settled in the Caucasus that one historian refers to that range as "the graveyard of nations.") In the Appalachians, the peaks and ridges were not more attractive than such features anywhere else, so the new American highlanders settled the upland valleys, usually on a clan-by-clan basis. As late as the 1930's, there was one forty-mile stretch of the Kentucky River that was populated by people who all bore the same last name.

The clans stuck to their own valleys, pulling more and more tightly into family relationships, intermarrying and inbreeding (and paying the genetic price for it), generating their own internal distrust of outsiders. Contrary to the folklore surrounding our Hatfields and McCoys, the loyalties—and the feuds—developed on a valley-versus-valley basis rather than by bloodline. "Ridge-runners" were not only night-riding outlaws (who in some areas performed Ku Klux Klan-type vigilante actions against blacks and other interlopers), but were also rebels against the valley, refusing to accept its isolation: sowers of trouble, valley to valley. For the bulk of the population, people who ventured up on the ridges were not to be trusted.

Despite the ridge-runners, the deliberate maintenance of isolation in the Southern Appalachians is remarkable, with a larger number of true subsistence farms still in operation there than anywhere else in the country. Academics finally began penetrating those valleys in the 1930's, and discovered a dumbfounding collection of what were, to the academics anyway, living artifacts. An almost Shakespearean language had survived, and arts and crafts virtually unchanged from Elizabethan times were common. Seventeenth-century ballads were sung, sometimes with a verse or two added to reflect some narrow view of American history. In at least one case the crossbow was still in use for hunting small game. The recently published *Foxfire* books—begun as a high school project to preserve and record the mountain crafts and skills that play so large a part in the self-sufficiency of the region—can be read as a snapshot of the primitive isolation of mountain life, as well as of its peculiar rewards. Rewards are undoubtedly there. While "Appalachia" has become a synonym for a way of life that is, by every social measurement, a national disaster, the *Foxfire* books continue to push to the top of the bestseller lists. *Nostalgie pour la boue, montagne* department, perhaps. But social scientists have never had much success measuring quality.

In the more "civilized" Alps, the other side of the coin can be seen: the rugged individualism is of the group rather than of the single mountaineer. All the inhabitants of a single Alpine valley share the same climate, the same growing season, the same set of resources, however meager. The dangers of avalanches, floods, and other catastrophes are common dangers. Those threats are resisted by community effort: the mountain pasturage is owned in common (it can't accurately be divided anyway), the forests are managed in the public interest. Many Alpine valleys have become virtual syndicates, with tightly knit social organizations in each valley, in common bond against the difficulties of mountain life.

Until the 1850's, when Europe went on an orgy of road building and track laying, the Alps steadily gained in population. With the coming of easy transportation between 1850 and World War I, the Alps lost somewhere between 20 and 30 percent of their population, and lowland cities nearby swelled by like amounts. (The joys of mountain life evidently didn't stand up too well against the actual possibility of escape.) Nowadays, with communication and transportation almost universally available, the Alps are again gaining in population. It remains to be seen how this artificial boom will withstand the soaring costs of energy and transportation in the coming century.

Switzerland described as a scattered collection of communally organized valleys and Switzerland described as Europe's first self-governing democracy, are two pictures that do not gibe in my American vocabulary, where "individualism" tends to be characterized as either "rugged" or "two-fisted." Roderick Peattie resolves my confusion:

A government of mountain valleys having the same economic and political problems is more rational than the government of mountain valleys by unsympathetic plains people. In their external relationships mountain groups have all the independence that writers have ascribed to the individual mountaineer. The confederation of valleys into a state is a matter of singleness of economic purpose and the need for protection. It is worthy of note that in Switzerland the communes are older than the cantons and the cantons existed before the confederation. The confederation was created, indeed, as a defense of communal and cantonal autonomy.*

That Switzerland should have evolved so rational a confederation while the Appalachians are stuck with "the government

* Peattie, *Mountain Geography*, p. 217.

of mountain valleys by unsympathetic plains people" seems distressing to our own chauvinistic notions of home rule and American democracy. The Swiss formed their confederation in 1291, after uncounted centuries of more or less successful habitation of those mountain valleys. The Appalachians have held white settlement for less than four hundred years. There's time enough yet for our mountain people to learn a way to live together more peaceably than their past history would predict. There's even time for the government of the unsympathetic plains people to learn to defend the autonomy of those mountain people rather than try to assimilate them into nonmountain ways of life. It's an approach that always leaves us puzzled—witness our bewildered irresolution over our native American Indians—but we may yet learn to have the magnanimity and trust to allow such revolutionary ideas to work.

Some part of the beholder, even some vital part, seems to escape through the loose grating of his ribs as he ascends.
—HENRY DAVID THOREAU, *The Maine Woods*

Chapter *17*

The Center of the Universe

The center of the universe is a mountain, El Huerfano, near Chaco Canyon National Monument in New Mexico, not too far from Farmington. I can't find the height of El Huerfano in any atlas. Huerfanito is there—"little orphan"—at 7,475 feet, but no senior orphan is indicated, which is perhaps appropriate for so sacred a mountain.

The Holy Mountain of the East is Wheeler Peak, about 120 air miles away, just above Taos; at 13,160 feet it is the highest point in the state. According to Indian legend, it should be made of sand and white shell. The sacred Blue Lake, the "church" that the Taos Indians have been trying to protect from Anglo interlopers for over three hundred years, is on the flank of Wheeler Peak.

The Holy Mountain of the West—yellow-red sand and abalone—is somewhere in the San Francisco Peaks of Arizona, above Flagstaff. The Holy Mountain of the North, of black sand and jet (lignite), is an unnamed peak in either the La Plata or San Juan ranges of southern Colorado. The Holy Mountain of the South, legendarily of sand and blue-green turquoise, is Mount Taylor, 11,390 feet, in the San Mateo Mountains northwest of Albuquerque. These five peaks mark the center and the approximate boundaries of the Four Corners country, where the borders of Utah, Colorado, New Mexico, and Arizona meet.

The Four Corners area is the ancestral home of several Indian tribes, including the Navajo, Hopi, and the various Pueblo groups; it is the Navajo who have identified these sacred mountains. El Huerfano is also known as the Mountain Around Which Moving Was Done, the Mountain Surrounded by Mountains, or the Encircled Mountain. According to Hopi authority Frank Waters, it could well be that El Huerfano is only a religious metaphor for the center of the universe: "Its original prototype, its greatest physical image, may well have been, not El Huerfano, but the Colorado Pyramid, the high hinterland heart of America"*—that is, the entire massively uplifted Colorado Plateau, through which the Colorado River has carved the Grand Canyon. The Hopi consider the Canyon to be the womb of the world.

Or perhaps the center of the universe is a mountain named Sun Chan, in the province of Sinkiang; the Chinese there have so designated it. My information about Chinese mountains is extremely sketchy, but on the west of Sun Chan is another sacred mountain called Hua Shan; on its east, T'ai Shan; and on the north and on the south, two peaks sharing the same name, Heng Shan. A wandering dragon named Kung Kung was responsible, in Chinese legend, for the Flood. It violated the northern Heng Shan, tipped the heavens in the process,

---

* *Masked Gods* (New York: Ballantine Books, 1970), p. 166.

and brought down the Deluge. These five sacred mountains are all in Sinkiang; just to the south in Szechwan there is another sacred mountain, O'mei (10,150 feet), sacred enough to have fifty-six pagodas and thirty-five Buddhist monasteries erected on it.

One source tells me that to both Hindus and Buddhists, Mount Kailas (22,028 feet) in Tibet is the Throne of Shiva and therefore the center of the earth. Frank Waters says that in Tibetan Buddhism the center of the universe is a Mount Meru. The only Mount Meru I've been able to find in the atlas is in Tanzania, 14,977 feet high, just about forty miles from Kilimanjaro. Considering that Mount Kilimanjaro is the highest point in Africa, and that nearby lies the fascinating geology of the Great Rift Valley—as well as the Olduvai Gorge, which continues to provide us with the earliest known remains of man—Mount Meru has a certain appropriateness as the point of origin of us all, for Tibetan or any other creation legends.

But that's the wrong Mount Meru. The Tibetan Buddhists' Mount Meru is really much more of a metaphor than El Huerfano, as Waters clearly explains. It is eighty thousand miles high and eighty thousand miles deep, surrounded by seven concentric circles of mountains and four "continents," only one of which is represented by our entire planet. Parallels between American Indian mystical systems and those of Buddhism are endless, as Waters has developed with great care. One interesting example is that the four continents around Mount Meru have symbolic color schemes similar to those of the Four Corners Indians: white on the east, blue on the south, red on the west, and yellow (rather than black) on the north. Tiny coincidences abound, and it doesn't do to make too much of them, perhaps. I was nevertheless startled to find, as I was searching the maps of New Mexico for El Huerfano, that there is a "Chacra Mesa" very close to the center of the Four Corners universe. In Buddhist disciplines, a *chakra* is a focal center in the body through which psychic energy flows.

There is a sacred mountain in just about every geographical area of the earth that has ever held human habitation. The natives have usually at some time in their history decided that there were gods, or at least spiritual forces, up there. A non-Indian's first view of 6,288-foot Mount Washington in New Hampshire was recorded in 1524, when Verrazano spotted it from the sea; but it was first climbed in 1642—well before mountain climbing had come to be regarded as sane behavior in Europe—by one Darby Field, of Exeter, New Hampshire. He inveigled two Indian "companions" to make the climb with him, but only after considerable persuasion. They did not serve as guides; they had never been up there. Mount Washington was Agiocochook (Mountain of the Snowy Forehead) or Waumbeket Methna (Home of the Great Spirit), and one did not intrude on the Great Spirit lightly. Thus Field's climb is not only the first recorded ascent, but very likely the first of any kind, as the Indians avoided summits.

Western Indian attitudes were consistent. The Utes have been accused of deliberately setting forest fires to burn off the summits of many Colorado mountains, as a scorched-earth policy to express their rage at white encroachment. It may be true, but I rather suspect lightning. Indians who would abandon the trail of promising game rather than intrude on the gods of the upper mountains would seem unlikely to risk the ire of those gods with spiteful arson. A mature Plains Indian—before white settlement intruded—would spend about half of his waking hours in religious observances, so tightly bound to the spiritual was his life, and a respect for the natural world was a basic tenet of that religious life in all of the 315 North American tribes.

There is no flippancy intended here about centers of the universe. For a given mystical system, particularly that of an untraveled, hence "unsophisticated," people, the center of the universe is bound to be identifiable within the known territory. What is remarkable is the consistency with which those centers have been located at specific mountains throughout mankind's history. The Greeks placed their gods on Parnassus (8,064 feet) and Olympus (9,550 feet).* When God handed down the Ten Commandments, Moses was standing on a mountain to receive them: Mount Sinai on the Sinai Peninsula, now in the atlases as Gebel Mûsa, 7,497 feet. Buddha ascended to Heaven from a mountain; Noah repopulated the earth after landing the ark on Mount Ararat (16,946 feet) in Turkey. Mohammed saw the Angel Gabriel on Mount Hira. David chose Mount Zion as the place to build his capital. Isaac was sacrificed to Jehovah on a mountain. Jesus withdrew into "the wilderness"—surely a desert mountain area—for forty days and nights, then returned and laid down the basis of His teaching in a sermon preached from . . . The Mount. He then underwent His Transfiguration—when He underwent spiritual change, after which "His face did shine as the sun, and His raiment was white as the light." It happened "on a mountain high apart."

Nowhere is the connection between the mountain world and matters of the spirit clearer than in the two societies which have taken the highest altitudes as their home territory. In the high Andes between 1100 and 1550 A.D., the Incas achieved the most sophisticated civilization of any native people of the western hemisphere. The Inca empire was an absolute theocracy: its 380,000 square miles, its entire population (estimated at sixteen million), and its intricate network of stone temples were all devoted almost obsessively to spiritual matters. The temples were connected by paved highways, hand-built at altitudes above fifteen thousand feet, products of unimaginable physical labor.

Their supreme ruler, the Inca, was understood to be the Son

* One Bolivian scholar has held that the name "Olympus" is a corruption of the name of Mount Illiampu, a twenty-three-thousand-foot peak in the Andes, and that the forebears of Greek civilization migrated from South America—using the lost continent of Atlantis as a stepping stone, of course.

of the Sun, and his priests outranked both the nobility and the military, overseeing the administration of a fabulously wealthy empire. Peasants contributed a third of their product to the priests for maintenance of the temples and for religious observances, and a third to the upkeep of the secular administration; the remaining third was owned in common by the local population, in a truly communistic social organization. It was the preoccupation with, and absolute faith in, the top-heavy Inca religion that brought the downfall of the empire. Once Pizarro had captured the reigning Inca, Atahualpa, in 1533, the headless empire quickly crumbled to the invading Spaniards.

Tibet is perhaps even more devoted to the life of the spirit, although what it has developed in the way of civilization may still be considered a bit primitive by modern Western standards. Before the Chinese takeover in 1951, it was estimated that about half a million Tibetan males were monks, or lamas, out of a total population of less than a million and a half. Thus one Tibetan male in three is a monk. There were as many as seven thousand monasteries in the tiny kingdom, although the Chinese are reported to have forced the abandonment of some of them. The Dalai Lama, now in exile but still head of the sect, is, to Tibetans, a living god. In Tibetan Buddhism young males are accepted into full-time religious training well before puberty, and may spend fifty years in study in preparation for various levels of priesthood. Prayer wheels, whirling and clacking in the breeze, are still ever-present throughout the nation, symbolizing the Tibetan's dedication to religious observance. Like the Plains Indian, he spends a considerable portion of his daily time in prayer, chanting, and meditation. Blessings, advice, and augury are sought from the priesthood for almost any undertaking, no matter how inconsequential.

Tibetan Buddhism is an ecstatic sect: heady, extremely mystical, characterized by trance states that elevate its practitioners to altered states of consciousness. It gets its practitioners "high" without the use of drugs, without even requiring particularly antisocial behavior. Perhaps for this reason, perhaps simply as an outgrowth of increased interest in Eastern religions in general, it has developed a growing following among the postdrug elements of the counterculture in this country and throughout the Western world. With only the gentlest and most unobtrusive sort of evangelism, Tibetan Buddhist missionaries have been able to establish successful missions in several places: Scotland, Vermont, Colorado, New Mexico. In the mountains.

The great mystics of history have traditionally gone into the mountains alone in times of spiritual crisis, to seek truth, insight, revelation, understanding. The solo trip to the mountains has been institutionalized by many primitive cultures, including American Indians, as an initiation rite, usually at puberty. (Where mountains are available, they're used, the "site of choice" so to speak; if there are no mountains, wilderness or simply isolation will do.) There, initiates commonly experience visions or dreams which predict their future, establish their adult identities, and the like. Admittedly, the mountain mystical experience is enhanced by solitude, fasting, and other sensory deprivations, but there seems to be evidence that the mountain vastness, the heights and depths, are directly contributory. As the drug psychologists are fond of saying, set and setting are everything.

Drug use in the mountains, not quite incidentally, may be more extensive than in the flatlands. The Andeans have their coca (of which cocaine is a manufactured derivative), the Tibetans their chung and rakshi. The Aztecs and Mayans had their pulque and mescal—alcoholic beverages, the latter the source of the name of the Mescalero Apaches—and hallucinatory mushrooms. A Four Corners tribe from the Taos Pueblo was the group who secured federal dispensation for use of peyote in rituals of the Native American Church. The mountains have historically been left to primitive peoples, and the shamans, sorcerers, and witch doctors of mountain peoples have always been experts in the collection, preparation, and dispensation of psychoactive natural products. Note Carlos Castaneda's Don Juan Matus, who may or may not be a hoax, but who certainly knows his organic pharmacology.

(A decade or more before marijuana gained its recent popularity—well before the advent of the drug culture—an experienced mountain climber told me of its recreational use by "some" of the climbing fraternity. The rationale was that it was a gentle relaxant that could be enjoyed without any discernible deleterious effect on subsequent physical conditioning. I have no idea how widespread this use—or this rationale—was or is, but the fellow who thus described it had been a member of a successful Everest expedition.)

In short, there seems to be some connection between getting "high" and getting—physically—high. It is in the language: when we are "high" we have an "elevated" mood, our spirits are "raised." We overuse the terms now, awash in mood-altering substances: we even say we get high on alcohol, which is physiologically a depressant. Drug-culture terminology puts a finer point on it, dividing such stuff into "uppers" and "downers." The directions indicated, if not the slang, have come down to us through antiquity. Up is good, down is bad; it's a cultural inheritance.

(As a precondition for mystical experience, some emotional *dislocation* seems necessary, whether from drugs or from any other source. Despite the emotionless, matter-of-fact approach that much modern-day theology prefers to take, all religions have their origins in mystical experience. Ecstatic experience. It is only with rationalization and codification that the ec-static—"primitive"—component is removed. Religious rituals develop out of instructions for attaining ecstatic states. Too bad the rituals work so seldom for us anymore. No new religion is developed through linear, rational intellection. Some twentieth-century ideologues might take lessons from the shamans.)

It's easier to be high in mood when one is high in physical location for several rather self-evident reasons. At high altitudes there is: less oppressive atmospheric pressure, clearer and cleaner air to breathe (if less of it), more light, brisker temperatures—an assortment of environmental characteristics that we've traditionally regarded to be a veritable tonic for the spirit. That one often arrives at higher altitudes in a state of mild fatigue, suffering from the dizzying and disorienting effects of reduced oxygen, is not necessarily a handicap: those effects, too, can stimulate euphoria. In fact almost anything that serves to violate the numbing everydayness of lowland existence can bring a positive mood change.

As, for instance, height. The perception of depth, a sense of scale, can itself have a druglike effect. That very "prospect" that went "unnamed" before the romantic poets began selling it to us is a force that works on the mind to alter mood dramatically. Psychologist Bernard S. Aaronson ran experiments using hypnosis and posthypnotic suggestion to augment depth perception with startling results. A control group had the perception of depth deliberately diminished by posthypnotic suggestion. They were told that upon awakening from the hypnosis, the dimension of depth would be gone, the world would seem two-dimensional. The other group was told that the dimension of depth would seem expanded, heightened, as in scenes viewed through a stereoscope.

Subjects perceiving reduced depth reported that in the two-dimensional posthypnotic world, colors, shapes, and sounds all seemed less intense; sensitivity to touch was diminished; the world had become a boring place. Observers reported, for example, that one reduced-depth subject became withdrawn: "he became apathetic . . . he showed little affect. He did not seem hostile, but felt that his environment had become alien and the people around him dehumanized." Trained psychologists compared the result to the onset of mental illness: "marked schizophreniform behavior with catatonic features" was reported.

By contrast, "when the dimension of depth was expanded, a psychedelic state resulted similar to that described by Huxley in *The Doors of Perception.* Lines seemed sharper, colors intensified, everything seemed to have a place and to be in its place, and to be esthetically satisfying. The hand of God was manifest in an ordered world." One subject began to talk about how "everything around him seemed to have been shaped into a world of super-reality and unspeakable beauty. 'The landscape was at once a gargantuan formal garden and a wilderness of irrepressible joyous space,'" he reported.

Aaronson's discussion draws the conclusion that mountain lovers will find inescapable:

The data suggest that expanding depth yields a psychedelic experience, while ablating depth yields a schizophreniform response. . . . The contrast between the response to the expanded depth and the ablated depth conditions involves a contrast between mystic experience and psychosis. . . . Far from being the same, mystic experience seems characterized by profound involvement and expansion of the boundaries of self, psychotic experience by profound alienation and shrinking of the self boundaries. . . .

The fact that expanded depth is associated with mystic experience recalls the observation of William James (1929) that most mystic experience tends to occur outdoors. The traditional predilection of religious devotees for mountain tops and desert places may not be merely a desire to get away from the distractions of the social world, but a movement to a place where experiences of enhanced depth are possible. The traditional association of mountain tops with the abode of Deity may be less because they are higher than the areas around them than because they make possible those experiences of expanded depth in which the self can invest itself in the world around it and expand across the valleys.*

As there is "rapture of the deep" caused by the specific chemical imbalance known as nitrogen narcosis, so there are also raptures of the heights, some forms of which are undoubt-

* Bernard S. Aaronson, "Hypnosis, Depth Perception, and Psychedelic Experience" (a paper presented to the Society for Scientific Study of Religion, New York, 1965).

edly caused by exhaustion and oxygen deficiency. Maurice Herzog, in his account of the French ascent of Annapurna in 1950—the first eight-thousand-meter (26,250-foot) mountain ever climbed—describes his own mental state in the agonized final stages:

> I felt as though I were plunging into something new and quite abnormal. I had the strangest and most vivid impressions, such as I had never before known in the mountains. There was something unnatural in the way I saw Lachenal [his climbing partner] and everything around us. I smiled to myself at the paltriness of our efforts, for I could stand apart and watch myself making these efforts. But all sense of exertion was gone, as though there were no longer any gravity. This diaphanous landscape, this quintessence of purity—these were not the mountains I knew: they were the mountains of my dreams. . . . I had never seen such complete transparency, and I was living in a world of crystal. . . . An astonishing happiness welled up in me . . . everything was so new, so utterly unprecedented.[*]

That is at twenty-six thousand feet with a fading oxygen supply; it is hardly necessary to go that high, to work that hard, before something similar—less chemical, and indeed, less befuddling, but similar nevertheless—starts happening to you.

In short, wonder and delight await, up there. (Mixed, sometimes, with a dollop of terror.) On any mountain summit, from any point of prospect. Air feels like a whole new element, bathing the body and cleansing the brain. Space seems much more coherent, a palpable presence. Solid ground becomes almost a source of pressure, an active part of the environment—a physical metaphor for trust. And the light, always the light, shimmering yet sharp edged, providing a visual acuity that borders on pain, promising . . . clarity. That's all there, for anyone willing to open up his senses, his experiential—primitive—brain to it. Elbowroom for the soul. All you have to

---

[*] *Annapurna* (New York: E. P. Dutton, 1953), p. 206.

do is suspend judgment and analysis long enough simply to be there, on the mountain, experiencing it. (A long hard walk to get there is remarkably effective for damping out all that jittery brain noise that elsewhere gets in the way.) It's easy: let your senses go. Let it happen. *Be* high, while you are on the mountain.

It may not unite you with God, it may not overwhelm you with revelation of the secrets of the universe—but it can give you a glimpse. It can let you understand how holy men have brought back from the mountains their sustaining faith. It can show you why mountains are holy, if you will only be sensitive to them.

And if that kind of talk makes you distinctly uncomfortable, as it always does me, there are more coolly rational messages to be contemplated. It is not for me to try to tell anybody how to think about mountains, but I'll tell you why I think the mountains have such capacity to move us. I think it is because mountains are always so new. Never mind the billions of years that are implicit in every cliff face, the slow geologic increments by which—according to the scientists—the earth builds its mountains. Forget that for a moment; just look. Gradient *is* the elixir of youth.

The flatlands are dead; it is all over for them. Where there is zero declination, where the slope stops, where erosion slows down to a stagnant, meandering trickle, there the earth feels worn out. Worn down to sea level, the lowest common denominator, the ultimate dull average. How weary, stale, flat, and unprofitable indeed, the uses of such a world.

Static versus dynamic. What the mountains tell us, in their soaring arêtes and frozen knife ridges and plummeting scarps, is that, yes, the land is cut low, time and time again. It is always restored. Mountains tell us that, in the course of geologic time anyway, the earth is a renewable resource. That's reassuring. There are new mountains to come, everywhere, so long as there is an earth to thrust them up. Mountains more magnificent, perhaps, than all that have ever been before.

Ah, but we can't know that for sure, and the ones we have now are coming down, pebble by sand grain. The mountains we have are unique; they may be surpassed, overshadowed, but they'll never be duplicated. Perhaps we'd better go pay them some attention now, while they are here to inspire us.

Appendix

For further reading:

Walter H. Bucher, *The Deformation of the Earth's Crust,* Hafner Publishing Co., New York, 1957.

André Cailleux, *Anatomy of the Earth,* World University Library, McGraw-Hill, New York, 1968.

Nigel Calder, *The Restless Earth,* Viking Press, New York, 1972.

John Cleare, *Mountains,* Crown Publishers, New York, 1975.

David F. Costello, *The Mountain World,* Thomas Y. Crowell Co., New York, 1975.

Lord Energlyn, *Through the Crust of the Earth,* McGraw-Hill, New York, 1973.

Colin Fraser, *The Avalanche Enigma,* John Murray Ltd., London, 1966.

Ronald Fraser, *The Habitable Earth,* Basic Books, New York, 1964.

Preston E. James, *A Geography of Man,* Blaisdell Publishing Co., Waltham, Mass., 1966.

Tony Long, *Mountain Animals,* Harper & Row, New York, 1971.

Harvey Manning (Editor), *Mountaineering,* The Mountaineers, Seattle, Wash., 1967.

Lorus J. and Margery Milne, *The Mountains,* Time-Life Books, New York, 1962.

Marjorie Hope Nicolson, *Mountain Gloom and Mountain Glory,* W. W. Norton, New York, 1963.

Roderick Peattie, *Mountain Geography*, Greenwood Press, New York, 1936.

Peter Randall, *Mount Washington*, University Press of New England, Hanover, N.H., 1974.

John A. Shimer, *This Changing Earth*, Harper & Row, New York, 1968.

John A. Shimer, *This Sculptured Earth*, Columbia University Press, New York, 1959.

A. C. Spectorsky (Editor), *The Book of the Mountains*, Appleton-Century-Crofts, New York, 1955.

Wallace Stegner, *Beyond the Hundredth Meridian*, Houghton Mifflin, Boston, 1962.

Arthur N. Strahler, *Physical Geography*, 4th ed., John Wiley & Sons, New York, 1975.

Walter Sullivan, *Continents in Motion*, McGraw-Hill, New York, 1974.

William D. Thornbury, *Regional Geomorphology of the United States*, John Wiley & Sons, New York, 1965.

Glenn T. Trewartha, *An Introduction to Climate*, McGraw-Hill, New York, 1968.

Jerome Wyckoff, *Rock, Time, and Landforms*, Harper & Row, New York, 1966.

Index